LIBERALS AND COMMUNITARIANS

Stephen Mulhall and Adam Swift

BLACKWELL
Oxford UK & Cambridge USA

Copyright © Stephen Mulhall and Adam Swift, 1992

The right of Stephen Mulhall and Adam Swift to be identified as authors of this work has been asserted in accordance with the Copyright, Designs and Patents Act 1988.

First published 1992
Reprinted 1993

Blackwell Publishers
108 Cowley Road
Oxford OX4 1JF
UK

238 Main Street, Suite 501
Cambridge, Massachusetts 02142
USA

British Library Cataloguing in Publication Data

A CIP catalogue record for this book is available from the British Library.

Library of Congress Cataloging in Publication Data

Mulhall, Stephen, 1962–
   Liberals and Communitarians/Stephen Mulhall and Adam Swift.
     p.   cm.
   Includes bibliographical references and index.
   ISBN 0–631–18377–9 — ISBN 0–631–18378–7 (pbk.)
   1. Rawls, John, 1921–   Theory of justice. 2. Justice. 3. Liberalism.
   4. Libertarianism. I. Swift, Adam. II. Title.
   JC578.M78 1992   91–41507
   320′.01′1–dc20   CIP

Typeset in 10 on 12pt Palatino
by Graphicraft Typesetters Ltd., Hong Kong
Printed in Great Britain by Biddles Ltd, Guildford and King's Lynn

This book is printed on acid-free paper

Contents

Preface   vii
Acknowledgements   xv
Abbreviations   xvii

Introduction: Rawls's original position   1

The basics of justice as fairness   3
The agenda: claims modelled by the original position   9
   The conception of the person   10
   Asocial individualism   13
   Universalism   19
   Subjectivism or objectivism   21
   Anti-perfectionism and neutrality   25

PART I
COMMUNITARIAN
CRITIQUES   35

INTRODUCTION   37

1 Sandel: the limits of liberalism   40

Liberalism and deontology   42
Rawls's theory of the person   45

The original position 47
The flaws in Rawls's theory of the person 50
Liberalism and moral subjectivism 55
The difference principle 59
Agreement in the original position 63
The limits of liberalism 66

2 MacIntyre: morality after virtue 70

The predicament of contemporary morality 71
The emotivist self 74
The Enlightenment project 77
Aristotle and the virtues 80
The concept of a practice 82
The narrative unity of a human life 86
The concept of a tradition 89
MacIntyre and liberalism 92

3 Taylor: the sources of the liberal self 101

The status of moral intuitions 102
The self in moral space 105
Selves and self-interpretations 107
The self and the community 110
Orientation and narration 112
Hypergoods and practical reasoning 114
The priority of right 118
Taylor and the communitarian critique of Rawls 120

4 Walzer: justice and abstraction 127

Rawls's methodological abstraction 129
Against methodological abstraction: the conceptual
  argument 132
Against methodological abstraction: the democratic
  argument 134
The relativity of social meanings 139
Complex equality 146
The desirability of complex equality 151
Walzer contra Rawls 154

Concluding summary   157

Family resemblances: the criticisms of liberalism   157
Family resemblances: the communitarianism of the critics   160

PART II   RAWLS'S RESPONSE   165

5 *Rawls's political liberalism*   167

Justice as fairness as political   170
   Society as a fair system of cooperation between
      free and equal citizens   173
Why political?   181
   Eliminating two reasons: not scepticism or pragmatism   183
   Public justifiability and political values   189
Rawls the communitarian   198
   Non-political community and identity   199
   Political liberalism as communitarianism   201

6 *Political liberalism: for and against*   206

Respecting the limits of the political   206
Defending the limits of the political   220

PART III
LIBERALISM, POLITICS
AND PERFECTION   227

INTRODUCTION   229

7 *Rorty: liberalism without foundations*   232

Foundational theories of the person   235
Alien vocabularies   237
Concepts, truth and reality   239
Communitarianism and correspondence   242
Metaphysics and politics   244

8 *Raz: the politics of perfection*   249

Raz's perfectionist autonomy   252
    Ideals qua valid not qua beliefs: perfectionism
        against scepticism   255
    Not coercive imposition   260
    Autonomy and value pluralism   264
Autonomy, social forms and state perfectionism   267
    Well-being depends on social forms   267
    Social forms require perfectionist political action   272
    Autonomy only conditionally valuable   281
Raz and communitarianism   282

CONCLUSION   289

Bibliography   295
Index   298

Preface

It is our aim in this book to provide an introduction to a set of debates in political theory that have come to be grouped together under the label of the communitarian critique of liberalism. These debates became central to the discipline during the 1980s and continue, in one way or another, to inform a great deal of contemporary theory. By now, however, the dust is beginning to settle, and we feel that the time is right for a survey of the battleground intended to render it more accessible to the uninitiated, whether undergraduate or graduate.

The contents pages convey the shape of the book. After a first chapter outlining what we regard as the paradigm statement of contemporary liberal theory, the theory of justice as fairness articulated by John Rawls in his book *A Theory of Justice* (*TJ*), and establishing an agenda of issues to recur throughout the book, we present, in turn, the ideas of four thinkers generally regarded as communitarian critics of liberalism: Michael Sandel, Alasdair MacIntyre, Charles Taylor and Michael Walzer. Having identified the themes that these theorists have in common, the ways in which they differ, and their relation to the agenda already established, we go on to examine Rawls's more recent restatements of his position, what is commonly called 'the new Rawls'. Arguing that, on some readings at least, the new Rawls can be understood as attempting to formulate a liberal position that is sensitive to aspects of the communitarian critique, we then turn to two other theorists who can also be read as communitarian liberals, Richard Rorty and Joseph Raz, before concluding.

Such an account of what is to come, however, begs a number of questions that need to be dealt with, or at least acknowledged, at this early stage. Given our theme it would seem important to start by identifying what liberalism and communitarianism are. Unfortunately this is not as easy as it sounds for, as we shall see, there is a great deal of disagreement about what exactly one has to believe in order to qualify either as a liberal or as a communitarian. While it may be possible to recognize as constitutive of liberalism a commitment to a vague and general value such as the freedom or autonomy of the individual, and to relate this to the substantive political concern that individuals should have freedom of conscience, of expression and of association, this does not really get us very far. Similarly, our preliminary characterization of the communitarian critique as one that questions the liberal understanding of the relation between the individual and her society or community, and argues that the emphasis on individual freedom and rights that follows from that understanding is misplaced, leaves a deal of room for further specification. In both cases it is hard to be more precise without begging questions that can only properly arise later, and by the end of this book we shall of course have filled out these characterizations in much greater detail.

The problem is that both 'liberalism' and 'communitarianism' mean different things to different people. Even in the language of everyday politics the term 'liberal' means different things in the United States and in the United Kingdom, and it may be that our deliberately loose formulation in terms of individual freedom or autonomy already fails to capture that connotation particularly apparent in the North American usage which associates liberalism with support for a fairly generous redistributive welfare state. The point here is that in ordinary usage the term 'liberalism' tends to refer to a *package* of beliefs or policies which can be analytically separated from one another, and, as we shall see shortly below, our initial characterization undoubtedly reflects the fact that the communitarian critique, and hence this book, is primarily concerned with some of these and not others. As might be expected, things are even more complicated at the level of self-consciously theoretical debate, for here we find that, even with respect to those liberal beliefs or policies to which we do devote our attention, different liberals endorse them for different reasons. Thus one theorist's reasons for his belief in the right to freedom of expression may be quite different from another's, or two theorists both regarding themselves as liberals may have quite different conceptions of, for example, something apparently so central as autonomy or the proper relation between the state and the individual. This point is particularly important because a standard move by liberals in the face of the communitarian critique has been to deny that they assert, or need to assert, what it is that communitarians deny. Communitarians are thus accused of attributing to liberals, and then attacking, claims that liberals do not in fact make and which are not required for their conclusions. If this is right, if liberals do not commit the theoretical sins with which communitarians charge them, then this would seem to raise the possibility of a liberalism which does not conflict with, and perhaps can even take on board, the arguments which communitarians have to offer.

Not that 'communitarianism' is any more straightforward. If anything the reverse is true, and here it may be helpful to think in terms of two distinct but related issues. The first concerns the extent to which it makes sense to talk about *the* communitarian critique at all. The label 'communitarian', although often used to characterize the four theorists whose ideas we examine in the second part of this book, is not one which they themselves employ to any great extent, and it is certainly not part of their self-understanding in the same way as the term 'liberal' is for liberals. As we shall see, the four theorists whose ideas we discuss address apparently different issues and certainly disagree in their substantive political conclusions. So one of the aims of our examination of their ideas is precisely to see exactly what, if anything, they share that would justify their being grouped together under a common label.

The second concerns the question of how we are to distinguish the communitarian critique of liberalism from the various other critiques that may be found in political-theoretical debate. For we should be clear that we focus quite specifically on this particular strand of criticism, all but ignoring the challenge to liberalism from conservatism, from Marxism, from feminism and from libertarianism.[1] Given this, it would seem important that we should be able clearly to identify the differences between the communitarian and these other critiques, but here again things are very complex. For example, we ourselves raise the issue of whether communitarianism is necessarily conservative in its implications, and, despite the claim of one communitarian that his position leads to demands for quite radical social and political change, there are clear affinities between these two strands of thought. Similarly, the etymological links between 'communitarianism' and 'communism' should suggest ways in which our area of concern might overlap with the Marxist critique of liberalism. Even more confusingly, it may be that what communitarians dislike about liberalism is something that liberalism shares with libertarianism. Indeed in many ways it makes sense to regard libertarianism as a strand of liberalism rather than its outright rejection.

This last point is worthy of attention at this preliminary stage, for one way of explaining how we understand the communitarian critique of liberalism is precisely to contrast it with the libertarian critique forcefully presented by Robert Nozick in his *Anarchy, State and Utopia* (1974). Such a contrast will also enable us to identify more clearly that particular aspect of liberalism that shall be our especial concern. We have said that we regard Rawls's theory of justice as fairness as the paradigmatic statement of contemporary liberalism and, while there are various defences of that claim that we might offer, the most immediately relevant is that which observes that Rawls's theory contains both of the two components which standardly go together as the liberal package: the commitment to the freedom of the individual embodied in the standard liberal support for civil liberties, and that belief in equality of opportunity and a more egalitarian distribution of resources than would result from the market alone which leads to support for a redistributive welfare state. The simple (and simplifying) point that we wish to make here is that the libertarian and the communitarian critiques focus on the different components of this package.

The essence of Nozick's objection to Rawls's theory is that its redistributive aspects involve a violation of the individual's rights to property and to self-ownership. In Nozick's view, Rawls, and all who support a redistributive welfare state, fails to take the individual seriously enough, since he is prepared to envisage a taxation system, analogous to forced labour, that involves using the talents that belong to some individuals as means to the ends of those other individuals who lack them. Nozick's libertarianism, then, involves a demand for more respect for individual liberty than Rawls acknowledges, and presents itself primarily as a rejection of those distributive and quasi-egalitarian aspects of Rawls's theory that correspond to the welfare state component of the liberal package. In contrast to this, the communitarian critique queries that priority accorded to the individual over the community upon which Nozick insists, and presents itself primarily as a rejection of the liberal emphasis on the freedom of the individual that corresponds to the civil liberties' component of the package. In a sense, then, the libertarian and the communitarian critiques are at once coming from different directions and concerned with different implications of contemporary liberal theory. Very crudely, for libertarians the distributive aspect of Rawls's theory shows that he does not take individuals and their freedoms seriously enough, while for communitarians the importance he gives to individual liberties reveals a mistaken prioritization of individuals over their communities.

Such a schematic opposition, though useful for introductory purposes, requires immediate qualification. First, as has already been suggested, in many ways Nozick's libertarianism is best understood as a version of liberalism rather than a rejection of it. Indeed, insofar as the essence of that classical liberalism of which Locke is the best-known example is a claim about self-ownership, then it may plausibly be argued that Nozick is the true liberal, Rawls the revisionist. This would fit well with that reading of the communitarian critique that sees it as equally cogent, if not more so, when aimed at Nozick's libertarianism as at Rawls's liberalism. Second, we should be clear that the distributive aspects of Rawls's liberalism can also be put in terms of a claim about the relation between the individual and the community. But here Rawls, in taking people's talents to be in some sense common property, is the communitarian. Thus it may be that Rawls can best be understood as communitarian on distributional questions but liberal on questions concerning the freedom of the individual in relation to his or her community.

Usually, however, as we shall see, the communitarian critique has concerned itself rather with these freedom-related aspects of liberalism than with its equality-related or distributive aspects. In terms of substantive political issues, what this means is that where the debate between redistributive liberals and libertarians centres on the justifiability of the welfare state and the taxation required to pay for it, that between the liberal and the communitarian concerns itself rather with the importance of the individual's right to choose her own way of life and to express herself freely, even where this conflicts with the values and commitments of the community or

society of which she is a member. It is this latter debate which is
our concern in this book.

Two concluding prefatory points both arise out of the discussion
above. First, mention of Locke and 'classical' liberalism raises the
question of the relations between contemporary liberalism and
communitarianism and the intellectual traditions from which they
emanate. When we think of the liberal tradition we think of such
theorists as Locke, Kant and Mill, each of whom made a distinct
contribution to the heritage of modern liberalism. On the communitarian side our minds may perhaps turn to Aristotle, to Hegel,
and even to Gramsci, although here, as the very heterogeneity of
the list suggests, there is less of a self-conscious tradition, a point
that corresponds to our earlier observation about how our four
communitarians have tended not to define themselves as such.
Nonetheless, there is no doubt that each of the theorists whose
ideas we consider in this book owes a great deal to figures such as
these, and it is very interesting to see the way in which the different
theories that they come up with reflect the various strands of thought
available to them from the traditions which they are continuing.
Interesting, but not our concern in this book. While occasionally we
shall make reference to such seminal thinkers, usually where the
present-day theorists make much of the connection or where it is
helpful for exegetical purposes, we shall not give much time and
space to the intellectual-historical task of tracing the links. The
arguments that our liberals and communitarians have to offer will
be primarily assessed in their own terms and without very much
reference to those who might very properly be regarded as their
progenitors.[2]

We do not, however, and this is our second and final point, go
so far down the analytical route that we consider the various ideas
and arguments that we discuss altogether without reference to the
wider systems of thought of which they form a part. What this
means is that, rather than directly organizing our discussion around
particular issues and themes, we adopt, as our title itself indicates,
an author-based approach. The basic reason for this has already
been given: the importance of identifying the different kinds of
argument put forward by different theorists tells strongly in favour
of an expository strategy which allows such differences to stand
out. But there are other reasons too. First, it may be useful for
students, who necessarily approach primary material in the author-

based form in which it is written, to be able to go directly from a particular contribution to the debate to our attempt to identify, and present in accessible form, its key points. Second, we believe that the best way to understand what the various theorists are saying is to consider their positions as a whole. The attempt to isolate and address specific propositions in a theory without reference to their context can be misleading, if only because one may be neglecting the theoretical background necessary if one is to appreciate the reason for asserting, and thus a large part of the meaning of, the propositions in the first place. It may of course turn out that the propositions are false or unhelpful but at least one will have understood why the theorist was led to assert them, and they are thus far less likely to look absurd.

As this last observation suggests, this author-based approach to exegesis is intended only as a first step towards understanding, and it by no means precludes the possibility of stepping outside a thinker's presentation of his own arguments so as to be able to compare and contrast them with those of others. Clearly, our aim of identifying the differences between different theories involves just such a process of comparison, and this requires us to develop a theme- or issue-based approach to complement our primary mode of presentation. Indeed, as we have said, in our first chapter we seek precisely to formulate an agenda or map of issues to which we shall make frequent subsequent reference. In a sense, then, we seek to combine the exegetical advantages of an author-based approach with the analytical clarity to be had from an issue-oriented presentation. That we are able to do this is partly due to our decision to restrict our attention in the way already indicated. By concentrating exclusively on the communitarian critique of liberalism we are able to do that critique justice, to give ourselves the opportunity of a proper and careful examination of communitarian and liberal ideas that is not possible for those who seek in a single book to compass a greater variety of themes.

Notes

1 As good places to start on these critiques we suggest the following: Scruton, *The Meaning of Conservatism*, Buchanan, *Marx and Justice*, Jaggar,

Feminist Politics and Human Nature, and Nozick, *Anarchy, State and Utopia*, the last of which we discuss very briefly below.

2 In the case of liberalism, two books that attempt this intellectual-historical task alongside their own analytical discussions are, sketchily, Gray, *Liberalism*, and, at rather greater length, Arblaster, *The Rise and Decline of Western Liberalism*. For communitarianism, Stephen Holmes's article 'The Permanent Structure of Antiliberal Thought' polemically discusses aspects of what he (somewhat controversially) regards as the ancestry of anti-liberalism.

Acknowledgements

We first indulged our interest in these issues in two classes held in Balliol College, Oxford, in the springs of 1990 and 1991. Andrew Williams was the third member of the teaching team, and we owe him a great deal of thanks for his efforts in helping us to appreciate – in those classes, in private discussions, and in helpful written comments – the complexity of many of the issues we discuss, we hope in not too simplistic a manner, in this book. The chapters on the new Rawls and Raz in particular have benefited from his untiring assistance. We are grateful also to those students whose contributions and questions in those classes forced us to get our thoughts straighter than they would otherwise be. Joseph Raz managed to combine personal and moral concerns by reading a draft of the chapter devoted to his work and indicating passages where it might be improved, and Will Kymlicka's constructive suggestions were also much appreciated. And we owe a great debt of thanks to Deborah McGovern, the Fellows' Secretary at All Souls, for her cheerful and efficient help in the preparation of the manuscript: there were no technical difficulties she could not resolve, and no deadlines she could not meet.

We are pleased to have the opportunity to acknowledge also the support of a number of institutions. Stephen Mulhall is grateful to All Souls for the luxury of a Prize Research Fellowship, and Adam Swift to the Kennedy Memorial Trust, the Economic and Social Research Council, Nuffield College, and Balliol College, each of whom kept him for a period while he worked on matters discussed in these pages.

While it is impossible clearly to identify the individual origins and authorship of particular chapters, especially in the context of a collaboration that goes back, in one form or another, to our arrival at Balliol as undergraduates in October 1980, this is a book about a debate, and the reader will not go too far wrong if she takes Stephen Mulhall to be the communitarian and Adam Swift to be the liberal in the argument. That we claim to detect a synthetic resolution of the conflict perhaps reflects the fact that each cannot believe the other completely misguided.

One co-author dedicates this book to Danny Swift, who was born halfway through chapter 5, and to Lucy Butterwick, who makes all the difference; for the other, that difference is made by Alison Baker, to whom the book is also dedicated.

The authors and publisher wish to thank the following for permission to quote from material in copyright: Joseph Raz and Oxford University Press for extracts from J. Raz, *The Morality of Freedom* (1986); Basic Books for extracts from M. Walzer, *Spheres of Justice* (1983); and Harvard University Press for extracts from J. Rawls, *A Theory of Justice* (1971).

Abbreviations

AV   A. MacIntyre, *After Virtue*
MF   J. Raz, *The Morality of Freedom*
SJ   M. Walzer, *Spheres of Justice*
SS   C. Taylor, *Sources of the Self*
TJ   J. Rawls, *A Theory of Justice*

INTRODUCTION:
Rawls's original position

We emphasized in the preface that there are different kinds of both liberalism and communitarianism, and it follows from this that any particular liberal thinker with whose theory we might begin must be regarded as no more than a starting-point. This is especially true because we seek in this chapter only to identify some of the key themes and issues that we can think of as forming an agenda for the rest of the book. Since, however, we must begin somewhere, John Rawls's theory of justice as fairness is the obvious choice. The commonplace observation that the publication of Rawls's *A Theory of Justice* was the single most important stimulus to the renaissance of political theory during the 1970s and 1980s is not our particular concern, although the extent to which his theory established the terrain upon which subsequent political-theoretical battles were to be fought is clearly to the point. Both communitarian critics and defenders of versions of liberalism other than that offered by Rawls have formulated their positions in terms that make explicit reference to his theory, so that in many ways Rawls simply *did* define the agenda and continues to do so. It thus makes a lot of sense for us to begin with a basic exposition of his theory.

That our exposition be basic is demanded not only by the introductory role in which we are casting it but also by the fact that the theory of justice as fairness is subject to different interpretations. Most significantly, Rawls himself has published a series of articles subsequent to the appearance of *A Theory of Justice* that seem to change the way in which he would have us understand his position, although, as we shall see in our chapter on the new Rawls, opinions differ as to the extent of the change involved. The point relevant here is that since we do not wish to address the difficult issues raised by this variety of interpretations until later on, we must, if we are to avoid begging questions, present the theory in its barest outline, giving only that level of detail that is required for us to be able to relate it to the agenda of themes that it is our primary purpose to present. Doubtless our presentation will be both selective and simplistic, and the reader already familiar with the variety of theoretical issues at stake will be uncomfortable at our glossing over difficult matters of interpretation. We can only remind the reader of our intended audience and hope that our awareness of the complexities around is apparent by the end of the book.

It is equally important that we present the theory in a way that will allow us to understand what it was about it that communitarians regarded as problematic. This is because we believe that the changes in interpretation that Rawls's more recent writings seem to suggest can best be understood as responses precisely to the sorts of criticism that communitarians brought against the theory as originally formulated. Whether one regards these later articles as constituting significant alterations of position or as little more than restatements of the original theory with slight shifts of emphasis, in either case it makes sense to see these subsequent additions as motivated by Rawls's desire to acknowledge the validity of at least some of the points that communitarians were making. As well as providing another very good reason to start with Rawls, this belief necessarily affects the way that we present his theory. Even if we were to decide in the end, along with his most sympathetic interpreters, that the communitarians simply mistook their target – that Rawls's restatements do render the theory immune from communitarian criticism and do not constitute a significant shift in position from that which he offered originally – still we should want to see what it was that communitarians took him to be saying, for this would be the best way of understanding both their arguments and his responses. Our exposition of justice as fairness, then, aims on the one hand to be minimal, so as not to beg questions of interpreta-tion, and, on the other, to bring out those aspects of the theory that communitarians read as objectionable. Regarding *A Theory of Justice* as an agenda-setter, we leave open for the present the questions both of whether Rawls was indeed arguing what it was to which they objected and whether, if he was, their objections were cogent.

The chapter consists of two sections. In the first we present an elementary exposition of the theory of justice as fairness, and in the second we draw out from this exposition a list of those themes or issues on which communitarian attention has focused and to which we shall make frequent reference in the course of our subsequent discussion. We expect our readers already to be familiar with Rawls's theory to some extent, and accordingly do not regard ourselves as required to give an account of it that could serve as a useful introduction for those to whom it is completely new. Those who are in this position should probably begin elsewhere, either to Rawls's own presentation in *A Theory of Justice* or to a secondary source that gives a more systematic exegesis than is provided here.[1] We aim only to remind readers of the bare outline of the theory so as to be able quickly to turn to the agenda which is our central concern.

The basics of justice as fairness

The twin ideas at the heart of justice as fairness are that of the original position and the veil of ignorance. For Rawls, the way to think about what would be a just or fair organization of society is to imagine what principles would be agreed to by people who were denied knowledge of certain particular facts about themselves. Principles of justice, which are 'to govern the assignment of rights and duties and to regulate the distribution of social and economic advantages' (*TJ*, p. 61), should be understood as what would emerge as a hypothetical contract or agreement that would be arrived at by people ignorant of particular aspects of their own beliefs and circumstances. The intuition being captured here is that which links fairness to ignorance. If I don't know which of the five pieces of cake that I am cutting I am going to end up with, then it makes sense for me to cut the pieces fairly. Similarly, if people don't know who they are going to be, then it will make sense for them to choose fair or just principles to regulate their society.

Since the content of the principles of justice that emerge is clearly a function of the characterization of the original position, it makes sense for our attention to focus initially on that characterization.

And here our vague attempt to identify the essence of the theory in terms of the cake-cutting analogy only of course immediately raises two crucial and related questions. First, what exactly is it of which people are ignorant in the original position? What information, that is, does the veil exclude? Second, why should we consider it appropriate to regard them as ignorant in such ways for the purposes of thinking about justice? What substantive theoretical claims about justice does the veil of ignorance embody? The answer to this more foundational second question is that the original position aims to model the sense in which it is appropriate, when thinking about justice, that people should be regarded as free and equal. Since this can most easily be understood in more concrete terms, let us immediately tie this in with the answer to the first question by noting that, in very crude terms, there are two kinds of thing, roughly corresponding to freedom and equality, that the people in the original position do not know about themselves. We indicated in our preface that we shall be more concerned with the freedom- than with the equality-related aspects of the theory, but it is nonetheless useful to say something about both of these now, and we shall begin with the equality-based strand in the theory.

In the first place, then, they do not know what position in society they will occupy, whether they will be at the top or the bottom of social ladder; nor do they know what their own talents or natural endowments will be. In real life, of course, people are born into particular families which are unequally placed in the distribution of advantage and, by a combination of natural and environmental factors, they have different abilities or disabilities which also lead to inequalities. The original position is intended to capture the idea that, when we think about justice, these differences are or should be irrelevant and that people should be regarded as equal. Now this has a great deal of intuitive appeal. There is a sense in which we think that, since people are not responsible for the fact that they were born into one family rather than another, or for the fact that they are talented or untalented, it should be the aim of a theory of justice to take no account of such differences. If I cannot be said to deserve my talents, how can I deserve the advantage that they can bring me? As Rawls puts it, the distribution of these attributes is 'arbitrary from a moral point of view' (*TJ*, p. 15).

In denying the people in the original position knowledge about their social location and their natural endowments, then, Rawls is trying to ensure that the principles to which they agree are not distorted by those chance inequalities that in the real world might be thought to bias distributive outcomes. One way of thinking about what happens in the original position is as a kind of bargaining process, in which each person, acting rationally in her own self-interest, seeks to get as good a deal as possible for herself. If, in that situation, people were allowed to know their own position in the distribution of these chance attributes, then the agreement reached would reflect the unequal bargaining power of the people involved and not justice or fairness. While this may well be what happens in real world negotiations, as between, say, employers and workers, the moral recognition that for the purposes of thinking about justice we are all equal despite our chance differences means that people in the original position should be denied knowledge of those inequalities likely to distort the outcome in favour of the lucky. Justice requires a bargain made under fair conditions, and this is why knowledge of inequalities is ruled out.

If their ignorance of circumstances is intended to capture the sense in which we are all equal, the people in the original position's ignorance of their own conceptions of the good is intended to model the sense in which, for the purposes of thinking about justice, it is appropriate to regard ourselves as free. What does it mean to say that they do not know their conception of the good? And how does this relate to an understanding of people as free?

To take the first question first, a person's conception of the good is her set of beliefs about how she should lead her life, about what makes her life worthwhile. Catholics have different conceptions of the good from atheists, those who devote all their leisure to the pursuit of excellence in, or perhaps just watching, a particular sport have a different conception of the good from those who prefer to spend their free time visiting art galleries. When we say that the people in Rawls's original position do not know their conceptions of the good, what this means is that they do not know what their beliefs are about how they should lead their lives. Considering this alongside the previous couple of paragraphs, we should be able to see how this will feed into the principles of justice that get chosen. Just as justice requires that no attention be paid to the different talents of different members of society, so, it would seem, it requires that no attention be paid to the particular conceptions of the good held by those members.

But, in contrast to the previous, here surely the argument seems rather mysterious. One way of thinking about the veil of ignorance is that it models the substantive moral claim that certain reasons should not be considered relevant to our thinking about justice. Now, as we argued above, it makes some intuitive sense to think that the social position into which a person happens to be born, or the talents or disabilities with which she happens naturally to be endowed, should be ruled out of such thinking. But in the case of conceptions of the good, things are more problematic. If one believes that some ways of life are better, worthier or more valuable, than others, why should one hold that it makes sense to ignore those beliefs when it comes to thinking about justice? The idea that we should arrange our society so that it be fair as between the talented and the untalented has a certain plausibility, but the idea that it should be organized so as to be fair as between someone who believes in the value of a life spent pursuing beauty and truth and someone who prefers alcohol, heavy metal rock music and counting blades of grass may seem less attractive. And in any case, we still have the question of what this has got to do with the point that it is their ignorance of conceptions of the good that constitutes the sense in which the original position models people as free.

The link between ignorance of conceptions of the good and freedom is as follows. Rather than being attributed particular conceptions of the good, and seeking to reach an agreement as favourable as possible to those particular conceptions, the people in the original position are taken to be motivated above all by an interest in protecting their capacity, as Rawls puts it, to 'frame, revise, and rationally to pursue' such conceptions. Of fundamental importance on the Rawlsian scheme are not the conceptions of the good that people have but something that lies behind such conceptions, their freedom to decide upon their own conceptions of the good, to act upon, and to change those decisions. In denying people in the original position knowledge of their beliefs about what makes a life worthy or valuable and attributing to them rather a 'highest-order interest' of this kind, Rawls is modelling the substantive moral claim that, when thinking about justice, what matters is people's freedom to make their own choices, and to change their minds, not whatever it is that they choose.

And the reason to exclude from our thinking about justice beliefs about which ways of life are better than others may now seem less bizarre than it did at first. If one thinks that what matters from the perspective of justice is not so much that people make good choices as that they are free to make their own choices, then the idea that the articulation of a conception of justice should ignore those reasons that lead us to hold some ways of life more valuable than others makes some sense. The connection between freedom, the value of our capacity to choose and change our minds about how we live our lives, and the exclusion of certain considerations about which ways of life are better than others, may still, perhaps, be less immediately intuitively appealing than the link between equality, chance, and the arbitrariness of talents that underlies the distributional aspect of Rawls's theory. The fact that someone occupies a particular social position is fairly straightforwardly not a good reason for them to support a way of arranging society that favours that position. But the fact that someone believes some ways of life to be more valuable than others may well seem a good reason for them to support a way of arranging society that favours those conceptions of the good. Indeed, a large part of this book will be devoted to thinkers who regard the exclusion of reasons of this second kind as deeply problematic (and one of them, Raz, is a liberal). But at least we now have a rough idea of the ground on which the debate will take place.

In Rawls's view, people in the original position, denied knowledge of their talents and endowments, motivated not by a particular conception of the good but by their interest in their capacity to frame, revise and rationally to pursue such conceptions, would agree that their society should be regulated by the following principles of justice. First:

> Each person is to have an equal right to the most extensive total system of equal basic liberties compatible with a similar system of liberty for all.

Second:

> Social and economic inequalities are to be arranged so that they are both (a) to the greatest benefit of the least advantaged, and (b) attached to offices and positions open to all under conditions of fair equality of opportunity. (*TJ*, p. 302)

They would agree, moreover, to a clear system of priorities among these principles: the first principle, that of equal basic liberties, has lexical priority over the second, which means that there can be no trade-offs between those liberties and the other forms of advantage that come under the second principle; and, within the second, (b) the principle of fair equality of opportunity has priority over (a) the part that says that inequalities must benefit the least advantaged, which latter is the difference principle.

It should be clear how these principles derive from the characterization of the original position. In terms of our previous simplifying distinction between the distributive or equality-related and the liberty-related aspects of the theory we can see how each of the principles concerns itself with a different aspect. The principle of equal basic liberties derives directly from the people in the original position's ignorance of, and concern to protect their freedom to choose, change and pursue their own conceptions of the good, while the second principle, and especially the difference principle, derives from their ignorance of their own likely position in the distribution of social and economic advantage. Given that ignorance, according to Rawls, it is rational for them to maximin, to ensure that the worst position is as good as it can be, and this leads them to support equality unless inequality will actually help that worst-off position. In fact, and this is one way of seeing how our distinction between the distributional and the liberty-related aspects of the theory is somewhat artificial, Rawls regards the liberties that are given priority in the first principle as among the goods (primary goods) that are to be distributed in accordance with the agreement reached in the original position, and their priority similarly follows from the application of maximin thinking. They are prior because the capacities that they protect are of such fundamental importance that the people in the original position will not envisage their being compromised for the sake of any of the other primary goods.

We have talked about the principles of justice being 'derived' from the original position, but the reader may suspect that this gives a rather misleading picture of the relation between these two components of the theory. The question of how to understand the original position and the nature of the agreement reached there is one that has occupied interpreters of Rawls for a long time, and our brief and selective account has attempted to steer clear of such matters as far as is possible. At various points our exegesis has suggested that one way of thinking about it is to see the principles of justice as what would be agreed to by individuals acting rationally in pursuit of their interests but ignorant of certain aspects of their situation. This strand, which relates the concept of justice to that branch of economic theory concerned with what it is rational for people to do in conditions of uncertainty, is clearly central in Rawls's own presentation, but it is obviously combined with a separate, more substantive strand, which is what leads to the original position being set up in the particular way that it is in the first place. Thus, even if it were rational for people characterized in a certain way to choose the principles of justice that Rawls says that they would choose, this would still leave the question of why we should characterize them in that way to begin with.

Clearly the original position embodies substantive normative claims. We recognized as much when we said that it is intended to model the sense in which it is appropriate to regard people as free and equal when thinking about justice. And since the principles that emerge as 'conclusions' are to some extent built into the very construction of the thought-experiment from which they are then 'derived' – it is hardly surprising, for example, that we end up with rights to equal basic liberties if the people making the agreement are attributed a highest-order interest in their capacity to choose, act on and change their minds about their own conceptions of the good – it is clear that we should see the weight of the theory as residing in that construction. The issues upon which critical attention has focused concern the substantive claims that are embodied in Rawls's characterization of the original position, and it is to an agenda of such issues that we now turn.

The agenda: claims modelled by the original position

There is a variety of questions that we might ask about the original position. We have already given a summary sketch of the sense in which the original position tries to model the idea that principles of justice should be understood as those which would be agreed to by people who are free and equal, and showed how this involves the claim that certain sorts of reasons are inappropriate when thinking about justice, but this leaves open a host of problems. In the rest of this introductory chapter we identify five themes upon which the debate between communitarians and liberals, and between different kinds of liberal, has focused. Because the aim here is to establish an agenda for the book as a whole, and because Rawls's position, however understood, by no means exhausts the theoretical resources available to liberalism, some of these issues are only indirectly raised by Rawls's theory, especially by that bare outline of his position which we have offered above. Nevertheless, while we aim here to introduce themes that go beyond both Rawls's own arguments and those that have been presented explicitly as objections to them, we hope to be able to show how the various issues relate to the idea of the original position, thereby justifying our claim that it was Rawls's theory that set the agenda for the debates that followed.

The conception of the person

A great deal of communitarian thought has presented itself in terms that make explicit reference to, and involve the explicit rejection of, the conception of the person that they regard as underlying liberal political theory. We shall see that Sandel and MacIntyre both formulate their objections to liberalism in these terms, and it is important to think about how these critiques might or might not relate to Rawls's original position. The general shape of the communitarian claim is that liberal political theory takes people to be distinct from their ends (or values, or conceptions of the good) in a way that simply fails to correspond to the way in which they actually do relate to those ends. For the communitarian, the liberal picture of the person as someone separate from her conception of the good ignores the extent to which people are constituted as the people that they are precisely by those conceptions themselves. Who, the communitarian asks, is the shadowy 'person' that exists independently of, and able freely to choose, the ends that give her life meaning and value?

Whatever we end up concluding about this issue – whether we decide that Rawls's theory does not actually involve such a conception of the person, or that even if it does other versions of liberalism need not, or that it does and, contrary to the communitarian critique, this can be justified – we should at least be able to see how the original position puts the question of conceptions of the person at the centre of political-theoretical debate. While one might seek to downplay the metaphor of the original position insofar as that seems to involve us in imagining an actual process of negotiation between people characterized in terms quite unlike how people really are, and without any of that particularity that might serve to differentiate them, it is clear, and Rawls does not seek to deny, that the theory is built around a conception of the person. We can emphasize that reading of the original position that sees it merely as a device of representation for the idea that certain reasons should be deemed irrelevant to questions of justice, but this still leaves us with the question of why those reasons should be ruled out, and the answer to this surely leaves a claim about what is important about, or in the interests of, people at the centre of the theory. Even if the oddly disembodied selves who populate the original position are not intended as metaphorical portrayals of our essence as people, they explicitly stand for the claim that, when it comes to thinking about justice, people should be regarded as distinct from their particularity, both their particular natural endowments and social position and their particular conceptions of the good, and, of especial importance to us, possessed of a highest-order interest in their capacity to frame, revise, and rationally pursue conceptions of the good. We can address not the particular dramatic model but the substantive claims that it represents and still be left with a debate that properly focuses on the issue of the conception of the person, where this involves claims about what is important about people, what is in their interests, what constitutes their well-being, and so on.

Given that the conception of the person embodied in the original position is indeed central to Rawls's theory, the issues that arise concern, in an intricately interconnected web, the validity or coherence, the scope and status, the source or origin, and the desirability of that conception. On the first, the question is whether we can sensibly think of ourselves as relating to our conceptions of the good in the way that Rawls seems to suppose. The identification of our highest-order interest seems to presuppose that we are indeed individuals capable freely of forming, and changing, our own views about how we should live our lives. It is this capacity that the rights that are prioritized in the first principle are there to protect. But is this true to our moral experience? Can we really step back from the particular values that we have and change them for new ones, or are we rather made the very people that we are by the values that we endorse, so that such detachment is impossible?

The second set of issues concerns the precise scope of the conception of the person. Is it intended to be a conception pertinent when thinking about all aspects of our moral lives or might we think of it as restricted in its scope of application? We have consistently talked about the characterization of the original position as attempting to represent the way in which it is appropriate to conceive people *when thinking about justice*, and, if we contrast this more limited understanding with a fuller or more comprehensive one which involved claims about people per se, we see that this is one way in which we might construe the conception as deliberately narrow, as appropriate to some issues, specifically those concerned with justice, and not others. Another concerns not the areas of moral and political theory in which the conception might be thought appropriate but the range of cultures to which it might be thought applicable. However we read the claim about people being conceived as free and equal, is it a claim that is supposed to hold across cultures? Do those who have a highest-order interest in their freedom to frame, revise and rationally pursue their own conceptions of the good have it even if they have never heard of it, do not think that they have it, and would not want it if it were explained to them? Or is its being their highest-order interest rather in some way conditional on the sort of culture in which they live?

Clearly these questions about the scope of the conception of the person tie in closely with those relating to its status. Is it a conception of the person that, whatever its scope of application, attempts to capture our metaphysical essence? Is it even to be regarded as 'true' in any sense, or is the point rather just that it is a way of thinking about themselves to which people can agree? These in turn are intimately connected to the issue of its source or origin. Where does this conception come from? By what route does it come to play such a central role in the theory? If it is a conception that enters Rawls's liberalism because he takes it to be valid or correct in its own terms then its source would seem to be some independent moral justification. But if, on the other hand, the point, for Rawls, is not so much that it is true as that people believe it, that it is something to which people can agree despite their other differences, then the conception of the person enters the theory not as a substantive moral claim about what is important about people (whether restricted in scope or not) but as an empirical sociological claim about the beliefs of the citizenry of certain societies.

The fifth and final set of issues raised by the conception of the person is rather different in kind, and in a sense rather more straightforward. If the previous four questions were methodological in nature, the fifth, the question of desirability, is substantive. Whatever our conclusions about its validity, scope, status and source, however we end up specifying the precise claims modelled by its representation in the original position, there will still remain the question of whether the conception of the person at the heart of Rawls's theory is desirable. Even if, suitably delimited and understood, it can be reckoned valid or coherent, this does not mean that we must regard it as attractive, as capturing aspects of our self-understandings that we would wish to see developed into a theory of justice that is to regulate the social and political structures in which we live. Perhaps, that is, Rawls's, and liberalism's, prioritization of individual freedom is coherent but undesirable, unwarrantedly emphasizing one aspect of moral life at the cost of neglecting others.

Some of these remarks may be obscure at this stage. Perhaps all of them are. Such obscurities are unavoidable in any attempt to introduce a wide range of difficult theoretical issues in reasonably concise fashion, and the reader should be assured that we return, at much greater length, to all of the points identified above. That, indeed, is the reason why we identify them here. Our hope is that, as we present communitarian criticisms and liberal responses, at least the reader will have a rough idea of what to look out for.

Asocial individualism

A second theme in the communitarian critique of liberalism concerns the claim that the latter misunderstands the relation between the individual and her society or community, and, more specifically, ignores the extent to which it is the societies in which people live that shape who they are and the values that they have. Obviously this strand of argument overlaps considerably with some of the points that we considered under the previous heading, for it can readily be put in terms that make it a complaint about Rawls's conception of the person, but the precise angle identified here is sufficiently distinct and important to warrant a separate introduction. The charge is not the general one that the original position misrepresents the way that people relate to their conceptions of the good, regarding ends as chosen by a self that is defined prior to such conceptions, but the more specific one that the contractual approach to political theory, of which it is a modern example, embodies the mistaken view that people's ends are formed independently of or prior to society, which is regarded as the outcome of negotiation between individuals whose ends are already given. For the communitarian, this conception overlooks the way in which it is the kind of society in which people live that affects their understandings both of themselves and of how they should lead their lives.

The idea that society, and particularly its political arrangements, can be understood as the outcome of a contract between individuals has been a major theme in the history of liberal thought, and Rawls's theory clearly continues this contract tradition in many important ways. It would be foolish to deny that liberalism regards the individual as of ultimate importance, and the way in which justice as fairness involves the idea of people agreeing to a contract certainly reflects this strand. Part of the point, for Rawls, of conceiving justice as the outcome of an agreement reached between individuals characterized as free and equal is that such a conception rules out the possibility that some people, even a large majority in a particular community, will use others as means to their ends. In contrast to utilitarianism, Rawls's theory aims to take seriously the separateness of persons, and this is one way of thinking about the kind of individualism that is captured by the original position. Whether, however, his version of the contract is vulnerable to the kinds of criticism that some other accounts have attracted must remain an open question. If it is the idea that individuals in a pre-social state of nature come together in pursuit of their individual interests to form society that is considered objectionable, then we may think that Rawls's theory, which has no obvious place for such an understanding, is straightforwardly immune to such criticism, and Nozick's attempt to derive the legitimacy of a minimal state from strongly individualistic premises may seem a more appropriate target.

The fact that Rawls's liberalism has a significant place for the idea of society as contract makes it important for us to distinguish between two points that the contractual metaphor encourages us to run together. While both are aspects of the communitarian charge that liberalism is guilty of an inappropriately asocial individualism, it will be helpful to be clear at this early stage that they are indeed different. On the one hand, then, there is the sociological-cum-philosophical point that people necessarily derive their self-understandings and conceptions of the good from the social matrix. Whether this is put as a quasi-empirical claim about socialization processes, or as a conceptual claim about the impossibility of language, thought, or moral life outside a social setting – and it is these philosophical themes that communitarian theorists have given particular attention – the emphasis here is on liberalism's neglect of the way in which the individual is parasitic on society for the very way that she thinks, including the way that she thinks of herself as an individual. With this first point, the communitarian is insisting on recognition of the necessarily social or communal *origins* of the individual's self-understanding and conception of how she should lead her life, and it is a point that applies to *any* such understanding and conception.

The second strand of communitarian criticism that arises under this heading of asocial individualism is quite separate and concerns not the *source* of people's conceptions of themselves and of what makes their life worthwhile, but the particular kinds of *content* which, on the communitarian account, liberalism ignores and encourages. In contrast to the philosophical-cum-sociological point, the quite general applicability of which indicates that it is essentially methodological, this second point is straightforwardly substantive: the charge here is that liberalism builds upon, fosters, and promotes a particular understanding of the individual's relation to her community, and in so doing neglects, undermines, and even rules out, alternative ways of thinking about that relation. According to this communitarian objection, the liberal sees society as nothing more than a cooperative venture for the pursuit of individual advantage, as an essentially private association formed by individuals whose essential interests are defined independently of, and in a sense prior to, the community of which they are members. Conceptions of the good that are more strongly communal in content, that have as part of their very nature an insistence that social bonds are valuable in themselves, over and above their value as means to the attainment of other, merely individual, goods, are thereby downgraded. It is here, as we shall see in our discussion of Sandel, that it becomes impossible to separate the question of asocial individualism from that of liberalism's conception of the person, for one way of putting this communitarian point is to talk about the liberal's neglect of constitutive attachments, of the sense in which the individual may understand her own identity and interests to be constituted by her relations with others in ways that relate her more closely to the communities of which she is a member than this merely associational model can allow.

That the communities of which people are members are indeed plural is an important point, if only because it raises the possibility that different ways of conceiving the relation between those communities and the individuals who compose them may be appropriate in different cases, and it may be that the liberal can respond by asserting the significance of these differences. As members of families, for example, or of religious faiths, we may well have conceptions of the good that are indeed strongly communal in content; we may believe that what makes a life valuable or worthwhile is that it be lived in and for community with others in a way that precludes an understanding of that community as a mere scheme of cooperation. But perhaps the liberal can acknowledge this, and grant the propriety of such conceptions, whilst at the same time insisting that this is not a legitimate or proper way to understand political community. While there are substantive conceptions of human flourishing that regard the good life for human beings as that devoted to participation in political life, so that the content of individual well-being is inherently communal – and communal at the level of political society – the liberal may defend her individualism at least to the extent of denying that it is appropriate to conceive the relation between the individual and the state in this way.

These last remarks will make more sense when the reader has reached the end of the second part of the book, but the distinction between the two strands of the charge of asocial individualism should at least be clear. It is easy to see why these two points will tend to be run together, for the understanding of society as the outcome of a contract or a process of negotiation between people concerned to protect and promote their individual interests seems to presuppose that those interests are themselves pre-social, given to the individual prior to her membership of society. Indeed, it may seem that the two stand or fall together, that recognition that we derive our self-understandings and our goals from the social matrix precludes any understanding of society as a mere association. We cannot pursue the matter here, but it is worth holding onto our initial suggestion that the two points are actually quite different in kind, for this may lead one to regard this move as too quick. While we may wish to reject any form of liberalism that takes the state of nature or contract picture of society seriously as a historical account, or even as a model of the relation of priority between the individual and society, it is not clear that this is fatal to *any* contractual component to liberal theory. The liberal, perhaps, can accept the sociological-cum-philosophical point that her ends and self-understandings are derived by the individual from the social matrix but argue that their content is such as to make certain aspects of the contractual approach appropriate when thinking about justice.

It is in any case by no means clear that the liberal emphasis on the importance of individual freedoms neglects the significance of the social matrix which communitarians stress. While it is true that one way of getting to the importance of individual liberties might be by taking people's ends as fixed or given prior to society, so that people can be thought of as agreeing to cooperate in society only if they can continue to live their own lives without interference from others, this is not the only way. Indeed, it might be thought that if people's ends were fixed pre-socially, there would be no reason to care about guaranteeing them the social conditions necessary for them to be able to change their minds.[2] Some theorists argue for the standard individual rights and freedoms precisely because they recognize the importance of the kind of society in which they live to the capacities that people develop and the choices that they make. Rather than grounding those rights in the pre-social individual, they defend them by pointing to the value of a community that permits individuals to question not only the conceptions of the good that are dominant but also their own previous commitments. A liberal society is justified precisely because it fosters certain capacities, and perhaps even certain choices.

Recognition of the extent to which it is the kind of society in which we live that shapes our self-understandings, our capacities, and our conceptions of the good, would only be a problem for the liberal if it could be argued that a society with a liberal framework, such as one governed by Rawls's principles of justice, in some way undermined either those very capacities and self-understandings upon which liberals place so much importance or the value of the ways of life which are available to be chosen. In the first case, the claim would be that liberal theory is in some sense incoherent, since liberal conclusions guaranteeing the freedom of the individual would be said to lead to a society which did not foster the capacities and self-understandings that liberals take to be of such value and that themselves generate those conclusions. In the second, the claim would be rather that the capacity to make one's own choices is only as valuable as the choices that one can make, and that a liberal framework leads to a society in which valuable options, or at least some of them, are likely to wither away. While the second is less immediately problematic, since, as we shall see, the liberal does not have to agree that it is appropriate to worry about the value of the choices available to those choosing them, both lines of argument might be thought to tell against liberalism's apparent disattention to the social conditions necessary for the sustenance of those individual-level features in which it *is* interested. Of course, the onus is very much on the critic of liberalism to indicate the precise ways in which the liberal framework does undermine itself or lead to unpalatable consequences. It is hard *prima facie* to see how the guarantee of individual freedoms could lead to the withering away of individual capacities or valuable ways of life (indeed in the pre-vious paragraph we suggested that the liberal might argue exactly the opposite), but we shall see that some do seek to argue something like this.

For now, our aim is just to point out why liberalism's emphasis on the individual might be thought to involve a neglect of the extent to which it is the society she lives in that makes her the individual that she is and makes available to her the kinds of life that she might live. While the contractual metaphor can lead us to confuse the two, we have made explicit the distinction between a claim about the *origins* of people's self-understandings and conceptions of the good (with the communitarian insisting on the extent to which these are necessarily derived from the social matrix) and a claim about its *content* (where the communitarian charge is that the liberal neglects or discriminates against those that are strongly communal in nature). In terms of Rawls's theory, both of these might seem to be suggested by the idea that principles of justice are understood as what would be contracted to by mutually disinterested individuals motivated to protect and promote their own interests, though we have suggested that to emphasize this aspect of theory may be to read Rawls as closer to the state of nature strand in the liberal tradition than a careful reading of his argument, and the role of the original position in it, would justify.

Universalism

The third theme we identify here is one that has already been mentioned under our heading of the conception of the person, and it is clearly closely interrelated with questions to do with the source, status, and scope of that conception. The specific issue here concerns whether liberalism claims that its conclusions apply universally and cross-culturally, or whether it might rather have room for the idea that different ways of organizing society are appropriate, and morally justified, in different sorts of culture, so that a liberal political framework is only argued for in societies of a certain kind. A significant strand of communitarian thinking has been directed at liberalism's alleged failure to attend to cultural particularity, to the ways in which different cultures embody different values and different social forms and institutions, and to the consequences that these differences might have for political theory.

It should be easy to see why Rawls's theory might be thought to involve pretensions to universality. We have already stressed the sense in which the original position involves abstraction from particularity, for the people behind the veil of ignorance are denied knowledge not only of their own social position but also of what their society is like and of their own particular beliefs about how they should lead their lives. There is a clear attempt to identify the respects in which we are all the same underneath, to characterize people in a way that detaches them from what it is that makes actual people different from each other, so it is not at all surprising that Rawls has been taken to neglect the variety, and the moral importance, of the different cultures in which people live and in whose terms they conceive themselves and the meaning of their lives. The emphasis on rationality in the original presentation of the theory suggests that Rawls is seeking to identify some conception of the rational essence of human beings, and his description of the original position as representing an 'Archimedean point' (*TJ*, pp. 260, 584) supports the suspicion that we are being offered a theory that is meant to apply cross-culturally. Certainly communitarian critics, and most obviously Walzer, who insists that an appreciation of cultural particularity is central to a proper understanding of how a community should arrange itself politically, have taken Rawls to be claiming, and have objected to, pretensions to universality.

If, as we have argued, the original position embodies claims about people's highest-order interests, then the question is really how universal those interests are taken to be. Do all people, whatever their cultural background and self-understandings, have an interest in their capacity to make their own choices about how they lead their lives, or is this an interest only of those living in certain sorts of society? If the latter, does that mean that liberalism is not the answer for those societies that do not have the appropriate institutions and practices already in place? Clearly difficult issues of moral and cultural relativism are raised by such questions, with communitarians, because of their emphasis on the senses in which it is the community and its traditions and practices that should be regarded as the locus of moral value, tending to be more relativistic than liberals. A major strand in the liberal tradition since the Enlightenment has been the idea that social arrangements and conventions should be subjected to rational and critical examination, not simply conformed to and respected, and contemporary liberals have tended very much to pursue this line.

It is especially interesting, therefore, to note that in his more recent writings Rawls himself seems to be denying that his theory makes any universalistic claims. We shall explore the various different ways of understanding the new Rawls in a later chapter, but on any interpretation it is clear that he is now endorsing a brand of cultural particularism of his own. If the conception of the person, and the identification of people's interests that it stands for, at the heart of Rawls's theory is taken itself to be a culture-specific understanding, and to derive its place in the theory because of its status as such, then it would seem that the liberal theory of justice as fairness that results is similarly culture-specific. To anticipate points that will be spelled out more fully later, we have said that it is the abstraction in Rawls's theory that seems to involve it in claims to universality and a neglect of cultural context, but it may be useful to distinguish between two senses in which that concept might be applied. On the one hand there is abstraction from people's particular social positions and particular conceptions of the good, and this Rawls's theory certainly does involve. But this does not necessarily imply a second kind of abstraction, that which separates people from their particular cultural traditions or social practices. It may be not only that Rawls's theory does not involve this second kind of abstraction, but also that this is precisely the reason why it does involve the first kind.

If it is our particular cultural understandings that identify people's highest-order interests in a way that requires us to abstract from their particular conceptions of the good, then Rawls's liberalism can hardly be accused of disattending to cultural particularity.

Some liberals do not like what they would characterize as this retreat from universalism, and they seek to argue that liberalism's claims about the importance of people's interests do indeed capture something which is true of all people, whatever their cultural self-understandings and values. There thus occurs the slightly strange situation whereby other theorists seek to defend Rawls's theory in versions apparently stronger than those to which he himself is happy to subscribe. What matters at this stage is just that we should be prepared for this question of liberalism's pretensions to universality to come up at various places later on in the book.

Subjectivism or objectivism

If the original position and the conception of the person represented there models the claim that people's highest-order interest is in their capacity to frame, revise and rationally pursue their own conception of the good, attention must at some point turn to the theoretical assumptions that underlie that claim. What other sorts of beliefs about moral values must one hold in order to think that this is what is particularly important about people? More specifically, does their emphasis on the individual's choosing her own way of life mean that liberals must believe that such choices are arbitrary expressions of preference, that value is in the eye of the beholder, that moral judgements are completely subjective? Or is it possible, and perhaps even more coherent, to prioritize the individual's freedom to make her own choices while at the same time maintaining that some choices are very definitely better than others and that reason can help people discriminate between worthy and unworthy ways of life? Can one, that is, be a liberal and believe that judgements about value are objective? This is the fourth theme in the debate between liberalism and communitarianism that will recur in the rest of this book.

The reasons why one might take liberalism and moral subjectivism or scepticism to go together are reasonably straightforward. If no way of living is better than any other, if people's choices are simply expressions of preference, with no rational grounds available to justify claims about their value, like choices between flavours of ice cream, then it would seem crazy for the state to do anything other then let people make their own choices. In the absence of any right answers, or even rational criteria for thinking about how to come to right answers, about how people should lead their lives, the state would seem to have no justification for encouraging some ways of life and not others. If a life devoted to the pursuit of beauty and truth is no better than one spent playing video games, then it seems that we would be committed to a political framework that leaves people free to make an unbiased choice between the two.

We believe that a lot of people's commonsense intuitions supportive of liberalism derive from a vague sceptical belief that one choice is as good as any other, or more likely, and in effect just a variant on the sceptical theme, that even if some are better than others we cannot know which are which. The fact that people disagree in their conceptions of the good, in their views about what makes a life worthy or valuable, and are unable to provide each other with conclusive arguments for their own point of view, is often taken as evidence for the claim that there is no rational way of judging who is right, and the inference drawn is that people should make up their own minds. The reason to stress this pervasiveness of moral subjectivism at the level of commonsense intuitions relates to our earlier observation that communitarian critics of liberalism do not necessarily regard academic political theorists as their primary targets. Sometimes, and we are thinking here particularly of MacIntyre's worries about emotivism, their focus is rather on aspects of contemporary liberal culture more generally understood, with political theorists invoked merely as specific symptomatic illustrations of the more general disease afflicting that culture. This is important because, even if we were to decide both that liberalism need not be grounded in a sceptical claim and that particular liberals charged with so grounding it do not in fact do so, still we might think that the communitarian critique was pointing to something central to our contemporary self-understandings and conceptions of moral and political life that warranted criticism.

Since we regard subjectivism or scepticism as widespread, it is important to be clear about the *scope* of the moral scepticism that might seem to fit neatly with liberal politics. We are imagining a liberal who thinks that the fact that moral judgements are merely subjective expressions of preference means that the state ought to be liberal, ought to leave people free to make their own choices. But what is the status of this claim that the state ought to be liberal? It is surely a moral judgement. Does that mean that it is itself no more than a subjective expression of preference? Surely this would be incoherent and self-defeating, for if she allows this, then the liberal has to say that there is no rational basis for her endorsing a liberal state rather than a totalitarian one; that it is just a matter of taste, like the ice creams, which kind of political regime is better. When this is pointed out to her, the subjectivist liberal will tend to retreat from this self-defeating global scepticism to a more restricted version, arguing that there is a difference between judgements about how people should live their lives, which are indeed merely subjective, and judgements about how people ought to be treated by one another and by the state, which are objective. The claim now is that the fact that judgements of the first kind are subjective gives one an objective reason to leave people free to make such judgements for themselves. The liberal can stand up for the objective judgement that liberalism is right, but ground that judgement in the belief that judgements about how people should lead their lives are merely subjective.

We shall not pursue this matter here. Clearly a great deal of the subjectivist liberal's position depends upon the validity of the distinction between these two kinds of judgement, and, in our final chapter on Raz, we shall look at a liberal who rejects outright this attempt to divide moral judgements into two qualitatively different categories. For our purposes it is important just to be clear that when we discuss, in what follows, the relation between liberalism and subjectivism, it is not the (self-defeating, incoherent) global brand of subjectivism that we are talking about, but the more plausible view that judgements as to how people should lead their lives lack rational justification.

The important theoretical question is whether one has to endorse even this more limited form of subjectivism if one is to reach liberal conclusions, for it is clear that some liberals argue for those conclusions as consistent with, and perhaps even as implied by, the claim that judgements as to how one should live one's life are objective. A weak version, claiming only consistency, might hold that even though some ways of life are, and can be known to be, better than others, it is so important that people make their own choices that we should ignore that knowledge when thinking about how to organize our society politically. A stronger idea, arguing for a connection between liberalism and objectivism, might be that some ways life are indeed better than others and that a framework of liberal rights is needed precisely to provide the conditions under which people can make informed and rational judgements about which are which. Here the argument merges with what we were saying earlier about how some liberals recognize the importance of social conditions in fostering certain self-understandings and conceptions of the good, for the claim is that liberal conditions – freedom of expression, of association, and so on – are required if people are to be able to find out what is valuable in life. Indeed, liberalism's insistence on the freedom to revise one's commitments, to change one's mind, only make sense, it might be argued, if we can be wrong about our goals and can come to see that they can be changed for the better.[3] If they really are arbitrary, why should the liberal accord such importance to our capacity to change them?

It is important to be clear about what this argument for the compatibility of liberalism with the claim that some ways of life are objectively better than others does or need *not* entail. Clearly, it does not commit one to the view that there is a single way of life that is uniformly right for everybody, but, perhaps more interestingly, it need not even maintain that for each individual there is a single conception of the good that is objectively superior to all others, as if reason could guide the individual to see exactly how she ought to live her life. The point here is that the claim that reason can tell us that some lives are worthier than others does not contradict the claim that there is, even for each individual, a plurality of conflicting and incompatible worthy ways of life. As we shall see in our chapter on Raz, it is perfectly coherent to argue that we can judge the life of an artist to be objectively more valuable than that of a gambler, without being able to judge whether the life of an artist is more valuable than that of a farmer.

There is, finally, another point which naturally arises under this heading, although the fact that it does so can be rather misleading since it concerns not so much the higher-order issue of the status of moral judgements as the substantive question of what makes a life good. The point here is that the claim that some choices are better than others most certainly does not mean that one can make someone live a better life by getting them to live a life that they have not themselves chosen or do not themselves endorse. This, of course, is the liberal bit of the objectivist liberal position, the idea that what matters is that people are free to choose for themselves. It does not follow from the claim that I can be mistaken in my beliefs about what makes my life valuable or worthwhile that someone else, or an institution such as the state, can improve my life by making me do things other than those in which I currently believe. But nor, for the objectivist, is it the case that whatever I choose is *ipso facto* valuable, as if all there was to a life's being valuable was that it had been willingly endorsed. People can freely choose a way of life, can believe it to be worthwhile and valuable, and be mistaken. While one cannot make a person's life go well by forcing them to live a life they have not in some sense chosen, one does not, for the objectivist, guarantee that their life goes well just by letting them choose it for themselves.

The connection between liberalism and subjectivism is an important item on our agenda because a significant strand in the communitarian critique of liberalism takes the form of a rejection of the moral subjectivism that is thought to underpin it. Even with the distinction between global and restricted subjectivism taken into account, however, we have suggested that the two need not necessarily go together, and that it is possible to support liberal politics despite a belief that some ways of life are objectively better than others. That said, we should at least be able to see that there is an affinity between the two, and why it might look as if the doctrine that (some) values are only subjective underwrites the claim, embodied in Rawls's original position, that our highest-order interest is in making our own choices.

Anti-perfectionism and neutrality

The fifth and last theme to recur in the book concerns the question of whether it makes sense to exclude, when thinking about politics and political morality, considerations that might be thought pertinent to individual private conduct. By now we have enough of our agenda in place to enable us to make connections between this and previous themes, and this, combined with the fact that the matters that fall under this heading are particularly complicated, requires us to treat this issue at slightly greater length. The central idea here is that rather than seeking to act on those perfectionist ideals that guide people when they live their individual lives and pursue their own conceptions of the good, the state should deliberately ignore some or all of such ideals. At the extreme, if it excluded all perfectionist considerations, the state could be thought of as committing itself to being neutral between the different conceptions of the good held by its citizens. Rather than making its own judgements about how people should lead their lives, the argument might go, the state should deliberately eschew such judgements, and seek only to provide a neutral framework within which people can make their own choices.

We should be clear that this is an issue of direct concrete political relevance. At present, in the United Kingdom, the state uses money that it has raised through general taxation to subsidize a variety of activities that are believed to be worthy, and it taxes others that are believed to be unworthy. For example, those people whose conception of the good is a life spent gambling are penalized, in the form of duty levied on bets, to support, through state subsidy, those whose conception of the good is a life spent watching the Royal Shakespeare Company. If we were to decide that it was illegitimate for the state to act in accordance with judgements of this kind as to the relative merits of different ways of life, it would seem to follow that decisions about which forms of life thrived and which withered away should be left to the free market, the great virtue of which, it might seem, is precisely that it is the way of allocating resources that reflects only the judgements of individuals. Rather than deciding politically that some ways of life deserve encouragement and others discouragement, it might seem plausible to argue that we should just see what it is that people are willing to pay for. If opera lovers are not prepared to pay the real cost of a night at Covent Garden, then why should others be forced, in the form of taxation, to give resources to help them out? Of course it might be argued that the free market reflects the judgements of the wealthy rather more clearly than it reflects those of the poor, but this will hardly help the case for state subsidy of opera, where it is the lifestyle of a cultured and relatively well-off elite that requires assistance. More generally, the way to identify one's intuitions on this precise issue of anti-perfectionism and neutrality is to think about whether one would reject the free market, and support subsidy, if everybody had equal shares of resources to begin with. For in that case, the market really would reflect people's different choices equally.

While the above example concerns the ways in which the state might or might not be justified in distributing society's resources, thereby indicating the artificiality of our earlier distinction between the equality-related and the liberty-related aspects of contemporary liberalism, we should be clear that state anti-perfectionism also has implications of other kinds. The current British state recognizes only one form of marriage – a monogamous union between a man and woman – and this, as well as having great symbolic effects, feeds through into many aspects of its legislation: tax policy, inheritance rights, and so on. Since this is favouring one form of life over others, over, for example, that valued by homosexuals, it is clearly not anti-perfectionist. The state is making the judgement that some forms of life, and not others, are worthy and warrant state support and encouragement. Here again, any conclusion that the state should be anti-perfectionist, and hence thoroughgoingly agnostic on such questions, would have substantial concrete implications.

In our initial presentation of Rawls's theory we noted that one way of thinking about the veil of ignorance was that it excluded certain sorts of reason from thinking about justice, and we should now be able to see how it is the exclusion of beliefs about particular conceptions of the good that represents the sense in which his theory is anti-perfectionist. The force of denying people in the original position knowledge of their perfectionist commitments is that it models the claim that political morality should take no account of the reasons people might have for such commitments. The idea that justice is derived by thinking about what people would choose who did not know their conceptions of the good is a way of presenting the claim that those conceptions are somehow inappropriate to questions of justice.

Now it is important to see how this claim might relate to *political* morality specifically, and this because of the way in which Rawls has attempted to defend his theory from communitarian objections. The reader will recall that one of the communitarian criticisms of the conception of the person at the heart of Rawls's theory was that it misrepresented the way in which people relate to their ends or values, that in fact we do not think of ourselves as independent from, and able freely to choose, those commitments which give our lives meaning and value. We suggested in our earlier discussion that one way in which Rawls might try to deal with this objection would be to deny that his conception of the person is intended to capture something about our moral experience in general, but rather seeks to model the way in which it is appropriate to think of ourselves *when thinking about justice*, and we can now tie this point in with the emphasis on the specifically political focus of the theory. The claim of the anti-perfectionist is not at all that we should exclude perfectionist ideals from our thinking about how we should lead our lives as individual private citizens. That would be crazy. Rather it is that those moral considerations that quite properly guide us in our private lives are not appropriate to questions of political morality, to questions of how we should organize the political arrangements of our community in the form of the state. Thus, it might be argued, the communitarian criticism of the conception of the person as failing to be true to the phenomenology of our actual moral lives, to our moral experience, misses the point that the conception is not intended to be true to that experience we have as private individuals, but is intended to model the way in which it is appropriate to think of ourselves specifically when it comes to politics and justice.

Whatever the strengths or weakness of this move, and we may have doubts about the schizophrenia that would seem to be involved in this idea that people can bracket or suspend, when it comes to politics, those values to which they are committed as private individuals, the central issue is clearly that of *why* we should exclude reasons from political morality in this way. Here it may be helpful to think about how the question of anti-perfectionism relates to our previous discussion of objectivism and subjectivism. It seems that (restricted) subjectivism quite readily yields the conclusion that the state should not make, or embody in its political arrangements, judgements about which conceptions of the good are better than others, for the simple reason that subjectivism precisely denies that such judgements can be objective or rational. If one citizen's opinion about how to live her life is as good as any other's, or if there is no way of knowing who is right, then it would seem to make sense for the state simply to treat those opinions as equally valid. If there is no objective ground by which to judge a life with theatre more valuable than one with video games, then state subsidy for the Royal Shakespeare Company would seem to have no justification. Here anti-perfectionism follows from the denial that perfectionist ideals are anything more than subjective expressions of preference.

Things get more interesting, perhaps, if one believes in the objectivity of judgements about which ways of life are better than others. Given that belief, can it be coherent to hold that reasons that guide people as individuals should not guide the political community in which they live?

Various possible moves might be made by the objectivist anti-perfectionist. One would be to insist upon the point that a life must be freely chosen if it is to be valuable, and to point to the ways in which state perfectionism undermines that freedom. Taxation ultimately rests on the coercive power of the state (those who don't pay get locked up), so that every time I, who value video games, am taxed to pay for somebody else's theatre, my freedom is being infringed. Perhaps it might be argued that state promotion of some, and discouragement of other, ways of life distorts the choices that I make, so that I am denied the information about the actual costs of my choices that I would need to consider my choices genuinely free. Another would be to say that what matters is that we live in a society to whose political arrangements we can all agree and, since we clearly disagree about perfectionist ideals, the only way to achieve this is to leave them out of the picture. If we think of this as a moral response to disagreement, in that it is the value of a society to which we can agree that drives the anti-perfectionism, there might alternatively be a practical response to that disagreement, which would take the form of saying that unless we regard our differing conceptions of the good as irrelevant to our political life, there will be continual trouble in the form of conflict and perhaps even civil war. Yet another move might be to insist that while there is nothing wrong in principle with the state embodying decisions about how people should lead their lives, there is little reason to think that it will embody the right decisions, or that it is dangerous to give it power of this kind. We do not seek here to assess the relative merits of these various arguments. Our aim remains that of giving an introductory overview of the issues to come up in the body of the book. In our chapters on the new Rawls and on Raz we consider the ideas of two kinds of liberal, one anti-perfectionist and the other perfectionist, and there we shall go into these issues in greater depth.

We have talked about the idea of a neutral state, and since this is a dangerous concept, full of ambiguity, it may be helpful to end our discussion by saying something about the sense of 'neutrality' that is involved here. In the first place, it is clear that the liberal does not seek a political system that is neutral in all matters. The neutral state, which protects the rights of its citizens to pursue their own conceptions of the good, obviously is not neutral between the religious fundamentalist and the secular liberal, for it supports the belief of the latter in a strict separation between church and state. Nor, clearly, is it equally accommodating to the mass murderer and the law-abiding citizen. The point here is that the anti-perfectionist liberal does not argue that the state should be neutral on questions of justice or the right. On the contrary, her view is that the state is justified precisely in acting to protect people's rights, to ensure that justice is done, and this is what permits and requires it to uphold freedom of religion and to protect people from murderers. The kind of neutrality for which she will argue, is neutrality not with respect to questions of the right or of justice, but with respect to questions of the good, with respect to judgements about what makes a life good or valuable. Indeed, it is in order to ensure that all citizens are treated justly and accorded their proper rights that the state is required to be neutral with respect to such judgements. Were the state to get into the business of acting in favour of some ways of life and against others, the anti-perfectionist might argue, it would be failing to treat its citizens justly, failing to protect their right to make their own choices.

Now our examples already make clear that even in the case of those matters with respect to which the liberal state might seek neutrality, conceptions of the good, the neutrality sought is not neutrality of *effects*. A state which acts to protect people's rights will have the effect of favouring some ways of life and not others even if the *justification* of its action is neutral in the sense that it does not involve reference to judgements about the relative merits of those different ways of life. While it is true that the state can prevent someone from committing murder on the right-based grounds that the intended victim has a right to life, and not on the good-based grounds that a life with murder is worse than one without, the effect is the same: neutrality of justification will not be neutral in its effects. If the case of murder seems too stark, consider also the point that the decision of a state to eschew judgements about which ways of life are valuable or worthless will have the effect of favouring inexpensive ways of life over expensive ones. If the anti-perfectionist state is not permitted to subsidize opera, for example, and if opera is relatively expensive, then those whose conceptions of the good include opera will be disadvantaged, at least in comparison to the current situation in which state subsidy does go on. For the anti-perfectionist, this non-neutrality of effects is not a problem: the right is prior to the good in the sense that the rights which people have, and which it is the job of the state to protect, come first and stand as constraints on the conceptions of the good which people can choose to pursue.[4] If some ways of life cannot survive in a society in which everybody has what justice demands, and without per-fectionist political action on their behalf, then that is unfortunate for those who favour such ways of life but no reason for the state to help them. Rather, they will have to revise their conception of the good to fit the constraints imposed by the priority of the right.

The anti-perfectionist liberal, then, argues for a state that is neutral in a specific and restricted sense: it is neutral between conceptions of the good and not on matters concerning justice or the right, and even with respect to the former it is not neutral in its effects, only in its justifications for action. We conclude by indicating two distinct kinds of objection that the perfectionist, whether, liberal or com-munitarian, may raise against the demand for this particular kind of state neutrality: a worry that valuable ways of life will not survive without state support, and a more deep-rooted rejection of the very distinction between the right and the good upon which the claim that the liberal state is neutral in *any* sense seems to depend.

On the first, the reader will recall our initial characterization of communitarianism as concerned to assert the importance of the community in which the individual lives, in contrast to liberalism's apparent prioritization of the individual and her freedom to choose her own conception of the good, and we have seen, under the heading of asocial individualism, that one aspect of this counter-emphasis focuses on the extent to which it is the community in which people live that provides the cultural resources in terms of which individuals come to understand both themselves and the value of different ways of life. The implication of this in the context of a discussion of anti-perfectionism is that communitarians suspect that some valuable ways of life simply would not survive unless they were promoted by the state. On the one hand, as in the opera example, the free choices of individuals to spend their resources as they prefer might aggregate so as to leave valuable and worthy components of our culture to wither away. On the other, the argument might be that unless a particular valuable form of life, such as monogamous marriage, is given symbolic recognition by the state and embodiment in its public institutions, then it will gradually perish. If, and it is a big if, one thought both that a withering away thesis of this kind was plausible, and that the state was likely to judge correctly about which ways of life are worthy and which not, then considerations of this kind might lead one to argue for some form of state perfectionism.

The second objection is rather more fundamental, for it calls into question the very idea that we can distinguish between the right and the good in the way that the anti-perfectionist supposes. If this objection can be sustained, then the claim that the former is prior to, and requires that the state be neutral with respect to, the latter, will look problematic. Liberalism's pretensions to neutrality, its self-understanding as somehow above the substantive battle about how people should lead their lives may then seem highly misleading. Rather than acting as a neutral arbiter, it might be argued, the liberal state actually smuggles in, under the cover of its category of 'the right', its own particular understanding of how people should live, its own ideal of what makes a life a good one. Instead of eschewing judgements about what makes a life valuable, liberalism consists essentially of the claim that a good life is one which has been freely or autonomously chosen by the person living it. It is in accordance with this claim that the political community supports some ways of life and rules out or discourages others, such as those that require state perfectionism. Far from remaining above the fray, liberalism is built on a particular substantive view about what constitutes people's good, about what are people's essential interests, and talk about the priority of the right over the good only serves to conceal this crucial point.

Since we identified as the very core of Rawls's liberalism the identification of people's highest-order interest in their capacity to frame, revise, and rationally pursue their own conceptions of the good, it is obvious that his theory is substantive to some degree, and our discussion above indicates that pretensions to complete neutrality must be misguided. The question that remains concerns the precise extent to which liberalism can sustain its pretensions to neutrality. If talk about the priority of the right over the good, and claims to neutrality with respect to the latter, make it look as if the liberal can be completely agnostic with respect to the question of what makes people's lives valuable, then attention to the problems inherent in that distinction may reveal that such agnosticism is unavailable. And if it is liberalism's purporting to remain above the substantive battle about how people should live their lives that attracts people to that doctrine, then coming to see the senses in which, its presentation and self-understanding notwithstanding, it requires engagement in that battle may force them to think again. They may, of course, remain liberals, but their liberalism will involve claims that they had thought it able to avoid.

The questions raised by this issue of anti-perfectionism and neutrality are many and complex, partly because we are dealing here with the relatively concrete political implications of the various more abstract strands of argument that have gone before, and these strands can come together in a number of different combinations. As with the previous themes that we have identified, we aim to have done no more than provide a cursory overview of the arguments that are to be presented in greater detail in the bulk of the book. If the reader has a rough idea of what to expect, and of how Rawls's theory can be seen to raise the theoretical issues at stake, she is sufficiently prepared for the next part of the book, in which we consider in turn the ideas of four communitarian theorists.

Notes

1 Kukathas and Pettit, *Rawls*, is a recent book that devotes a few chapters to basic exegesis.
2 This is one of the many helpful points made by Kymlicka, *Liberalism, Community and Culture*, pp. 16–17.
3 Again, this thought is to be found in Kymlicka, ibid., p. 19.
4 Kymlicka, ibid., pp. 21–40, points out that Rawls uses the distinction between the right and the good in several different ways, and here we discuss only the sense that illustrates the specific communitarian objection under discussion. For Rawls's most recent observations on this distinction, see his 'The Priority of Right and Ideas of the Good', which we discuss in our chapters on his writings subsequent to *A Theory of Justice*.

PART I

COMMUNITARIAN CRITIQUES

Introduction

Now that we have an agenda of issues in place, we can begin to explore the dense and confusing terrain for which it is intended to provide some preliminary orientation. Our next four chapters will each be devoted to a detailed examination of the work of one of the four thinkers we have grouped together as communitarian critics of liberalism – Sandel, MacIntyre, Taylor and Walzer. In each chapter, we will be attempting to provide answers to three fundamental questions – answers without which it will not be possible to go on and adjudicate between the opposing sides in this dispute.

First, and most importantly, we will try to summarize the most fundamental and distinctive claims of the thinker under examination, insofar as those claims seem to relate, and to stand in opposition, to the main tenets of liberalism in general and to Rawlsian liberalism in particular. However, it is vital to see that this must involve a great deal more than simply offering a list of theses. For such a list would detach each thesis from the surrounding framework of thought from which it emerges, and so would leave the reader with little idea of why the relevant theorist should want to propound it in the first place; and – as with most human utterances – if we do not know why a given speaker has said something, we are to that degree in the dark about what he actually means by what he has said. For similar reasons, we cannot always assume that two people who say roughly the same thing are committed thereby to exactly the same set of presuppositions or implications. For example, MacIntyre and Sandel both accuse liberals of deploying a conception of the person that detaches the individual from her ends; but their reasons for making this accusation, and their sense of its consequences for liberalism, are significantly different – and as a result any critique of their positions may have to take a different form in each case. So, if we want to get clear on the plausibility of each communitarian's claims, the ways in which each might be vulnerable to criticism and the degree to which the four communitarians form a group, we must first get clear on *why* they say what they do as well as upon precisely *what* they say. This means that each chapter will involve a great deal of exposition; and it will sometimes embroil us in issues that do not seem immediately or obviously related to the central topic of this book, issues that may seem more philosophical than political. All that we can do is affirm that, in our view, what may look like detours are in fact integral to the thought of the theorist concerned, and that this will become clear by the end of the chapter even if it is less than clear halfway through it.

The two other questions that each chapter is intended to address are in a way implicit in what has already been said. For, of course, the topic as well as the title of this part of the book is 'communitarian critiques'; and this means that we need to demonstrate the sense in which the pertinent claims of each particular theorist appear to be both communitarian in nature and critical of Rawlsian liberalism (since, like many of the communitarians themselves, we are taking Rawls as our representative of the liberal tradition). With respect to both questions, the agenda of issues established in our first chapter will prove invaluable. For, amongst other things, that agenda specifies several concrete ways in which it might be thought that one's understanding of the concept of a community (and of the relation of the individual to the community) must play a central role in any political theory; and it also specifies several concrete ways in which Rawlsian liberalism might be thought to embody an inadequate understanding of these matters. Our attempts to answer these two questions with respect to each communitarian critic will therefore involve explicit reference to our agenda.

Establishing answers to those three questions is an essential preliminary to two further matters which must also be addressed, namely the question of whether the communitarians form a coherent group with shared views and aims, and the question of whether their criticisms of liberalism succeed in hitting and damaging their target. The issue of whether the communitarians form a group will be dealt with in the conclusion to this part of the book; and it will of course draw upon the work of the preceding chapters, since it is only after establishing the sense(s) in which each individual thinker can be called a communitarian that we can establish whether the four thinkers are communitarian in the same (or at least in a similar) sense. The issue of the cogency and power of their individual criticisms of Rawlsian liberalism will be dealt with in the chapter immediately following that conclusion, the one that deals with what we have been calling the new Rawls; and this, too, will presuppose the work of the preceding chapters, since it will amount to an assessment of the degree to which the appearance of anti-liberalism established in those chapters matches the reality – of the degree to which Rawls is really committed to views of which the communit-arians are critical.

To summarize: the four chapters and conclusion that go to make up this part of the book form a self-contained whole because they are designed to advance the general argument of the book through a clearly defined set of stages. The four chapters will attempt to provide the reader with answers to the following three questions:

1 What are the central claims of each communitarian thinker insofar as they bear upon the topic of this book, how do they emerge from the more general frameworks of thought in which they are embedded, and what degree of independent plausibility do they possess?
2 In what sense does each thinker count as a communitarian?
3 Why might it seem that each thinker is a critic of liberalism?

The conclusion will attempt to provide an analytical surview of this material, primarily in order to address the following question:

4 To what degree do the four communitarians form a coherent group?

Armed with answers to these questions, the reader should then be prepared for the next stage of the debate, namely an assessment of the degree to which these putative criticisms of liberalism hit their target. That, however, will be the business of chapter 5, on the new Rawls.

1

SANDEL:
the limits of liberalism

It seems clear that any attempt to understand the communitarian critique of liberalism as a whole must begin with an assessment of the work of Michael Sandel. In the first place, it was the publication of his book *Liberalism and the Limits of Justice* in 1982 that initiated the debate with which we are concerned: even though Alisdair MacIntyre published *After Virtue* the previous year, it was Sandel's book that first elicited the label 'communitarian' and brought about the retrospective recruitment of other writers to that flag. Moreover, Sandel's book is explicitly structured as a critique of John Rawls's work: our decision to use Rawls as our representative liberal is thus no more than a reflection of the choice of the original communitarian thinker. And since Sandel accordingly offers a detailed reading of the text of *A Theory of Justice*, presenting an exegetical summary of Sandel's position will simultaneously make evident the ways in which Sandel sees himself as a critic of Rawlsian liberalism; no inferential leaps or speculative extrapolations will be needed to get from an understanding of the former to an understanding of the latter. We can therefore dispose of two of our three key questions at one and the same time. What may be less evident is the answer to the third of those questions – the sense in which Sandel's position is a communitarian one; but this too will become clearer if we begin with a brief summary of the ways in which Sandel's position relates to our agenda of issues.

Sandel's critique of Rawls clearly involves some version or other of most of the themes on that agenda. First, he argues that Rawls is committed to a conception of the person that is metaphysically rather than substantively flawed. That is, he takes Rawls's substantive political theory to presuppose a certain conception of the essential nature of personhood, a conception that rules out the possibility of a person's being constitutively attached to her ends; and he argues that this conception is invalid and incoherent rather than undesirable – a misrepresentation of the nature of moral experience rather than the advocacy of an unattractive form of moral life. Second, Sandel accuses Rawls of asocial individualism, in that, for Rawls, a sense of community can at best describe a possible aim of antecedently individuated selves rather than a possible ingredient of their identity; in particular, the good of political community is at best participation in a well-ordered system of cooperation for mutual advantage, a system to which the individuals that populate it are in some way logically prior. Third, Sandel claims that Rawls reduces moral choices to arbitrary expressions of preferences, thus committing himself to the subjectivist rather than the objectivist view of morality. Fourth, and as the above points – if true – help to demonstrate, Sandel suggests that Rawls's claim to be neutral between competing conceptions of the good is in reality much less plausible than it may seem. But Sandel also adds a fifth and final line of attack, one not listed on our agenda; he accuses Rawls of implicitly relying upon an intersubjective notion of the self in certain parts of his work, a conception that is inconsistent with the antecedently individuated conception of the self to which he is committed in other areas of that work.

It is the first two of these five elements of Sandel's critique that reveal the sense in which he is a communitarian, since they imply a belief on his part that Rawls has no room in his theory for the idea that individuals might be or become constitutively attached to their community and thereby gain access to a type of human good that they could not achieve on their own. But a full comprehension of any of the elements of Sandel's critique cannot, as we warned earlier, be derived from a summary of the sort offered above, even if that summary provides a useful guide for the reader as she follows the details of our presentation. Such comprehension will rather depend upon coming to see just what Sandel's notions of antecedently individuated selves, intersubjective selves and of constitutive attachments to the community might mean; and that is the task to which this chapter is primarily devoted. Since, however, Sandel's critique is ultimately based upon a claim that Rawls's theory of justice is a contemporary example of deontological liberalism, we must begin by coming to grips with what Sandel means by 'deontology'.

Liberalism and deontology

For Sandel, deontological liberalism is a theory about the primacy of justice amongst other political and moral ideals, one which Rawls himself summarizes in the slogan that the right is prior to the good. As we saw earlier, this slogan is meant to encapsulate the following thesis. Society, being composed of a plurality of persons each with his or her own aims, interests and conceptions of the good, is best arranged when it is governed by principles that do not themselves presuppose any particular conception of the good; what justifies those principles is not that they contribute to maximizing social welfare or otherwise promote the good, but rather that they conform to the concept of right – a moral category which is given prior to that of the good and which is independent of it.

When formulated in this way, the way favoured by Sandel, we can see that deontological liberalism gives justice primacy in two different but related senses. First, it assigns a moral primacy to justice, asserting that the demands of other political and social values can never be allowed to trump those of justice, that the rights of individual citizens cannot be sacrificed for the sake of other goods or goals. Second, it regards the value of justice as having a privileged justification; the right is prior to the good not only in the sense that its claims take precedence, but also in that its principles are independently derived.

It is this second claim, a claim about the foundation of morals or the derivation of moral principles, that (according to Sandel) distinguishes deontological liberalism from other varieties of that political and moral doctrine. Like many other forms of liberalism, the deontological variety – understood as a substantive or first-order ethical doctrine – stands opposed to consequentialism in that it assigns categorical priority to certain duties and prohibitions. But deontological liberalism is distinctive in also standing opposed to teleology on a foundational or meta-ethical level, in that it derives those unqualified duties and prohibitions in a way that does not presuppose any final human purposes or ends, or any determinate conception of the good life for human beings.

The attractions of combining an assignment of moral primacy to justice with an assignment of foundational primacy are twofold. First, the foundational primacy of justice would justify or account for its unqualified moral primacy: the liberal would be able to claim that justice stands as categorically privileged with respect to particular aims, interests and conceptions of the good precisely because its ground or justification is independent of and qualitatively different from such values. For example, if we regard the ultimate ground of justice as its contribution to social welfare, then we would be forced to admit that the priority of justice was contingent or qualified, since in any circumstances in which unjust rather than just action would make the greatest contribution to social welfare, we would be obliged to act unjustly. Second, if the derivation of the principles of justice did make reference to particular conceptions of the good, then the primacy assigned to them would in effect constitute the coercive imposition of one conception of the good upon persons who might hold differing conceptions of the good. So, in order to establish that the moral primacy of justice is both secure and non-coercive, it would seem that we need to provide a derivation of the principles of justice that grounds them in something other than the multiplicity of competing and circumstance-dependent aims, interests and ends adopted by human beings.

Kant, the greatest of classical deontological liberals, provides that ground in his account of the nature of the human subject; it is his theory of the person or conception of the self that explains the categorical priority of the right over the good. For Kant, human beings are possessed of a will and are capable of exercising it freely; they are capable of autonomous action. It is this capacity, rather than the results of exercising it, that is most fundamental to the dignity and worth of human beings because it distinguishes humans from other animals and elevates them above the realm of causally determined nature. What makes them a human subject at all is not the particular aims, interests and conceptions of the good that they decide to adopt and follow, but rather the capacity to think and act autonomously which is made manifest in such decisions. In other words, on the deontological view Kant exemplifies, what matters above all for human beings is not the ends we choose but the capacity to choose that is thereby presupposed; and if that capacity must be given prior to any particular end it is employed to affirm, then what really matters about the human subject is given prior to its ends. In short, just as the right is prior to the good, so the subject is prior to its ends; the deontological assignment of absolute priority to justice is paralleled by its assignment of absolute priority to the subject.

With this brief account of the nature of deontological liberalism in place, we can see the intended force of Sandel's claim that Rawls is a deontological liberal. In the first place, this characterization highlights Rawl's attribution of absolute *moral* primacy to justice:

> Justice is the first virtue of social institutions, as truth is of certain systems of thought. A theory however elegant and economical must be rejected or revised if it is untrue; likewise laws and institutions no matter how efficient and well-arranged must be reformed or abolished if they are unjust . . . Being first virtues of human activities, truth and justice are uncompromising. (*TJ*, pp. 3–4)

Second, it also highlights his attribution of foundational primacy to justice:

> We should . . . reverse the relation between the right and the good proposed by teleological doctrines and view the right as prior. (*TJ*, p. 560)

And third, it highlights the fact that Rawls assigns this twofold priority to justice because of his conception of what is fundamental to human personhood. Rawls's commitment to the regulation of society by principles of justice that do not depend upon any particular conception of the good is the direct result of his view that what really matters about human beings is their capacity to set, pursue and revise their own conceptions of the good; it reflects his explicit claim that people have a 'highest-order interest' in protecting that capacity. A state which, when regulating the lives of its citizens, encouraged or discriminated against particular conceptions of the good life for human beings (beyond the exclusion of those whose pursuit would violate the rights of other citizens) would fail to permit the full and equal exercise by all citizens of their capacity freely to determine how they should live. In short, human beings understood as moral personalities are most fundamentally auto-

nomous choosers of ends, and society must be organized in such a
way as to respect this feature of personhood above any other.

Rawls's theory of the person

As it stands, Rawls's conception of the subject is a claim about what
is most worthy of respect in our treatment of human beings; it is a
substantive moral position, and one which (as we saw earlier) Rawls
explicitly acknowledges as central to his theory. According to Sandel,
however, this first-order ethical view of the locus of human worth
presupposes in turn a particular second-order theory of the self
and its constitution to which Rawls has not acknowledged his commitment; it presupposes a foundational account of the person, a
philosophical anthropology. Such a second-order account might most
generally be called metaphysical; it has to do with claims concerning
the essential nature of human subjectivity rather than with claims
about how people should be treated – its focus is upon what selfhood
consists in and how it is formed, fixed or bounded. In the case of
Kant, the metaphysical view of the self, which grounded his moral
claim that human beings had an absolute right to be treated as ends
rather than means, involved him in claims about a noumenal realm
beyond space and time in which all human beings participated
insofar as they were rational; human beings were dual-aspect beings,
a part of nature and yet simultaneously possessed of faculties that
transcended nature. Rawls wants to avoid this highly controversial
and seemingly unintelligible metaphysical framework. According
to Sandel, however, he is nonetheless committed to a very specific
set of views concerning the nature of the human subject and its
possible forms of identity – views which are most evident in the
way he pictures the relation between the self and its ends.
  As we have already seen, the Rawlsian emphasis upon the human
being as an autonomous chooser of ends leads him to assign an
absolute moral priority to the subject over its ends. What most
fundamentally deserves respect in human beings is their capacity
to choose their aims and ends rather than the specific choices they
make; and since that capacity must be given prior to its exercise, the
locus of moral worth in a human being must be seen as given prior
to its ends. According to Sandel, however, this assignment of moral

priority is both matched and explained by his assignment of a metaphysical priority. Sandel claims that, for Rawls, the essential unity or identity of the self is also something given prior to the ends that it chooses; and it is the absoluteness of this metaphysical priority that accounts for the absoluteness of the moral priority. What is this metaphysical priority, and why does Sandel think that Rawls is committed to it?

Sandel bases his claim on certain passages from *A Theory of Justice* that seem to have a metaphysical rather than a moral ring to them. For example, at one point, Rawls says that '. . . the self is prior to the ends which are affirmed by it; even a dominant end must be chosen from among numerous possibilities . . .' (*TJ*, p. 560). In other words, the subject's ends are hers because she chooses them, and so presumably there must be a self already around to do the choosing. It seems to follow that the constitution of the self (its shape or identity) cannot be the result of the ends it chooses, for its unity is established prior to its making any given choice during the course of its experience. And this is a consequence which Rawls seems happy to embrace: 'The main idea is that given the priority of right, the choice of our conception of the good is framed within definite limits . . . The essential unity of the self is already provided by the conception of right' (*TJ*, p. 563). According to Sandel, this antecedent unity of the self means that, no matter how heavily an individual is conditioned by her surroundings, she is always and irreducibly prior to her values and ends; her sovereign agency is not dependent upon such circumstance but guaranteed in advance. Thus, to go against the Rawlsian assignment of absolute priority to the right over the good is not simply to commit an error in moral reasoning – to go wrong on the substantive level. It is to go wrong on the metaphysical level, to contradict our essential nature as persons.

> What we cannot do is express our nature by following a plan that views the sense of justice as but one desire to be weighed against others. For this sentiment reveals what the person is, and to compromise it is not to achieve for the self free reign, but to give way to the contingencies and accidents of the world. (*TJ*, p. 575)

In other words, Rawls sometimes seems to claim that a human being's capacity autonomously to choose its ends is not just one amongst many equally valuable capacities or features but rather forms the essence of his or her identity. It therefore follows that respect for human autonomy is not just one value amongst many in human life, but an absolutely fundamental one which must always trump any other; for to fail to respect that capacity is to fail to respect a metaphysically fundamental feature of personhood. In short: a subject for whom justice is the first virtue is not just an autonomous chooser of ends but an antecedently individuated subject; a self for whom justice has absolute priority over all other values is a self whose bounds are fixed absolutely prior to its choice of ends.

The original position

Sandel's view is that this metaphysical picture of the self as antecedently individuated is not only required to account for the absoluteness of the priority that Rawls assigns to autonomy; its centrality also becomes manifest in the details of his theory of justice. In particular, it is a vital component of the original position, which is of course the fulcrum of Rawls's project of justifying his theory of justice; every argument in his book passes through that imaginative construct. If his metaphysical picture of the self is indeed embedded within the original position, then it is undeniably at the foundation of his thought.

Sandel claims that Rawls makes certain significant assumptions about how the parties to the original position view themselves and their society when they deliberate – assumptions other than the imposition of constraints upon their knowledge which is dramatized in the veil of ignorance. According to Sandel, such further assumptions are essential: for in order to determine what the parties will decide when considering how the basic institutions of their society ought to be constructed, we must attribute to them some conception of the nature of society and of what they want from it, and so some conception of how they stand in relation to it and to its other members.

These assumptions are held to emerge when, for example, Rawls summarizes the conditions that engage the virtue of justice (the circumstances of justice): 'One can say, in brief, that the circumstances of justice obtain whenever mutually disinterested persons put forward conflicting claims to the division of social advantages under conditions of moderate scarcity' (*TJ*, p. 128). According to Sandel, such a way of formulating the form and nature of the conflict that engenders the need for principles of justice makes sense only if Rawls is assuming that the parties to the original position will think of society as a cooperative venture for mutual advantage. For Rawls's talk of 'social advantages' seems to give exclusive weight to a conception of social membership as a source of personal advantage; it seems to imply that the sole (or at least the primary) reason people engage in social relations is to derive personal benefit from advantages that could not be accrued other than by such cooperation. Further, Rawls describes the parties as 'mutually disinterested', that is as concerned to advance their own conception of the good and no one else's, and as not bound to each other by prior moral ties when advancing those ends.

Again, as with the constraints of the veil of ignorance, Sandel is aware that Rawls is not claiming that the mutual disinterest and lack of prior moral ties attributed to parties to the original position hold for persons in real life. They are assumptions built into a device of representation, not sociological generalizations, and it is perfectly possible that when the veil of ignorance is lifted the parties may find that they are tied by sentiment and affection to others and want to advance their interests. According to Rawls, his assumptions simply have the merit of clarity, simplicity and weakness; assuming benevolence rather than mutual disinterest 'would defeat the purpose of grounding the theory of justice on weak stipulations' (*TJ*, p. 149). But Sandel finds such a justification of these assumptions insufficient. An assumption of benevolence would not be conceptually more problematic or contentious than one of mutual disinterest; and if Rawls means that assuming mutual disinterest is weaker in the sense of being more realistic, then he is embedding a controversial empirical generalization into a device of representation that is supposed to test our convictions about moral and political values. In reality, Sandel claims, Rawls builds these assumptions into the motivation of the parties because they flow from his conception of the subject and its relations to its ends.

Sandel attempts to justify this claim as follows. He points out that Rawls's picture of society as a system of cooperation between people each of whom possesses their own conception of the good is one way in which he stresses the fundamental plurality and separateness of individuals: '. . . the plurality of distinct persons with separate systems of ends is an essential feature of human societies' (*TJ*, p. 28). Of course, on this picture it is perfectly possible for one person's systems of ends to overlap or coincide with another; if it were not there could be no basis for cooperation. But such an identity of interests is not itself an essential or fundamental feature of human society; on the contrary, according to Rawls's formulation, it is the separateness of each person's system of ends which is essential, whereas the possible overlap of any of those systems is a happy accident that is sometimes actualized and sometimes not.

In short, according to Sandel, Rawls assigns a different degree of metaphysical importance to two obvious facts about human beings – the fact that each person is one distinct being amongst a multiplicity of other such beings, and the fact that the interests and goals of any given person can overlap or coincide with those of any other. He regards the plurality and separateness of persons as an aspect of the fundamental nature of human subjectivity (treating such separateness from others as just a part of what it is to be a person); but he regards any actual coincidence of their chosen ends as at best a happy fact about their circumstances. Metaphysically speaking, we are distinct individuals first and only later do we form relationships with others and engage in cooperative activity; so those relationships cannot be integral to our constitution as selves. On Sandel's view, regarding society as primarily a system of cooperation involves viewing its members as already constituted individuals when they enter into it for their mutual advantage; they need not be selfishly motivated when they do so, but they are essentially constituted as selves in advance of any such engagement with others. In this sense, the plurality of persons is prior to their unity.

Sandel argues that the assumption of mutual disinterest has similar metaphysical underpinnings. It is of course not an assumption that human subjects are motivated only by self-interest or selfishness; but it is, he claims, an assumption about the form of the relationship between a human subject and its motivations in general (whether selfish or selfless): 'Although the interests advanced by [their] plans are not assumed to be interests in the self, they are interests of a self that regards its conception of the good as worthy of recognition' (*TJ*, p. 127). All interests must be the interests of some individual subject; more specifically, they must be the interests of an antecedently individuated subject. They are the interests of a self in the sense that they are merely possessed by that self; the identity of that self is not constituted by any of those ends – my ends are always mine, never me. According to Sandel, Rawls assumes not just that all human beings are individuals, but that they are individuated (their identity is fixed) prior to the ends, desires or interests that they may possess; the self is prior to its ends: 'It is not our ends that primarily reveal our nature' (*TJ*, p. 560).

The flaws in Rawls's theory of the person

Let us suppose that Sandel has correctly identified the philosophical anthropology that underlies Rawls's theory of justice and his emphasis upon the moral personality of human beings as residing in their capacity to be autonomous choosers of ends. What objections does he make against this conception of the person as antecedently individuated? After all, it places no restriction upon the content of individual's desires and ends; Rawlsian selves are as likely to be benevolent as to be selfish when the veil of ignorance is lifted, and the fact that all interests must be interests of a self does not entail that they must be self-interested.

According to Sandel, there are three main reasons for concern. The first is that Rawls's conception of the person entails that a person's goals, aims and ends are always things that she chooses to attach herself to; they are related to her (and therefore presumably detachable from her) by an exercise of her will. This voluntaristic picture is not the only available way of characterizing our relation to our ends. For example, one might suggest that in many cases human beings relate to their ends through acts of cognition rather than acts of will; they come to commit themselves to a certain goal or life-project as the result of a process of self-scrutiny, and regard that commitment as a manifestation of a deeper self-understanding. On such a picture, establishing one's own ends is not a matter of choosing from a menu of available possibilities, but one of discovering what one's ends really are or ought to be; and then my fundamental preference, in morality as well as politics, would surely be for the conditions of self-knowledge rather than the conditions of choice. In short, Rawls's voluntaristic emphasis in his picture of the self's relation to its ends excludes *a priori* certain alternative emphases which have a long tradition in moral and political thought;

his conception of the self is thus neither neutral nor uncontroversial on this matter.

The second reason for Sandel's concern is more important, and has to do with how Rawls understands the ways in which a person might identify with the ends to which he or she is committed. If the self is antecedently individuated, then no matter how closely it identifies with a given end, that end can never become integral to the self's identity. The characterization of such values or interests must describe the objects that I seek, not the subject that I am; my identity is fixed in advance of my choice of ends, so that a certain distance between who I am and what I value must always remain.

> One consequence of this distance is to put the self beyond the reach of experience, to make it invulnerable, to fix its identity once and for all. No commitment could grip me so deeply that I could not understand myself without it. No transformation of life purposes and plans could be so unsettling as to disrupt the contours of my identity. No project could be so essential that turning away from it would call into question the person I am. Given my independence from the values I have, I can always stand apart from them; my public identity as a moral person 'is not affected by changes over time' in my conception of the good.[1]

Such a conception of the self rules out the possibility of being torn between several competing values in a way which I experience as the pull of competing identities within my self; in other words, it permits no intra-subjective understandings of the self. And by the same token, it limits Rawls's understanding of the relation between a self and any other-directed (in particular, any community-directed) end to which that self is committed. The problem Sandel detects here arises not because Rawls's conception fails to admit of the possibility that human beings may take as their goal or object the good of another or of a group of others; it arises because such ends must be held in a way that ensures that they can be no more than the interests of a person – they can at best be possessed by the self, they cannot be integral to it. Rawls thus excludes the possibility of purposes and ends held in common with others that inspire more expansive inter-subjective self-understandings, ones in which I identify myself with that community and regard my membership of it as essential to who I am.

In general, then, Rawls's conception of the self as antecedently individuated excludes any understanding of the relation between the self and its ends and circumstances that implies that the boundaries of the self might be disrupted, whether by personal commitment, by intra-subjective conflict or by intersubjective relationships. But human moral and political life and experience abounds with examples that can only be described in these ways. We need only think of people who build their lives around a cause and whose life is accordingly devastated by the failure of that cause; of people whose sense of themselves is torn apart by conflicting desires or aims; of our tendency to attribute responsibility and acknowledge obligations to family, tribe, class or nation as well as to individuals. What this suggests is that, if Rawls's conception of the self *is* an antecedently individuated conception, then it simply cannot account for some of our basic human experiences of, and attitudes towards, agency and self-reflection; it is incapable of coping with the full range of human moral circumstance and self-understanding.

Sandel's third reason for concern is in effect a more specific version of his second worry: this is his belief that Rawls's conception of the self commits him to an impoverished understanding of *political* community. As we have just seen, on Rawls's view a sense of community describes a possible aim of antecedently individuated selves, not an ingredient of their identity. Essentially communal goods thereby find their place only as one type of contender amongst many within the framework decided by the principles of justice. So, individuals who happen to espouse communitarian aims in the political sphere can pursue them, but only within a well-ordered society as defined by Rawls's theory of justice; they cannot question whether that society is itself a community in the constitutive sense. For Rawls, the good of political community is participation in a well-ordered system of cooperation for mutual advantage; the possibility of a public life in which the identity as well as the interests of the participants might be at stake is, according to Sandel, ruled out in advance. The idea that a political community might specify the subject as well as the objects of shared aspirations is thus excluded from any society that accords absolute priority to justice. Once again, this hardly seems to be a weak or uncontroversial assumption about society.

On Sandel's view, then, the constraints imposed by Rawls's conception of the self are multiple and significant. That conception commits Rawls to ruling out in advance anything other than a voluntaristic relation between a self and its ends, any end whose adoption or pursuit might engage with or transform the self, and any possibility that the good of community might consist in a constitutive dimension of this kind. This makes his conception of the self radically inadequate as a reflection of human moral circumstance; and as a result, it entails that any society constructed on Rawlsian principles of justice will be much less neutral between competing conceptions of the good than might have seemed to be the case.

Of course, liberals have never attempted to deny that a society organized according to its principles of justice would discriminate against *some* conceptions of the good that are held by its citizens; it would necessarily and explicitly exclude any such conception whose implementation would violate the rights of other citizens as specified by those principles. But this is essential if autonomy is to be upheld as a general value, for it alone can ensure that any citizen's exercise of her freedom does not interfere with the right of all citizens to exercise that same freedom; any given citizen's autonomy is in this respect limited only by the need to protect the autonomy of all citizens. Apart from this, people in a liberal society are free to choose and live according to any conception of the good that they please; and the structure and policies of that society would not be built upon, and could not be justified by invoking, any particular conception of the good. This does indeed seem to suggest that a liberal society would be maximally neutral between competing conceptions of the good. But Sandel is arguing that the *absoluteness* of the liberal respect for autonomy which underpins their commitment to this neutrality, the unqualified priority of justice which liberalism presupposes, can be justified only by presupposing a commitment to a certain conception of the person. And this commitment has consequences which might significantly alter our conception of the kind and degree of neutrality to which liberalism can validly lay claim.

These consequences are of two different kinds. First, Sandel claims, commitment to this degree of neutrality (between competing conceptions of the good) in the realm of politics is founded upon a surprisingly high degree, and a surprisingly implausible kind, of non-neutrality (about the nature of human selfhood) in the realm of metaphysics. And second, this metaphysical non-neutrality seeps back into, and materially diminishes the amount of neutrality displayed in, the realm of politics and morality. For if Sandel's claim to have identified a set of necessary presuppositions about personhood at the basis of liberal thinking is correct, then a far wider range of conceptions of the good than might have been supposed will in fact be discriminated against in a truly liberal society. Why? Because a vision of the self as antecedently individuated excludes any conception of the good which allows for or presupposes constitutive personal attachments to values, projects and communities; a society built with antecedently individuated selves in mind cannot provide a home for those whose conceptions of the good are built around such constitutive attachments and so founded upon a very different conception of the person.

In the first place, it cannot provide a home for those committed to strongly communitarian conceptions of politics, ones in which a person's membership of a given political community is understood to be a constitutive attachment, a vital aspect of their well-being and identity rather than an attribute or end which they merely happen to possess. According to Sandel, a Rawlsian polis would force its citizens to think of themselves as participants in a scheme of mutual cooperation, deriving advantages they could not have gained by their own efforts, but not tied to their fellow citizens by bonds whose severance or alteration would change their identity as persons. Moreover, the conception of the person that grounds this limited conception of politics also distorts our understanding of non-political social relationships – ones in which the relevant others stand to us not as citizens but as fellow party-members, religious believers or relatives. For example, antecedently individuated selves would be unable to develop and sustain constitutive attachments to members of their family: although a mother might have the good of her children as her primary goal in life, it would not be integral to her sense of her own identity – it could only be an end she happens to have, not an aspect of who she is. If a political community is shown to be founded on a conception of the self that has no room for such non-political attachments, it may thereby lose some of its attractiveness as a vision of politics; and it might also fail to provide a framework within which those who found their conception of human well-being upon such non-political relationships with others can flourish. In short, whether the bond in question is political or non-political, Rawls's theory of justice seems to offer little scope for those who understand their relationships with others as constitutive of their identity as persons.

Sandel is not claiming something that is palpably untrue, namely that liberals have never perceived that such consequences flow from their understanding of what justice requires; for example, the ways in which family structures differentially influence the opportunities of children is a familiar topic in liberal politics. Moreover, the liberal theorist has a justification for regarding such consequences as a price that ought to be paid; for she might, if she wishes, argue that these undeniable goods must be sacrificed to the greater good of justice and the protection of individual rights. Sandel's aim is rather to point out that the sacrifices demanded in the name of justice may be a great deal more significant and extensive than liberals tend to admit, and to argue that any such sacrifices are ultimately made in the name of a conception of the person as antecedently individuated (as metaphysically asocial) which may lack the coherence and attractiveness that the liberal moral claims that it supports seem to possess.

In short, according to Sandel, Rawlsian liberalism is subject to a sort of metaphysical myopia. A certain range of conceptions of the good will be unable to flourish in a truly liberal society because the individualist and asocial metaphysical foundations of liberal principles of justice generate an inability to perceive or acknow-ledge the varieties of human moral experience around which those conceptions of human good are crystallized and their true worth displayed. What this myopia entails is that the Rawlsian liberal's claim to preserve and maximize the area within which a person's autonomous will may be exercised conceals the imposition of strong and implausible restrictions upon the range of values, projects and conceptions of the good from which that person is permitted to choose. The prime virtue claimed by the proponents of justice as fairness seems to have been put under seige by Sandel's examination of its metaphysical presuppositions.

Liberalism and moral subjectivism

What the preceding section has attempted to demonstrate is that Sandel's critique of liberalism includes versions of three of the five themes or topics on our original agenda of issues. According to Sandel, Rawls is committed to an incoherent conception of the person as antecedently individuated, and thus lacks any awareness of the ways in which our goods or ends contribute to the constitution of our identity as persons: this is a version of the first theme on our agenda. As a consequence, he believes that Rawls ignores the constitutive importance of social or communal human goods, of goods held in common through which people develop constitutive attachments to others, and so regards the political community in particular merely as a system of cooperation between mutually disinterested individuals rather than as a possible focus of constitutive attachments. This is a version of the second theme on our agenda, that of asocial individualism; but it is a version of only one of the two main strands of argument that we located under that general heading. For Sandel's point is not so much that Rawls ignores the social *origin* of our conceptions of the good (which would be a philosophical/sociological error about the importance of the social matrix for our acquisition of any of our individual ends or goals), but rather that he is blind to the constitutive importance of conceptions of the good whose *content* or focus is inherently social (which is a failure to see the true significance of those specific ends that regard our links to others as helping to fix our individual identity). And by making these two points Sandel casts doubt upon the liberal claim to maximal neutrality between competing conceptions of the good – which is the fifth theme on our agenda.

As we have seen, the source of all these liberal ills, for Sandel, is the Rawlsian conception of the person. The Rawlsian view of the relation between society and the individual, and the degree to which the Rawlsian state fails to live up to its claim to neutrality, are not just dispensable adjuncts to Rawls's central concerns but rather make manifest that which drives his theory as a whole; they result from the conceptual blinkers imposed upon that theory by its conception of the person as antecedently individuated and so incapable of constitutive attachments. In this section, we will trace out Sandel's reason for thinking that this conception of the self also leads Rawls into a particular picture of the process by which an individual chooses her ends or conception of the good – one in which such choices are seen as arbitrary expressions of preference, and which seems to imply that moral judgements in general are entirely subjective (the fourth theme on our agenda).

When Rawls discusses the question of how individuals would set about exercising the freedom that a liberal society provides for them – how they would choose a conception of the good, for example – his picture of the exercise of rationality in this domain is as follows:

> We can say that the rational plan for a person is the one (amongst those consistent with the counting principles and other principles of rational choice once these are established) which he would choose with deliberative rationality. It is the plan that would be decided upon as the outcome of careful reflection in which the agent reviewed, in the light of all the relevant facts, what it would be like to carry out these plans and thereby ascertained the course of action that would best realize his more fundamental desires. (*TJ*, p. 417)

Sandel fixes upon this final emphasis on desire, and interprets it as having two crucial consequences. In the first place, Rawls seems to be restricting the focus of deliberation to the self's desires without leaving room for deliberation about the self understood as the subject of these desires. Apart from conforming to the basic tenets of instrumental rationality (for example, employing more rather than less effective means to a given end), the full extent of the individual's decision-making process seems to amount to determining the various plans or goods that are available and their likely consequences, and establishing the existence and relative intensity of her own desires. If this is so, then the agent's self-reflection seems to go no further than a sort of introspection – in order to decide how to live, one need only weigh the relative intensity of one's existing wants and desires. In other words, although the self's desires and wants are to be inspected, the self as subject of those desires is not; we can reflect upon the kind of desires we have, but not upon the kind of selves we are. Self-reflection does not seem to extend to asking who we really are – it only involves asking what we really feel.

Sandel regards this emphasis as entirely to be expected, given Rawls's conception of the person. If the self is antecedently individuated, then the kind of beings we are is given entirely independently of any form of reflection or agency and so not subject to revision by them; indeed, if all of our ends, goals and beliefs are at best contingent attributes of the self (things that we possess or have rather than features that are integral to our identity), then there can be nothing in the self to reflect upon – it is barren of constituent traits. For Rawls, the identity of the subject can never be at stake in moments of choice or deliberation, for the bounds that define it are beyond the reach of the agency that would contribute to its transformation.

Sandel's second reason for focusing upon Rawls's picture of rational choice as a matter of weighing the relative intensity of desire is that it suggests to him that Rawls views the final stage of such deliberation as a matter of bare expressions of preference. This is a suggestion that seems to be supported by several remarks in *A Theory of Justice*. For example, according to Rawls, since the rational principles mentioned above do not specify a single best plan of life, 'a great deal remains to be decided . . . We eventually reach a point where we just have to decide which plan we most prefer without further guidance from principle . . . We may narrow the scope of purely preferential choice, but we cannot eliminate it altogether . . .' (*TJ*, pp. 449, 551, 552). Sandel points out that if decision is a matter of weighing existing desires and wants, then the process of choosing a life-plan is not really a matter of choice at all: the agent merely introspects, establishes the presence of a given desire and then acts upon it – it is a matter of taking a psychic inventory, not choosing the values she would profess or the aims she would pursue. Of course, Rawls could allow for the presence of second-order desires on a given person's inventory – that is, an agent could find that she possesses desires about her desires, perhaps a desire that she have certain first-order desires rather than others. But this second layer will not really alter the situation, since the agent would still have only the fact of this second-order desire to establish and its intensity to assess; her only ground for justifying or defending this second-order desire would be its existence and force. In particular, she could not affirm it as essential to her own identity as an agent, since on Rawls's view (according to Sandel) the identity of the agent is barren of constituent traits and so it simply cannot be argued that a given desire is integral or essential to it.

The main thrust of Sandel's critique here should by now be a little clearer. Rawl's picture of deliberation rests upon the notion of a psychic inventory of present desires and wants; and his conception of the person as antecedently individuated relegates those desires and wants to the status of ultimately contingent attributes of the self. But if my conception of the good is based upon such essentially contingent facts about me, then my commitment to that conception has no more worth or validity than they do; as the product of my desires, that commitment is no less governed by contingency than they are, and so has no deeper basis than the sheer fact that I happen to hold them with a certain degree of intensity. In short, my choices of ends or conceptions of the good are arbitrary; they give expression to my preferences, but can be given no less subjective and no more rational a basis than that. According to Sandel, Rawls's conception of the self pushes him into a position of general moral scepticism, and one which fits well with the liberal commitment to neutrality. For, of course, if no given conception of the good can be assigned a more rational or objective justification than any other, then it would simply be crazy to attempt to construct a society based upon any such conception. For Sandel, Rawls's reason for asserting that the state should treat any individual's choice of con- ception of the good as if it were an expression of personal prefer- ence is not (or not merely) that to do otherwise would violate the state's neutrality; it is his belief that this is all that such choices really are. 'That we have one conception of the good rather than another is not relevant from a moral standpoint. In acquiring it, we are influenced by the same sort of contingencies that lead us to rule out a knowledge of our sex and class.'[2]

The difference principle

One might think that the four Sandelian criticisms so far touched on, if valid, are sufficiently damning in themselves to demonstrate that Rawls's theoretical edifice is radically flawed; but Sandel wishes to press his critique further. He argues that, as well as presupposing an inadequate and controversial metaphysical conception of the self as antecedently individuated, Rawls's theory of justice must at other points presuppose a very different conception of the self if its principles are to be regarded as valid. In short, he wishes to demonstrate that Rawls is committed to two contradictory con- ceptions of the self at one and the same time.

The need for an alternative conception emerges most clearly in Rawls's defence of the difference principle. As we saw in our In- troduction, he argues that one of the key principles that would be agreed upon by parties to the original position is the following: that only those social and economic inequalities that work to the benefit of the least advantaged members of society will be permitted. Rawls defends the claim that such a principle determines a truly just distribution of social and economic resources by arguing that it would be unjust to permit a social system in which those endowed with social and economic advantages (wealth, status, power) or natural advantages (talents, abilities) benefit more than those who lack them. Such assets – whether social, cultural or natural – are not deserved by their possessors; the distribution of such assets is entirely a matter of contingency and so is wholly arbitrary from a moral point of view, no better than a lottery. No one deserves to be endowed with intelligence, any more than he deserves to be born into a wealthy or powerful family, or to be provided with high-quality education or training: 'There is no more reason to permit the distribution of income and wealth to be settled by the distribution of natural assets than by historical and social fortune' (*TJ*, pp. 73–4). Since my possession of these assets is arbitrary, it would be unjust to regard me as the rightful possessor of the rewards that flow from their employment; and the difference principle represents an agreement to regard the distribution of natural talents as a common asset, an agreement to share the benefits of this distribution whatever it turns out to be.

It is important to note that, if the notion of desert has no application to a person's assets, certain kinds of entitlement do play a role. Since it is in the general interest that I cultivate and exercise the talents I possess, so that society as a whole may benefit from their fruits, society is typically arranged so as to provide resources and incentives for their cultivation. Rawls is perfectly happy to say that I am entitled to my share of the resulting benefits when I have qualified for them under the terms specified. However, these claims are legitimate expectations created by institutions designed to elicit my efforts, not primordial rights based upon virtues I possess; they presuppose the existence of the cooperative scheme, and have no validity independently of those institutional arrangements. Rawls thus has a twofold reason for asserting that I do not deserve the fruits of my talents: to do so, I would have to possess the talent non-arbitrarily and have a pre-institutional right that society value this particular talent rather than some other one. On Rawls's view neither condition holds.

The possibilities opened up by this form of argument are worth contemplating; for example, Sandel notes in passing that it is often used – although not explicitly by Rawls – to justify policies of positive discrimination. With respect to this issue Dworkin has argued[3] that no individual can claim that her rights have been violated by an affirmative action programme that entails, for example, that some black candidates are admitted to medical school with lower qualifications than some white candidates who are excluded, because no one – black or white – *deserves* to go to medical school to begin with. Someone's possession of the relevant characteristics is a matter of good fortune and so simply does not constitute a basis for desert. At best, we can talk about entitlements or legitimate expectations; but these have no pre-institutional validity, and so cannot be determined independently of the existence and rationale of those institutions. No one is entitled to demand that medical schools reward any particular talent or characteristics they possess (for example, intelligence or medical aptitude), because what counts as a characteristic meriting such a reward depends solely upon the qualities deemed relevant to the social purposes the institution serves. In the case of medical schools, intelligence is clearly relevant to the purpose of saving lives, but a range of other characteristics may also be relevant to other purposes; and if it is decided that society wishes to utilize these institutions as means of increasing the number of blacks in socially strategic professions, then colour of skin will count as relevant as well. Just as whites are not excluded out of contempt but out of an instrumental calculation of the sort that justifies the more familiar criteria, so blacks are included not out of a belief that skin colour has intrinsic worth but out of the belief that in certain circumstances skin colour is a socially useful trait. This defence of affirmative action thus relies upon precisely the understanding of natural assets, desert and entitlement that underlies Rawls's defence of the difference principle.

According to Sandel, it is easy to see how this Rawlsian view of natural assets as failing to provide the basis of desert emerges very smoothly from a theory committed to a conception of the person as antecedently individuated. According to that conception, my specific talents, character and motivations are contingently given and wholly inessential attributes of my self – they are inessential to my being the particular self that I am. Such a self's identity is preserved by its invulnerability to transformation by experience or circumstance: if it is not defined or constituted by such things as its talents, then it cannot be transformed or redefined by their alteration or loss.

More specifically, a principle of distribution that regards those talents as common assets and redistributes their fruits to others cannot be said to violate the self by treating it as a means to social ends; for it is not persons but their attributes that are being so used. For a talent to constitute a basis for desert, it must be something that I possess in an undistanced, constitutive sense of possession: if I deserve a high grade in a course, for example, then it must be in virtue of some fact about me as a person. On Rawls's view, however, there are no such facts; there are no attributes I possess that are integral to my identity. And if there is nothing of that kind that I can be said to possess in the relevant sense, then nothing of that kind can provide me with a basis of desert. I do not deserve to benefit from the use of my natural or social endowments – not because they are arbitrarily given, but because they are non-constitutively possessed.

The fit between the difference principle and Rawls's conception of the self thus looks to be a very neat one. However, two immediate problems emerge if we follow Sandel and look a little more closely at the way these two claims hang together. In the first place, in order to defend his claim that people do not deserve the fruits of their talents, Rawls is forced to press very hard indeed on the distinction between persons and their talents, character, abilities and assets; he distinguishes so sharply between the self and its possessions that he risks falling into the Kantian trap of making the subject radically disembodied. The Rawlsian subject is so shorn of its empirical characteristics as to leave it little more than an abstract, pure consciousness that floats behind every one of its traits; and this seems incoherent. If the difference principle is indeed based upon such a conception of the self, this is hardly an argument in its favour. In the second place, even if we accept that the distinction between the self and its possessions does justify the conclusion that individuals do *not* deserve or possess their natural assets, it does not justify the conclusion that society *does*. After all, our bodily parts are in this sense natural assets and their distribution is arbitrary from a moral point of view; but we do not think that society has a right to redistribute them, for example to redistribute one eye from those lucky enough to have two to those unfortunate enough to have none at all. Is not the location of natural assets in the province of the community just as accidental and arbitrary from a moral point of view as their attribution to the subject? Why not simply regard them as unattached in advance to any particular subject?

In short, Rawls's conception of the self as antecedently individuated leaves the difference principle without an adequate justification
and open to the charge of presupposing an incoherent account of
personhood. The only way in which Rawls might justify his presumption that assets not possessed or deserved by individuals *are*
possessed and deserved by society is by making use of a very
different conception of the subject. Instead of claiming that the difference principle is justified because my assets rather than my person
are thereby utilized for others, Rawls might question the sense in
which those who share in 'my' assets are properly called 'others'.
If Rawls allowed that the relevant description of the self might
sometimes incorporate more than a single empirically individuated
human being, he could then argue that these assets are common
because they belong to a common subject of possession – the community. If my identity as an individual is partly constituted by my
membership of the community, if I identify with it and my fellow
members in a constitutive sense, then a redistribution of the fruits
of my labours to other members of that community is not a case of
using me as a means towards the ends of entirely distinct individuals.
I will then not experience redistributive taxation as a violation of
my integrity as a person because I have a sense of community that
is strong enough (sufficiently integral to my sense of my own
identity) to transcend such purely individualistic reactions.

Certain passages in *A Theory of Justice* suggest that Rawls is not
unaware of the trend of his own thinking on this issue. Indeed, at
one point he says: '... the difference principle represents, in effect,
an agreement to regard the distribution of natural talents as a
common asset and to share in the benefits of this distribution whatever it turns out to be' (*TJ*, p. 101). But Sandel's claim is that treating
natural assets in this way can only be justified by invoking an intersubjective conception of the self and a constitutive conception of
community – both of which Rawls is officially committed to rejecting.

Agreement in the original position

A similar need to invoke an intersubjective conception of the self
also seems to emerge if we return to the original position and enquire
more closely into the way Rawls imagines people coming to agreement on the principles of justice.

The original position is a dramatized expression of Rawls's con-
tractarian approach to social and political issues; his principles of
justice are defined as those that would be freely agreed upon by
everyone behind the veil of ignorance. However, just as the original
position is a device of representation rather than an actual location,
so the contract which is the outcome of deliberation in the original
position is a hypothetical rather than an actual contract. Like actual
contracts, hypothetical ones presuppose the plurality and distinctness
of the parties to the contract, and emphasize the element of choice
involved in consenting to them. Unlike actual contracts, however,
the Rawlsian hypothetical contract cannot turn out to be unfair:
because of the veil of ignorance there can be no differences of power
or knowledge amongst the parties, and there is no possibility that
a hypothetical agreement might be implicated in the (possibly unfair
or coercive) practices and conventions of a given actual society. If,
then, the parties are in a situation such that no unfairness could
result, the agreement reached in the original position will be an
instance of pure procedural justice; its outcome is fair no matter
what, purely by virtue of the fact that it is agreed to.

The important question for Sandel arises here; for if the original
position is constructed so as to *guarantee* that any agreement reached
in it is fair, then what scope is there for the exercise of choice by
people in the original position? Although they are theoretically free
to choose any principles they wish, their situation is such as to
guarantee that they will wish to choose only certain principles, upon
which they will unanimously converge. As Rawls puts it: 'The
acceptance of these principles is not conjectured as a psychological
law or probability. Ideally anyway, I should like to show that their
acknowledgement is the only choice consistent with the full
description of the original position. The argument aims eventually
to be strictly deductive' (*TJ*, p. 121). Sandel argues that the implications of this remark are wide-ranging.

In the first place, it follows that no bargaining can be said to go
on in the original position, because bargaining in any sense requires
some differences in the interests or knowledge or power or preferences of the bargainers, whereas the veil of ignorance removes any
such thing. Neither could any discussion coherently be thought to
take place between people, all of whom are assumed to reason in
the same way and draw the same conclusions and none of whom
has perceptions or concerns that distinguish him from anyone else.

And if bargaining and discussion are not possible, then agreement is not possible either; if everyone reasons in the same way and has identical interests and preferences, any given person need only reach a conclusion for him or herself in order to know that it has been reached by all. In effect, the agreement made in the original position is not a freely willed agreement made with others to abide by certain conditions, but an acknowledgement of the validity of a certain set of propositions (like coming to see that $2 + 2 = 4$). It is something we come to know rather than something we decide, agreement to a proposition rather than agreement with others; it is agreement in a cognitive rather than a voluntaristic sense.

If, however, Rawls's real emphasis in the original position is upon agreement in the cognitive sense, then our earlier assumption that the original position acknowledges and respects the plurality and distinctness of persons begins to look a little hasty. For the veil of ignorance removes every characteristic that distinguishes one person from another; and this means not that everyone is *similarly* situated but that they are *identically* situated – we have no means of distinguishing them one from another. There is no bargaining, discussion or agreement behind the veil of ignorance because the plurality of people which such notions presuppose is absent; what we find behind the veil of ignorance is not many persons but one subject – we find an intersubjective self of precisely the sort against which Rawls has officially turned his face.

Sandel summarizes his claim as follows:

> The secret to the original position – and the key to its justificatory force – lies not in what [the parties] *do* there but rather in what they *apprehend* there. What matters is not what they choose but what they see, not what they decide but what they discover. What goes on in the original position is not a contract after all, but the coming to self-awareness of an inter-subjective being.[4]

This may sound a great deal more ontologically speculative than it really is. Sandel is in essence arguing that Rawls's conception of the original position and its occupants – in other words, his conception of ourselves insofar as we are thinking about justice – seems to involve the attribution of a very strong (indeed, a constitutive) sense of community. Only if we think of ourselves as already bound to one another in our political community will it make sense for us to accept the constraints imposed upon us by the veil of ignorance and its associated features, and to deliberate within those constraints in the sorts of way that Rawls seems to imagine. In short, our propensity to accept the original position as an appropriately de-signed device of representation for deliberation about justice seems to presuppose an acknowledgement of moral ties binding us to others – ties of precisely the sort that we are forbidden to presuppose or draw upon *within* the original position, in which all parties are stipulated as being mutually disinterested.

This argument therefore precisely parallels Sandel's claim about the difference principle; in both cases he claims to detect a reliance within the Rawlsian theory upon a constitutive sense of community. And this sort of constitutive attachment to our community and to the other members of it, is of course precisely what Sandel thinks that Rawls's official conception of the person (upon which Rawls must rely if he is to justify the assignment of absolute priority to autonomy) forbids. As he puts it: 'We cannot be persons for whom justice is primary and also be persons for whom the difference principle is a principle of justice.'[5]

The limits of liberalism

With that final quotation, we can conclude this attempt to analyse the five main elements of Sandel's critique of Rawls. Having tried to establish Rawls's commitment to a conception of the self as in-dividuated antecedently to its choice of ends and so incapable of constitutive social or communal attachments of any sort, Sandel has gone on to argue that this general commitment results in a conception of the political community as a system of cooperation between mutually disinterested persons, a conception of moral judgements as arbitrary expressions of preference, and a degree of neutrality between competing conceptions of the good that is significantly lower than it might appear. For good measure, Sandel adds the charge that features of Rawls's own theory presuppose the existence of constitutive attachments to the political community whose very possibility is denied by the terms of his official con-ception of the self.

It should now be clear why Sandel's criticisms of Rawlsian

liberalism were labelled 'communitarian'. Rawls's conception of persons as antecedently individuated excludes the possibility that attachment to *any* good or end might ever be integral to one's identity as a person; but what Sandel particularly emphasizes is that it therefore excludes the possibility that any *communal* goods might have such a constitutive role – most specifically, that it commits Rawls to thinking of the *political* community as a scheme for the production and distribution of mutually advantageous benefits between mutually disinterested individuals, rather than as something with which such individuals might identify and through which they might develop and refine their sense of their own identity as individuals. The fundamental importance of such constitutive attachments to the political community is demonstrated, for Sandel, by the fact that some of the most intuitively attractive of Rawls's own political ideas can be seen to presuppose them. And this merely confirms what Sandel takes to be obvious in its own right, namely that our sense of identity is inseparable from an awareness of ourselves as members of a particular family or class or community or people or nation, as bearers of a specific history, as citizens of a particular republic; and that we look to participation in the political realm as a way in which we can develop and refine our sense of ourselves by developing and refining forms of community with which we can be proud to identify. In other words, the restrictions of Rawlsian theory ensure that '... it forgets the possibility that when politics goes well, we can know a good in common that we cannot know alone'.[6]

Of course, this does not mean that Sandel regards the values to which Rawls is so explicitly attached – the values of freedom and equality – as unimportant in politics. His worry is rather the degree to which Rawls's theory focuses so exclusively upon them, and the degree to which they are compatible. For, according to Sandel's critique, what commits Rawls to a conception of the self as antecedently individuated is his assignment of absolute priority to individual autonomy, to the individual's capacity to choose its own conception of the good; but Rawls's commitment to equality (for example as manifest in the difference principle) presupposes the very possibility of constitutive communal attachments that his official conception of the self prohibits. As Rawls himself acknowledges, his commitment to equality presupposes the existence and force of the value of fraternity amongst the members of the political community – he identifies the difference principle as an 'interpretation' of fraternity, of our capacity to identify with and care for other citizens (cf. *TJ*, pp. 105ff.); but according to Sandel, the absoluteness of Rawls's commitment to freedom (reflected in the lexical priority he attaches to the principle of equal liberties) prevents him from being able to accommodate that value – even in the lexically subordinate position he wants to give it. In short, Rawls's lexically secondary commitment to equality presupposes the very thing that his lexically primary commitment to freedom places under threat – fraternity. Moreover, setting equality aside, even if most of us would agree that it would be wrong to subordinate liberty entirely to fraternity (sacrificing individual freedoms in pursuit of the goods we can only know in common), it would surely be equally wrong entirely to subordinate fraternity to liberty. For Sandel, a balance must be struck which acknowledges them both; an absolute commitment to one cannot be the best response to the fact that such fundamental values can and do come into conflict in the arena of politics.

Perhaps the most important thing to note at the end of this consideration of Sandel's critique is the degree to which four of its five elements depend for their force upon the validity of the fifth element. We have quoted passages from *A Theory of Justice* that can, it seems, be read in ways that imply that Rawls holds a view of the political community as a cooperative scheme and a view of moral judgements as arbitrary expressions of preference; but a Rawlsian liberal might well dismiss these passages as lax formulations, or as views that are not at all essential to the main elements of Rawls's theory. From Sandel's perspective, what shows that such a dismissal is wrong – what shows that they manifest something integral to Rawls's theory – is primarily the fact that both views are a consequence of Rawls's commitment to a specific conception of the person. Similarly, Sandel's main ground for claiming that Rawlsian theory discriminates against conceptions of the good that focus upon constitutive attachments to projects, values and community is his claim that Rawls conceives of persons as antecedently individuated; and the notion that Rawls's commitment to the difference principle conflicts with other elements of his theory depends upon the claim that one of those elements is a conception of the person as antecedently individuated. In short, any attempt to defend Rawls against Sandel's critique must focus upon Sandel's attribution of this conception of the person to Rawls: if that attribution can be justified, then the other four elements of Sandel's critique will be massively buttressed, and if it cannot, then the critique as a whole will lack foundations.

The questions that must be answered will, therefore, all focus upon this issue. Does Rawls's conception of justice presuppose a particular conception of the person, and if so is it a conception of the sort that Sandel claims, that is, is it a vision of the person as individuated antecedently to its acquisition of any ends (particularly communal or social ones), and does it function as a general meta-physical claim about the nature of personhood (as opposed, for example, to a conception of the person that is suited to political matters but not moral or metaphysical ones)? If Rawls is not committed to such a conception of the person, then what is it that justifies his assignment of absolute priority to the autonomy of the citizens in his liberal society? How else might he defend his claim that people have a highest-order (not merely a high-order) interest in this capacity – that the right is prior to the good in a way that brooks no compromise whatever? These are the questions that we shall address in chapter 5.

Notes

1 Sandel, *Liberalism and the Limits of Justice*, p. 62. The qotation from Rawls cited in this passage is from 'Kantian Constructivism in Moral Theory', pp. 544–5.
2 Rawls, 'Fairness to Goodness', p. 537.
3 See Dworkin, 'Why Bakke has no Case', in *New York Review of Books*, 10 November 1977, pp. 11–15, reprinted as 'Bakke's Case: Are Quotas Unfair?'.
4 Sandel, *Liberalism and the Limits of Justice*, p. 132.
5 Ibid., p. 178.
6 Ibid., p. 183.

2

MACINTYRE:
morality after virtue

Alisdair MacIntyre's work (in *After Virtue* and succeeding volumes)[1] operates at a much higher level of generality and involves a much broader sweep of moral and cultural history than does Sandel's work. MacIntyre's critical analysis is focused not on one text in contemporary political theory but on the origins, development and decline of Western moral and political culture; so any conclusions of his that might be thought pertinent to Rawlsian liberalism will have application just insofar as Rawls's work can be read as a specific symptom of much deeper and wider cultural movements and attitudes. This means that our exegetical presentation of MacIntyre's framework of thought will necessarily involve the examination of many issues in moral philosophy whose connection with contemporary political theory will not at first be obvious; and it also means that we will afterwards have to indulge in a much higher degree of speculative extrapolation in order to show how MacIntyre's work might be thought to constitute a critique of Rawlsian liberalism than we did with Sandel. On the other hand, MacIntyre does make some references to liberalism in general and to Rawls's work in particular, so the speculations that will follow our exegetical presentation will not entirely lack a concrete textual basis; and the details of that presentation are essential to any attempt to establish why MacIntyre can be regarded as a communitarian thinker.

Even at this stage, however, we can give the reader some preliminary indication of which strands in MacIntyre's analysis will support the claim that he can be read as a communitarian critic of liberalism, by signalling in advance the way in which his conclusions relate to our original agenda of issues. Like Sandel, MacIntyre accuses liberalism of presupposing an incoherent rather than unattractive conception of the person (first theme), and of being committed to a form of scepticism about the possibility of rationality or objectivity in moral matters (fourth theme); in addition, and again like Sandel, he holds that liberalism misrepresents and underestimates the importance of communal life to the identity and integrity of the individual (second theme), and that liberalism is far less neutral than it claims between competing conceptions of the good life for human beings (fifth theme). However, the way in which MacIntyre sees these various criticisms as relating to one another differs significantly from that of Sandel; in particular, where Sandel regards the asocial individualism of liberalism as the result of its commitment to a conception of the self as antecedently individuated, MacIntyre sees things the other way round – he sees the liberal conception of the self as a consequence of liberalism's failure to perceive the importance of the community in the moral life of the individual. And this in turn means that the sense in which MacIntyre is a communitarian thinker is significantly different from the sense in which Sandel can be so categorized.

At the moment, of course, these comparisons and contrasts may be difficult to appreciate; but they are simply designed to give the reader advance warning of the aspects of our exegetical summary that will turn out to be of most importance for our specific purposes.

The predicament of contemporary morality

According to MacIntyre, contemporary moral and political culture is in a state of confusion. He begins *After Virtue* by noting that modern liberal democracies are beset with arguments between people holding opposing moral positions on such issues as the rectitude of abortion, the justifiability of doctrines of deterrence in a nuclear age and the structure of truly just societies; and as yet no widely agreed answer to these questions has emerged. What MacIntyre takes to be worrying about this, however, is not the mere fact that such arguments occur or that they have not yet arrived at a conclusion; his worry is that the form these arguments take guarantees that they can *never* be brought to a rational conclusion.

This is because the moral positions of the participants are fundamentally incommensurable. When a proponent of abortion rights attempts to justify her view, it is of course perfectly possible for her to highlight more basic and general premises that lead her to it; and those premises can themselves be traced back to more fundamental beliefs and values, until we reach the propositions that ground her moral view as a whole. However, when those truly basic premises are brought up against the basic premises of her opponent, it proves impossible to evaluate their relative worth or validity; within the parameters of their own position, each person's opinion is rationally derivable from his or her more fundamental premises, but the premises themselves are incommensurable with one another. Each invokes concepts that cannot be translated into the concepts invoked by opposing points of view: premises that invoke rights are contrasted with premises that invoke universalizability or the notion of a soul, and there is simply no overarching framework in terms of which these concepts can be compared with one another and the rational superiority of one demonstrated.

This incommensurability entails that any person's choice of basic premises or frameworks cannot be justified against those of her opponent; within a given framework, conclusions follow from premises, but the premises themselves are by definition ungrounded – they are what permits rational justification, and so cannot themselves be rationally justified or undermined. The invocation of one premise or framework against another is thus not something susceptible to rational evaluation; so the argument between proponents of different frameworks is incapable of rational termination. Moreover, if one person's choice of framework cannot be justified to another, then that person cannot justify it to herself either. It is purely and simply unjustifiable – a matter of purely personal preference.

This perception of the arbitrary nature of contemporary moral debate is, however, masked by a feature of the language employed by those who attempt to explain and justify their moral views. For our discourse retains a contrast between personal and impersonal reasons for doing something, and the reasons we offer to others for doing what we think is morally demanded fall into the latter category. An example of a personal reason would be something like

'Do this because I want you to': by saying such a thing I have given my interlocutor no reason for doing what I ask unless she has some other reason for doing what I want – if, for example, I am in a position of authority over her, or she is a relative of mine. An impersonal reason would be something like 'Do this because it is your duty': in this case, whether the reason given for the action is a good one is entirely independent of particular facts about the person speaking or her relationship with her interlocutor – it presupposes the existence of impersonal criteria, of standards which apply to all people regardless of their circumstances, wishes or desires. It is language of this latter sort to which people typically appeal when justifying a particular moral judgement.

In short, according to MacIntyre, the actual processes of moral argument exemplify the clash of personal wills and their arbitrary commitments, but the language in which the arguments take place invoke the existence of impersonal standards by means of which such disputes might rationally be arbitrated. According to a school of moral philosophy called emotivism, this paradox is easily explained: the essence of moral judgements is and has always been that of giving expression to one's personal feelings or attitudes and attempting to do so in a way that will bring others to align their feelings with your own; and the use of language designed to invoke impersonal standards is spurious – it is simply an effective way of bringing about the sought after realignment.

MacIntyre finds this account of the paradox inadequate. Understood as a thesis about the meaning of moral judgements it fails for the following reasons: first, it fails to explain in a non-circular way the precise nature of the feelings given expression by moral utterances. If one asks what kind of feelings are involved, it will not be sufficient to be told 'feelings of approval', since approval can be of many kinds; but the only way of further characterizing those feelings seems to be as 'feelings of moral approval', which simply reintroduces the term that this analysis was meant to explain. Second, emotivism seems to be engaged in a fruitless task from the outset, because its analysis conflates two kinds of expression whose function in the language (as we have seen) is determined precisely by the contrasts and differences between them. In effect, it collapses the difference between personal and impersonal reason-giving, and thus ignores what seems to be a significant difference in meaning. The reason for this error is to be found in the third of MacIntyre's criticisms, namely that emotivism confuses meaning and use. Emotivism is a theory about the meaning of sentences, but the expression of feelings or attitudes is characteristically a function not of their meaning but of their use on specific occasions. A schoolmaster might express frustration by screaming '7 × 6 = 42!' at his class, but this has nothing to do with the meaning of the proposition he utters.

In short, emotivism is false if understood as a theory about the meaning of moral utterances, but true if understood as a theory about the use to which such utterances are put in contemporary moral culture. According to MacIntyre, what has happened is that, over time, the meaning and the use of moral utterances have become radically discrepant: at present, we use them as modes of expressing our fundamentally arbitrary feelings and attitudes, but the meaning of the utterances we employ in this way retains traces of a prior historical period in which impersonal standards were available, and so their present use invokes those criteria in circumstances in which they can no longer be cashed out. Our present culture is indeed an emotivist culture, but it was not always like that.

It is this diagnosis that governs the structure of *After Virtue*; for it sets MacIntyre a twofold task. First, he must flesh out his claim that contemporary culture has become imbued with emotivist attitudes and practices; and second, he must investigate the history of that culture, in order to understand how it became emotivist and thereby to assess the possibility of restoring it to a state in which moral judgements might once again be able to claim real objectivity and impersonality.

The emotivist self

According to MacIntyre

> A moral philosophy . . . characteristically presupposes a sociology. For every moral philosophy offers explicitly or implicitly at least a partial conceptual analysis of the relationship of an agent to his or her reasons, motives, intentions and actions, and in so doing generally presupposes some claim that these concepts are embodied or at least can be in the real social world. (*AV*, p. 22)

In claiming that contemporary culture is emotivist, MacIntyre is therefore committed to claiming that this culture understands itself to be (and is, to some degree, in reality) structured in accordance with the sociology that this particular brand of moral philosophy presupposes.

MacIntyre argues that the social content of emotivism flows from its obliteration of the distinction between manipulative and non-manipulative personal relations. Emotivist moral philosophy regards all moral discussions as no more than attempts by one party to alter the preferences and feelings of another party so that they accord with their own; they involve using whatever means might be effective to bring about this goal. No distinction is drawn between reasons that will influence the person in the relevant way and ones that the person herself will judge to be good; there is no such thing as appeal to genuinely impersonal criteria whose validity the person must judge for herself regardless of her relationship to the speaker. By collapsing the distinction between personal and impersonal reasons, emotivism removes the possibility of treating persons as ends, as rational beings capable of making an independent assessment of what they take to be right; no moral debate can be anything other than an attempt to treat one's interlocutor as a means towards one's own goal, namely that of aligning her feelings to one's own.

If emotivist moral philosophy regards all moral discussion as an instance of a manipulative interpersonal relationship, then emotivist sociology will hold the same view of social relationships *per se*. We can see what the social world seen through emotivist eyes would look like by noting what MacIntyre calls the 'characters' of modern culture. A character is a fusion of a specific role with a specific personality type in a way that emblematizes certain moral and metaphysical ideas embedded in a culture; and the characters of modern emotivist culture are the Aesthete, the Manager and the Therapist. The Aesthete sees the social world as an arena for the achievement of her own satisfaction, a series of opportunities to gain pleasure and at all costs to avoid boredom; other people are the means by which she achieves this. The Manager's goal is to organize and direct her human and non-human resources in order to achieve her goals with maximum efficiency and effectiveness; but she explicitly eschews the task of fixing or evaluating the goals themselves – they are treated as givens (given to her by the market or her shareholders or her directors). The Therapist's concern is purely with the transformation of neurotic symptoms into energy that is redirected towards purposes deemed socially useful; like the Manager, her concern is with technique, efficiency and effectiveness, and she avoids the task of evaluating or advising her patients on the intrinsic worth of the ends they adopt. In short, modern characters agree in treating people as means towards others' ends and in regarding questions of ends as ultimately beyond systematic, rational or objective assessment.

It is by reference to role-models such as these that (MacIntyre claims) the modern individual works out her self-definition. This emotivist self cannot be unconditionally identified with any of the moral viewpoints it takes up; devoid of rational criteria for evaluating such viewpoints, it lacks any conception of limits to what can be evaluated – everything can be subject to criticism from the viewpoint it has adopted, including the viewpoint itself. To be a moral agent is thus to stand back from any and every situation in which one is involved and from every characteristic one may possess, and to regard them all as subject to judgement from a purely universal and abstract viewpoint, one detached from any social particularity. The capacity to be a moral agent is located in the self rather than in any of the social roles or practices that it adopts; the resources for the possession and exercise of moral judgement are to be found in that unencumbered self alone.

As a further consequence, any moral attitude or position that the self takes on must be seen as an expression of ultimately arbitrary and purely personal preference; since they cannot be justified by rational criteria, their only justification for the person who adopts them is the fact that she has freely chosen to do so. This entails regarding the self's relation to its ends as purely voluntaristic; and it also involves regarding that self's transitions from one position or end to another as an essentially arbitrary process. Such a person cannot be said to have a history; there is no way of telling a intelligible story of her movements through moral positions and through life – no narrative thread concerning the development or refinement of her self-understanding.

In effect, then, the modern self that hangs together with and is secreted from the social content of emotivism is fixed or bounded independently of any of its social embodiments or characteristics, and lacks a rational history. Neither its identity at any given time nor its identity over time are fixed by or dependent upon its attitudes, characteristics or life story; neither its personality nor its history are part of its substance; indeed, that substance assumes an abstract and ghostly character.

More generally, of course, this emotivist conception of the self is strikingly similar to the conception of the person as antecedently individuated that Sandel attributes to Rawls. At this stage of MacIntyre's argument, he makes no explicit reference to liberalism in general or Rawls in particular; but those references do emerge later, and it is easy to see why readers of Sandel should have assumed that MacIntyre's analysis of modern culture, and the critique that he builds upon that analysis, might converge with the analysis and criticisms of liberalism offered by Sandel. It seems clear that, for MacIntyre, contemporary forms of liberalism are simply further symptoms of the emotivist disease that he is attempting to diagnose and cure; the Rawlsian self is a version of the emotivist self.

The Enlightenment project

On MacIntyre's view, the emotivist self and the corresponding decline of moral debate into the conflict of arbitrary personal wills first became definitively established during the Enlightenment. More specifically, MacIntyre claims that the emotivist fate of modern culture was sealed when the Enlightenment project of providing a rational justification for morality failed. The attempts of Kierkegaard, Kant, Diderot, Hume and Smith were all uniformly unsuccessful; and although each of their attempts took its own form, MacIntyre is convinced that the reason for their failure was the same in every case.

All of these philosophers agreed to a surprising degree on the nature or content of the morality that they were attempting to justify; none denied that marriage and the family were fundamental moral structures, or that promise keeping and justice were inviolable values. Furthermore, they all largely agreed upon the form that a rational justification of such a morality would have to take: its key premises would characterize some feature or features of human nature, and the rules of morality would be justified as those that a being possessing such a nature would be prepared to accept. The trouble was that the moral rules that they were attempting to justify had originated in a historical and cultural context within which their function was very different from that imagined by those who had inherited the rules but lived in a very different environment.

Those rules had been developed within a wider moral scheme which had dominated the medieval period and had originated with Aristotle. Within that framework, there is a sharp and vital distinction between man-as-he-happens-to-be and man-as-he-could-be-if-he-realized-his-essential-nature; and ethics is seen as the science that enabled human beings to understand how to make the transition from the former to the latter state. What this presupposed is a distinction between potentiality and its fulfilment in reality (the sort of distinction we employ in order to relate an acorn to an oak tree, or a kitten to a cat), and an account of what the true end or fulfilment of human nature might be; it viewed human nature as initially discrepant with the precepts of ethics, and so in need of transformation through experience and the tutelage of practical reason until it fulfilled its potential (reached its telos).

It then follows, however, that the precepts that make up morality will require *both* a conception of untutored human nature *and* one of the telos or end of that nature in order to make any sense; they are intended to help people to achieve human-nature-as-it-could-be-if-it-realized-its-telos, to move them from their present state to a new one. But those Enlightenment philosophers we mentioned had (for a variety of reasons) dispensed with the idea of a human telos, and so of any sense that human nature as it happens to be might be discrepant or discordant with a higher or more fulfilled state. The abandonment of this notion left them with two elements of the older moral scheme whose relationship to one another inevitably became wholly unclear; for, since the moral injunctions that they wanted to justify were intended to alter, improve and reform human nature as it happened to be rather than to fit with it in its untutored state, it would never be possible to justify them by deducing them from or otherwise relating them to features of that present state. Indeed, it is much more likely that human nature thus understood would have a strong tendency to disobey the injunctions of morality. As MacIntyre puts it:

> ... the eighteenth-century moral philosophers engaged in what was an inevitably unsuccessful project; for they did indeed attempt to find a rational basis for their moral beliefs in a particular understanding of human nature, while inheriting a set of moral injunctions on the one

hand and a conception of human nature on the other which had been expressly designed to be discrepant with each other ... They inherited incoherent fragments of a once coherent scheme of thought and action and, since they did not recognise their own peculiar historical and cultural situation, they could not recognise the impossible and quixotic nature of their self-appointed task. (*AV*, p. 53)

We might put MacIntyre's conception of the importance of a human telos in the following way. He sees the concept as vital to morality understood as a rationally justifiable or objective enterprise, because it alone can license immediate transitions from statements of fact to statements of value or obligation – transitions from 'is' to 'ought'. We can move immediately from the knowledge that a knife is blunt and bent to the conclusion that it is a bad knife, and from the fact that it is sharp and evenly balanced to the judgement that it is a good knife, because we know that a knife is a tool for cutting things – we know, in other words, what the purpose or end (the telos) of such a thing is. Functional or purposive concepts thus seem to transform evaluative judgements into a species of factual statement; for then such judgements follow immediately from the object judged having, as a matter of fact, some particular characteristics. If we think of human nature as possessed of a telos, we can make similarly immediate transitions from 'is' to 'ought', since our grasp of the fulfilled or final state of human nature allows us to distinguish between character traits or behaviour patterns that do, and those that do not, contribute to the development and realization of that telos, and to regard the latter as 'bad' and the former as 'good'. We could therefore regard moral judgements as a species of factual statement as well.

So it seems that the reintroduction of the concept of a telos will be vital to any attempt to restore a sense of morality as an aspect of human life that can be said to be rational or objective in its content. This way of looking at human beings is of course central to Aristotelian ethics, but according to MacIntyre it is even older than that:

It is rooted in the forms of social life to which the theorists of the classical [Greek] tradition give expression. For according to that tradition to be a man is to fill a set of roles each of which has its own point or purposes: member of a family, citizen, soldier, philosopher, servant of God. It is only when man is thought of as an individual prior to and apart from all roles that 'man' ceases to be a functional concept. (*AV*, p. 56)

If one thinks of a person as a farmer, then one thinks of him as having certain purposes or ends by virtue of his role, and answers to the question of how he ought to behave – in relation to his animals, his crops, his fellow farmers and his fellow citizens – follow immediately from our grasp of the function it is his task to perform. For MacIntyre, then, the reintroduction of rationality to morality by means of the concept of a human telos can be brought about only by rejecting the abstract, ghostly emotivist self and regarding the person as necessarily implicated in and defined by his social, cultural and historical circumstances. These three elements (moral judgements as factual, a human telos, and the encumbered self) were central to the moral understanding of Ancient Greece, and formed the original and sense-conferring context for the incoherent fragments of morality with which modernity is left; so it is to that context that MacIntyre turns for advice on how to reconstruct such a framework within modern culture.

Aristotle and the virtues

In the Homeric world to which Aristotle's ethical system is a reaction, individuals were regarded as having a fixed role or status in virtue of the position they occupied in a well-defined and highly determinate social structure. As a consequence, knowing how any given individual ought to behave in a given situation followed immediately from knowledge of their role; in knowing that, we know what he owes to and what he is owed by others whose relationship to him is determined by the position they occupy in the same hierarchies of kinship, household and society. The concept of the virtues enters here as a term denoting those excellences of character that permit a man to carry out the duties incumbent upon him and that are manifested in his actions when he fulfils those duties. Furthermore, in knowing how he ought to behave, in knowing the role he occupies, the Homeric individual knows who he is; the idea of rejecting or distancing himself from that role could make no sense, since it amounted to the sloughing off of his identity. Thus, right action flows immediately from an individual's identity, and since that identity is defined by his social role, in Homeric society morality and social structure amount to one and the same thing; in other words, the emotivist self is no self at all, and evaluative questions are questions of (social) fact.

Aristotle understands himself as part of the Homeric tradition; the points just mentioned provide the framework of his ethical enquiry, but they do not so much fix its precise shape as form the landmarks in terms of which he will sketch his own significantly different map of the terrain. For example, Aristotle detaches the concept of the virtues and of morality from any tight connection with specific social roles, but not from all connection with any role; for him, the relevant role is that of 'human being' rather than 'king' or 'son'. Human beings are understood as having a specific nature which sets them certain aims and goals; and the virtues are those excellences of character that allow them to move towards that specifically human telos. However, those virtues are not merely a means towards the achievement of an independently specifiable end state:

> For what constitutes the good for man is a complete human life lived at its best, and the exercise of the virtues is a necessary and central part of such a life, not a mere preparatory exercise to achieve such a life. We thus cannot characterize the good for man adequately without already having made reference to the virtues. (*AV*, p. 140)

Moreover, the virtues as Aristotle understands them cannot be exercised outside the political community; their development and implementation in a complete human life requires that such a life be lived out in the polis, together with others all engaged in a common project of attempting to live the good life. Only the material and cultural resources of the city state allow this project to be implemented; and virtues such as courage, fidelity and friendship constitute both the framework conditions for any such community to maintain itself and an essential part of the form of life at which those in the community are aiming. This is the sense in which Aristotelian man is necessarily a political animal.

This exceedingly brief summary of MacIntyre's version of Aristotle identifies themes that will be vital if we are to understand his attempt to provide a reconstructed version of Aristotle's conception of ethics, in particular the central role accorded to the virtues and the need for a communal context for the living of the good life. However, MacIntyre has (at least) two main reasons for thinking that his prescription for modern morality must be a heavily reconstructed version of Aristotle. In the first place, Aristotle's own understanding of the human telos was dependent upon his metaphysical biology, and those proto-scientific theories are now entirely discredited – indeed, it was the discredit into which they had fallen that partly explained the Enlightenment's rejection of the very idea of a human telos. MacIntyre must therefore show that such a teleological understanding of human nature is justified or necessitated without relying upon such metaphysical presuppositions. Secondly, Aristotle places great emphasis on the constitutive role of the polis for morality, but the Athenian city state was a historically and culturally specific form of life which could not conceivably be revived in the twentieth century; so MacIntyre must find a way of invoking the concept of a community in morality without presupposing entirely utopian social and political changes.

His reconstruction attempts to meet both these challenges by deploying three central concepts – that of a practice, that of the narrative unity of a human life, and that of a tradition: the first and third of these in particular are, as we shall see, inherently social in nature, and all three are together intended to provide a rational framework for morality in which the concept of a virtue retains a central place. We shall look at each of these three concepts in turn.

The concept of a practice

According to MacIntyre, a practice is

> . . . any coherent and complex form of socially established co-operative human activity through which goods internal to that form of activity are realised in the course of trying to achieve those standards of excellence which are appropriate to, and partially definitive of, that form of activity, with the result that human powers to achieve excellence, and human conceptions of the ends and goods involved, are systematically extended. (*AV*, p. 175)

This requires a lot of clarification; but some of its implications are relatively obvious. For example, on this definition, noughts and crosses is not a practice (insufficiently complex) but chess is; kicking a football is not a practice (although it may be a component of a practice of playing football); planting turnips is not a practice (insufficiently complex or self-contained) but farming is.

The import of other terms in the definition is much less obvious, in particular the notion of a good that is internal to a practice. Internal goods are ones that cannot be achieved by engaging in any activity other than the practice itself; external goods are ones that can be derived from participating in the given practice, but that can also be derived from participating in other practices. Take chess as an example: power, fame and wealth can be achieved through excellence in chess playing, but they are external goods because they can also be achieved in other ways – they are not practice-specific; whereas certain highly particular kinds of analytical skill, strategic imagination and competitive intensity achievable by playing chess are goods internal to that practice, for they cannot be achieved in any other way. No activity that lacks internal goods can count as a practice; and those goods are the fulcrum of MacIntyre's first definition of the virtues:

> A virtue is an acquired human quality the possession and exercise of which tends to enable us to achieve those goods which are internal to practices and the lack of which effectively prevents us from achieving any such goods. (*AV*, p. 178)

This definition therefore links the possession and exercise of the virtues to participation in practices; and although MacIntyre's definition allows a wide range of things to count as practices, participation in any of them will necessarily have a certain character. In the first place, participation in the practice requires acceptance of the authority of the standards and paradigms operative in the practice at the time. If we stick with chess as an example: unless I begin by accepting correction from those more versed in the game and regarding certain games and certain players as paradigmatic of chess excellence, I can never hope to achieve even a modest version of that excellence in my own play and so cannot hope to achieve the internal goods of chess. In short, I must subject my own preferences, tastes and attitudes to the communal standards and authorities that currently define the practice.

It is this feature of MacIntyre's notion of a practice that has been taken to show that he is committed to a form of conservatism, to the view that criticism of the status quo within a given practice is ruled entirely out of court. But this is a misreading of his position; for the fact that entry into a practice demands the subjection of my personal preferences to the standards prevailing in it does not entail that, subsequent to my entry, I must unquestioningly accept every judgement made by the community of other practitioners. MacIntyre is happy to admit that such judgements will often be disputed, and will sometimes be disputed at a fundamental level; after all, practices have a history within which the participants' perception of its paradigms and standards (and so of its internal goods) will change, and such disputes are the motor of that change. The point is that such disputes will be subject to certain constraints.

For example, it will not be enough merely to *assert* that Capablanca was a better chess player than Karpov, for any such judgement must be justifiable by reference to the standards and paradigms that govern and partly constitute the practice. I must argue, for example, that Karpov's end-game play lacks a certain fluidity, that he is prone to loss of nerve at crucial points in his matches, that even his best games display a strategic imagination very limited in comparison with Capablanca at his best. Of course, my interlocutor might disagree, arguing that Capablanca's imagination is insufficiently disciplined, as his 1946 game in Paris demonstrated and so on; it may even be the case that the two of us never resolve our disagreement. But our debate can be said to be a rational one because its progress has a logic: the process of grounding and disputing our differing judgements is governed by certain shared canons of relevance. We might disagree about the limitations of Karpov's strategic imagination, but we agree that the quality of that imagination is vital in any assessment of his claims to chess greatness; we might disagree over Capablanca's status relative to Karpov, but we agree that it is against the likes of Capablanca that Karpov's claim to chess greatness must be measured.

The same point holds for any attempt on the part of participants in a practice to alter the direction or self-understanding of that practice: such criticism may be radical, but it must nonetheless make reference to some one or other of the practice's paradigms and standards, on pain of being unrecognizable as a piece of chess criticism at all. Anyone who accepted that a given player lacked all strategic imagination, analytical skill and competitive intensity, but continued to claim that the player was a new brand of chess genius, would not be demonstrating a very different conception of chess greatness – he would be displaying complete incompetence in the practice of chess. In other words, the standards of the practice, together with the players and games regarded as paradigmatically great, provide a framework within which reasoned argument may be conducted and agreement may emerge (although, of course, agreement is not guaranteed). The framework itself is subject to change, but not all at once and not in any way the reformer pleases; for that framework serves to constitute the practice, and its total rejection would constitute the total obliteration of the practice rather than a change in its trajectory. Even the revolutionary critic must be a participant.

Judgements within practices therefore cannot be regarded as purely subjective or arbitrary; they cannot be given an emotivist analysis. It is not up to the individual to determine in an entirely abstract and ultimately criterionless way what she will regard as the achievement of chess excellence. Although she can decide to place more importance on certain chess-playing virtues than on others, she cannot pluck any old character trait out of the air and transform it into such a virtue; although she is not forced to agree with every judgement made by her fellow practitioners, she cannot decide for herself what will count as a relevant ground for such a judgement or what will count as a relevant response or counter to the ground she invokes. This framework of agreed modes of argument and shared canons of relevance allows us to achieve an objectivity and impersonality of judgement that transcends purely personal expressions of preference.

It seems, then, that participation in such shared projects, acceptance of such communally and historically determined standards, initiates the individual into forms of life in which human judgements of worth are immune to the threat of emotivism. Moreover, the fact that there can be many and varied practices, and so a wide variety of internal goods and virtues, signifies a healthy pluralism in MacIntyre's conception of what is valuable in human life. However, that same multiplicity of practices also raises a worry: for, granted that within a given practice questions about value and worth can be settled in non-arbitrary ways, what of questions about the relative value and worth of practices themselves? The fact that there are so many practices makes it likely that any given individual will participate in several at the same time, and the demands they make upon her will inevitably come into conflict; the demands of practising to become a chess Grand Master will conflict with the demands of being a good parent and spouse, the demands of the artist's life will conflict with those of the sportswoman. But no single practice can provide an overarching framework within which the question of which demands should take precedence can be given a rational or objective answer; arbitrary retentions and renunciations of allegiances seem inevitable. In short, MacIntyre must face the threat that these competing allegiances will fracture the life of the virtues. His response is his account of the narrative unity of a human life.

The narrative unity of a human life

Human behaviour cannot be understood simply as stretches of bodily movements. In order for such movements to count as actions at all, we must characterize them in relation to the intentions, desires and goals of the person whose bodily movements they are (even if only by saying that what was done was unintentional); and if we are to make sense of those intentions, we must relate them to what MacIntyre calls the setting of the action. He takes the case of a man digging his garden. Such an action can be rendered intelligible by explaining it either as the result of his intention to prepare the garden for winter, or as the result of his desire to please his wife; in the former case, the action is related to a particular type of household-cum-garden setting, in the latter to the setting and history of a marriage. Of course, any piece of behaviour may relate to more than one setting at the same time: the digging could be embedded in both of the settings invoked by my explanations of it; and if we wish to know exactly what the agent is doing, we will need to find out which of these settings is primary for him. Would he, for example, continue to perform the action if he discovered that his absences in the garden irritated his wife? In other words, we will need to identify his short-term intentions about the digging, their relation to one another, and their relation to his longer-term intentions concerning his marriage and his garden. In effect, we relate the agent's history to the history of the settings to which it belongs.

It seems, then, that rendering an action intelligible is a matter of grasping it as an episode in the history of the agent's life and of the settings in which it occurs; we come to view it as another instalment in a nesting of narratives. In other words, narrative history of a certain kind is the basic genre for the characterization of human action. This holds both for our characterization of other's actions and for our characterization of our own; in offering an explanation of what we are doing, we relate it to our own intentions and thereby present it under the aspect of a further episode in the narrative of our lives. This is what explains the fact that both short- and long-term stretches of our lives can be and are characterized in terms appropriate to literary works. Events ranging from conversations through chess games, courtships and seminars to marriages and careers are all capable of having dramatic shape: they have beginnings, middles and ends, they are subject to dramatic reversals and eleventh-hour reprieves, they develop and decline, they have digressions and subplots, they belong to genres (the tragic, the comic, the farcical). And in the absence of such patterning, they become alienating and unintelligible, both to those participating and to those observing. Because action has a basically historical character, our lives are enacted narratives in which we are both characters and authors; a person is a character abstracted from a history.

Of course, we are not entirely sovereign authors. We are subordinate characters in the dramas of others, the settings in which our actions must take place are and have been shaped in ways not fixed by us, and the future will always be ultimately unpredictable. Despite such constraints and unpredictability, however, the narrative form of our lives gives them a certain teleological character (without invoking metaphysical biology):

> We live out our lives, both individually and in our relationships with each other, in the light of certain conceptions of a possible shared future, a future in which certain possibilities beckon us forward and others repel us, some seem already foreclosed and others perhaps inevitable. There is no present which is not informed by some image of some future, and an image of the future which always presents itself in the form of a *telos* – or of a variety of ends or goals – towards which we are either moving or failing to move in the present. Unpredictability and teleology therefore coexist as part of our lives; like characters in a fictional narrative we do not know what will happen next, but nonetheless our lives have a certain form which projects

itself toward our future . . . If the narrative of our individual lives is to
continue intelligibly – and either type of narrative may lapse into
unintelligibility – it is always the case both that there are constraints
on how the story can continue *and* that within those constraints there
are indefinitely many ways in which it can continue. (*AV*, pp. 200–1)

It is this narrative form that provides the framework within which
we can attempt to make rational choices concerning the conflicting
demands of different practices. In effect, MacIntyre is saying to the
person trying to decide between spending more time playing chess
and spending more time with her family: 'Don't think of this as a
choice which is made in a vacuum, as if you have to decide whether
chess *per se* is more worthwhile than family life *per se*. This is a choice
that is being made by a particular person at a particular stage in
her particular life – one in which it may be clear that you have
exceptional chess potential and that your marriage is in a stage of
terminal decline, or in which it is clear that the years of your married
life have transformed a once obsessional commitment to chess into
a satisfying but ultimately secondary subplot. Ask yourself not
"Which internal goods are best?" but rather "Which matter most
to me?" or "Which decision will introduce or maintain the shape
or form which my life has begun to develop?"; ask yourself "Who
am I really – a chess player or a spouse?" This shift of perspective
will not *necessarily* isolate the one right thing for you to do, but it
might do so; and even if it doesn't, it provides a context within
which both you and anyone who knows you can distinguish between
better and worse options. Perhaps your decision will never come to
seem clearly right or wrong, or perhaps it will do so only in retro-
spect; but what allows such clarity of vision will be the shape that
your life took (its unity, depth and coherence) as a result of that
decision.'

Of course, in urging that we approach such dilemmas by asking
'How best may I live out the narrative unity of my life?', MacIntyre
is arguing that the asking of the question is at least as important to
an individual's success in living the good life for human beings as
the specific answers which may or may not emerge. Systematically
asking the question, and attempting to answer it in word and deed,
are what provide the moral life with its unity – the unity of a
narrative quest for the good. For embarking on such a quest amounts
to embarking upon a search for a conception of the good life that

will enable us to order the other goods in our lives and to extend our understanding of the virtues; but the goal of the quest is not separable from the quest itself, in the sense that it is only in the course of the quest and in the course of coping with the events that threaten such a project that its goal is finally to be understood.

It is because a quest educates the person engaged upon it, about herself as well as about what she is seeking, that MacIntyre can define the good life for human beings as a life spent searching for the good life for human beings, and not be accused of leaving an empty circularity at the heart of his definition. And he is now able to offer a second, revised definition of the virtues:

> The virtues are therefore to be understood as those dispositions which not only sustain practices and enable us to achieve the goods internal to them, but which will also sustain us in the relevant quest for the good by enabling us to overcome the harms, dangers, temptations and distractions which we encounter, and which will furnish us with increasing self-knowledge and increasing knowledge of the good. (*AV*, p. 204)

The concept of a tradition

Of course, the shape of this quest for the good life is not the same for all individuals everywhere. To begin with, the historical specificity of practices means that the good life for an Athenian general will not be the same as that of a medieval nun or a seventeenth-century farmer.

> But it is not just that different individuals live in different social cir-cumstances; it is also that we all approach our circumstances as bearers of a particular social identity. I am someone's son or daughter, someone else's cousin or uncle; I am a citizen of this or that city, a member of this or that guild or profession; I belong to this tribe, that clan, this nation. Hence what is good for me has to be what is good for one who inhabits these roles. As such I inherit from the past of my family, my city, my tribe, my nation, a variety of debts, inheritances, rightful expectation and obligations. These constitute the given of life, my moral starting-point. This in part is what gives my life its moral particularity. (*AV*, pp. 204–5)

The fit with MacIntyre's narrative conception of the self is obvious: in effect, he is claiming that the possession of a historical identity and the possession of a social identity coincide. The idea is not that one cannot rebel against that identity; it is rather that in so doing one is adopting one mode of acknowledging it, and that after doing so one will be in no less particular a set of circumstances: *pace* the emotivist self, there is no way of finding a realm of truly abstract and universal principle which holds only of human beings *per se*. MacIntyre is thus stressing a central part of what makes us less than wholly sovereign authors of our lives, and which provides a texture and framework within which we might make better and worse decisions about how to carry those narratives forward.

One central part of this social inheritance will be a person's membership of what MacIntyre calls a tradition. A tradition is constituted by a set of practices and is a mode of understanding their importance and worth; it is the medium by which such practices are shaped and transmitted across the generations. Traditions may be primarily religious or moral (for example Catholicism or humanism), political (for example Marxism), economic (for example a particular craft or profession, trade union or manufacturer), aesthetic (for example modes of literature or painting) or geographical (for example crystallizing around the history and culture of a particular house, village or region). The communal understanding embodied in such traditions is neither hegemonic nor static; on the contrary, in a healthy tradition that understanding will be the subject of continuous debate at any given moment and across time. So, when an institution (for example a church, a university, a hospital, a farm) is a bearer of such a tradition, its common life will be partly constituted by a continuous argument as to what a good church or university or hospital or farm might be – an argument that is constrained by that tradition's best self-understanding but that can move forward in an indefinite number of ways.

Insofar as persons must be understood as partly individuated by their membership of traditions, the history of their lives will be embedded in the larger narrative of a historically and socially extended argument about the good life for human beings. Most importantly of all, this background will determine that individual's resources for making rational decisions about how to pursue her quest for the good, for it will be in terms of that tradition's best understanding of itself (both of its practices and of the ways in which those practices might be evaluated and criticized) that she will evaluate and criticize her own efforts to live the good life. Part of developing a conception of the good life for human beings is developing a conception of how one might evaluate and criticize one's attempts to enact and extend that conception; and just as the former is open to revision and redefinition, so the standards by which such revisions are justified and rendered intelligible are themselves open to reshaping. For MacIntyre, the view that there is an ahistorical, timelessly applicable mode of practical reasoning to which all individuals can or must commit themselves is no more intelligible than the idea that there is a universally applicable evaluation of an internal good, or a timeless essence of the self.

However, this third stage in MacIntyre's reconstruction of morality seems to leave us prey to relativistic worries of precisely the sort that arose with respect to practices. For contemporary culture contains a multiplicity of traditions, and even if we are born into one of them we can only regard a decision to remain within it or to leave it for another as a rational one if there is some way of evaluating the relative validity of one tradition with respect to its rivals. If, however, the only available conceptions of practical reasoning are tradition-specific, then we must either rely upon one of those conceptions and beg the question against rival ones, or be reduced to an arbitrary (because criterionless) choice between traditions.

In *Whose Justice? Which Rationality?*, MacIntyre attempts to allay these worries. He argues that the relative worth or cogency of a tradition can be settled by examining its performance when it meets an *epistemological crisis*. Any tradition has its own internal standards for assessing the degree to which it is progressing and deepening its own understanding of its doctrines and conceptions of the good, or alternatively failing to transcend its previous achievements and finding it impossible to reduce the number of unresolved difficulties left on its agenda. When a tradition tends towards the latter pole – riven by sterile conflicts and reiterating old formulae – it is in a state of epistemological crisis. It can overcome the crisis only by developing a new set of concepts or a new synthesis of old doctrines and ideas, a framework that meets the following three conditions: it allows the tradition to solve its outstanding problems, to explain how they arose and why they had not hitherto been solved, and to do so in a way that exhibits fundamental continuity between the old and the new synthesis.

The internal availability of such a conceptually innovative synthesis is never guaranteed, and yet no tradition can be immune from the possibility of crises that require it for their valid or rational resolution. So it is possible that a tradition may not only decline but definitively founder as a result of such a crisis. Alternatively, however, its proponents may experience such a crisis, be unable to transcend it from within, and perceive that a rival tradition has the resources to construct concepts and theories that – by the standards of the tradition in crisis – both permit the solution of the critical problems and provide an account of the emergence of the crisis. Of course, these solutions and explanations are discontinuous with the tradition's old synthesis; but that merely confirms that the rival tradition has established its rational superiority over the tradition in crisis. The proponents of the latter are obliged, by virtue of their commitment to their own standards, to admit that the alien tradition is superior in rationality and in respect of its claims to truth.

If the reader is interested in looking in more detail at specific examples of traditions coping or failing to cope with such crises, *Whose Justice? Which Rationality?* provides a wealth of historical information, concentrating in particular upon Aquinas's synthesis of Christianity and Aristotelianism. Of course, MacIntyre's particular interpretations of these historical episodes are highly controversial, as is his general notion of an 'epistemological crisis'; but we have no space to explore these matters in any depth here. What matters most for our concerns is that, from MacIntyre's perspective, he has the resources needed to establish that traditions as a whole *are* open to rational assessment: 'It is in respect of their adequacy or inadequacy in their responses to epistemological crises that traditions are vindicated or fail to be vindicated.'[2] And when there is no crisis, then *ex hypothesi* there is no good reason for any member of any tradition to put his allegiance to it in question, and every reason to continue within it.

MacIntyre and liberalism

The central weight that MacIntyre places upon the interrelated concepts of a practice, the narrative unity of a human life and a tradition should at least make it clear that he is a fundamentally communitarian thinker; for on his view, the very possibility of sustaining rationality and objectivity in the arena of moral and political evaluation depends upon locating individuals and their arguments with other individuals within an overarching and nested set of inherently social matrices. This gives the concept of 'community' a much broader and more vital role than it has in Sandel's work. On the latter's view, the liberal myopia about the possibility of individuals developing constitutive attachments to their ends entailed a failure properly to acknowledge *one* important sort of human good – the sort that is strongly communal in content, and so can only be achieved through constitutive attachments to the community. But on MacIntyre's view, failing to recognize the way in which human beings can be and are constitutively attached to their communities entails an inability to give a coherent account of the circumstances necessary to achieve *any* kind of human good (whether communal in content or not), for in the absence of such constitutive communal frameworks, the very idea of morality as a rational or intelligible enterprise drops out.

The important question for our purposes, however, is whether liberalism in general and Rawlsian liberalism in particular can or should be read as ignoring or denying the communitarian claims that MacIntyre makes. Why does MacIntyre think that liberalism – as opposed, say, to emotivism – is a legitimate target for his critique? In short, why and in what ways does he think that liberalism is a species or variant of emotivism?

We claimed earlier that MacIntyre criticizes liberalism under four of the five headings mentioned on our original agenda of issues. To begin with, he accuses liberals of being committed to an incoherent emotivist-style conception of the self as unencumbered, and – as a consequence – to the view that the moral judgements made by such a self are inherently arbitrary and subjective rather than being capable of rational or objective justification. In *After Virtue*, he clearly thinks that these two criticisms apply to liberalism generally, and so must presumably think that Rawls's theory of justice is vulnerable to them as well; but he provides little textual evidence to back up this claim. It therefore seems that those who wish to co-opt MacIntyre as a critic of Rawls will here have to take advantage of the fact that MacIntyre's versions of these two criticisms parallel those of Sandel. In other words, a communitarian might plausibly argue that Sandel's detailed textual arguments for the presence and importance in Rawlsian liberalism of a conception of the self as antecedently individuated themselves constitute the main grounds for concluding that Rawls falls under MacIntyre's critical fire. MacIntyre's unencumbered emotivist self and Sandel's antecedently individuated self are so similar that they stand and fall together: if Rawls can be shown to hold the latter, he can be taken to hold the former; and if he can be shown not to hold the latter, then he cannot be taken to hold the former.

Of course, as we noted at the very beginning of this chapter, although MacIntyre and Sandel both criticize liberalism for its conception of the person and its commitment to moral subjectivism, they differ in their diagnosis of the reasons for liberalism's commitment to these views. For Sandel, the liberal conception of the person is the defining characteristic of that mode of moral and political theory, and its commitment to moral subjectivism is a consequence of its cleaving to that conception. But for MacIntyre, both that conception of the person and the commitment to moral subjectivism are consequences of a more fundamental liberal myopia, namely their inability to comprehend or accommodate the importance of the community in maintaining the objectivity of all moral thought and the integrity of human identity. In short, a full comprehension of MacIntyre's first two criticisms will lead us on to a third charge – the claim that liberalism is essentially a form of asocial individualism in politics and morality. But in this respect as well, his attack on liberalism is different from Sandel's: for whereas, under this heading, Sandel restricts himself to the charge that liberalism is blind to the importance of human goods (both political and non-political) whose *content* is social or communal, MacIntyre's view is that liberalism is a reflection in politics of the general modern inability to perceive that every human good or end (whether communal in content or not) has its *origin* in social matrices – that all human goods derive from a framework of overlapping communal practices and traditions. And here MacIntyre does attempt to argue explicitly that Rawls's conception of politics and political theory is vulnerable to his attacks.

His ground for accusing Rawls of endorsing a political variant of this asocial individualism seems to be the role of the original position in Rawls's argument, and in particular the fact that this device of representation is a modern-dress version of the social contract, which encourages us to think of the structure of society as something about which people who already possess certain interests can come together and negotiate under certain other conditions of voluntarily imposed ignorance about themselves.

> For ... Rawls a society is composed of individuals, each with his or her own interest, who then have to come together and formulate common rules of life ... Individuals are thus ... primary and society secondary, and the identification of individual interests is prior to, and independent of, the construction of any moral or social bonds between them. (*AV*, pp. 232–3)

MacIntyre's claim is thus that, by positing the original position as an appropriate device of representation for thinking about justice, Rawls reveals his view that entry into society ought ideally to be envisaged as the voluntary act of rational individuals with prior interests whose question is 'What kind of social contract is it reasonable for me to enter into with these others?' Such a vision would, MacIntyre claims, entirely exclude the possibility that society is or might be a community whose primary bond is a shared understanding both of the good for human beings and of the good of that community, and within which individuals identify their primary interests by reference to those goods. It is, he thinks, a possibility that Rawls cannot envisage because of what MacIntyre calls his explicit presupposition that '. . . we must expect to disagree with others about what the good life for man is and must therefore exclude any understanding of it that we may have from our formulation of the principles of justice' (*AV*, p. 233).

But, of course, from MacIntyre's perspective, it is only by working to establish and maintain precisely the sort of shared communal understandings of the good that Rawls explicitly excludes from our deliberations about justice that we can confer any rationality or objectivity upon the course of those deliberations. For it is only by introducing a conception of desert in relation to the common tasks of the community in pursuing shared goods that we can provide the basis for rational judgements about social virtue and social injustice. In the absence of the strong social bonds that create space for such a conception of desert, MacIntyre argues that Rawls's task of developing a conception of justice upon which we can all agree is doomed to failure; and he asserts that Rawls's inability to justify

the importance he attributes to a principle of equality with respect
to needs against competing basic premises (for example Nozick's
principle of entitlement) merely exemplifies the incommensurability
that descends upon such matters when they are shorn of their communal matrix.

So, for MacIntyre, Rawls's asocial individualism ensures that he
will be incapable of giving his theory of justice the rational grounding
it requires, and his theory will accordingly be incapable of forming
the substance of a political consensus in his society – of filling the
very vacuum that leads him to forbid himself any reference in his
political theorizing to specific conceptions of the good. MacIntyre
thus associates Rawls with a long tradition of individualistic political
thought, in which it seems as if '. . . we had been shipwrecked on
an uninhabited island with a group of other individuals, each of
whom is a stranger to me and to all the others' (*AV*, p. 233). The
question of how far this characterization accurately reflects Rawls's
position and how far it merely caricatures it is one that, technically
at least, we will be leaving open until chapter 5; but even at this
stage, it is worth pointing out something of which MacIntyre seems
to take no account. As we suggested in our Introduction, whilst the
structure of the original position does show that Rawls places a
great deal of emphasis upon the individual, and upon that
individual's social structures being ones to which he or she might
be thought freely to consent, it does not necessarily embody the
claim that individuals are in some chronological or logical sense
prior to society, and so that their conceptions of the good are not
necesssarily social in origin. It is meant to be a device of representation, a way of thinking about justice in which people already in a
society ignore certain information about their social identity without having to imagine that they could actually be divested of their
membership of society and still remain capable of the sort of thinking
in which they are at present engaged. It therefore seems at least
possible that the original position is not so much an attempt to
represent society as a collection of individuals essentially lacking
any social bonds, but rather an attempt to represent precisely the
common assumptions about an individual's primary interests that
constitute the bonds that hold our particular liberal society together.
In short, it may well be that Rawls has designed the original position
to reflect the high importance that our political community attaches
to the liberty and equality of its citizens; in particular, his exclusion

of specific conceptions of the good may be designed to reflect the importance we attach to (what might be expressed in MacIntyre's terms as) the capacity freely to search for the good life for human beings without the state discriminating against certain forms of answer to that question.

We will take up this matter in more detail in later chapters, but it is worth raising at this point because it seems likely that an appreciation of this possibility on MacIntyre's part led him to alter the fundamental orientation of his attack upon liberalism in the seven years between the publication of *After Virtue* and that of *Whose Justice, Which Rationality?* In the earlier book, as we have seen, MacIntyre treats liberalism as a mode of thought whose presuppositions are such that it is incapable of understanding the true nature and source of morality and human identity, and so cannot really be thought of as a genuine *moral* position at all. In the later book, however, MacIntyre's conception of liberalism and his criticisms of it are placed in a much more detailed historical perspective, and he ends by claiming that contemporary liberalism is in fact a genuine and viable moral and political tradition. Of course, this does not make him any more enthusiastic about the elements that go to make it up; but now his criticism of it primarily takes the form of suggesting that the tradition-bound nature of liberalism ensures that it cannot be as neutral between competing conceptions of the good as it might appear to be – which is, of course, his fourth criticism of it, and a version of the fifth theme from our original agenda of issues.

The story MacIntyre tells is of a moral tradition that has its historical origins in the Enlightenment attempt to develop a morality that transcends tradition. He locates liberal political theory as part of a historical project of founding a social order in which individuals could emancipate themselves from the contingency and particularity of traditions by appealing to genuinely universal, tradition-independent norms. Initially the liberal claim was to provide a political, legal and economic framework in which assent to one and the same rationally justifiable principles would enable those who espouse widely different and incompatible conceptions of the good life to live peaceably together within the same society. According to MacIntyre, however, this goal necessarily entailed proscribing any attempts to reshape the life of the community in accord with any one particular conception of the good:

And this qualification of course entails not only that liberal individualism does indeed have its own broad conception of the good, which
it is engaged in imposing politically, legally, socially and culturally
wherever it has the power to do so, but also that in so doing its
toleration of rival conceptions of the good in the public arena is se-
verely limited.[3]

What MacIntyre includes under this broad liberal conception of the
good, and claims to locate in contemporary representatives of this
tradition such as Rawls, are such elements as the following: a
distinctive conception of a just order (a primarily procedural one),
of the modes of practical reasoning that are permitted within that
order (treating moral beliefs as expressions of purely personal
preference), and of the good life for human beings (one in which a
variety of goods is pursued, each appropriate to its own sphere,
with no overall good supplying any overall unity to life). It might
seem surprising to think of Rawls's position as including the third
of these elements; but MacIntyre cites a passage from *A Theory of
Justice* that confirms that it does so: 'Human good is heterogeneous
because the aims of the self are heterogeneous. Although to
subordinate all our aims to one end does not strictly speaking violate
the principles of rational choice . . . it still strikes us as irrational or
more likely as mad. The self is disfigured' (*TJ*, p. 554). Moreover,
for MacIntyre these elements are not only present in theories such
as that of Rawls: they are embodied, debated and carried forward
through the medium of a specific set of social, legal and cultural
institutions – the institutions of a distinctively liberal social order.
In other words, what began (with Kant and others) as an attempt
to found morality upon tradition-independent principles which any
human beings could accept insofar as they were rational, ended
with the creation and perpetuation of one more moral tradition:
'Liberal theory is best understood, not at all as an attempt to find
a rationality independent of tradition, but as itself the articulation
of a historically developed and developing set of social institutions
and forms of activity, that is, as the voice of a tradition.'[4]
    At first sight, however, it seems the very reverse of a radical
criticism of liberal political theorists to tell them that they are
proponents of a specific political tradition. Representing a tradition
is, on MacIntyre's own terms, an inevitable consequence of taking
any evaluative stance, and so cannot be seen as a weakness; and it

is difficult to imagine that contemporary liberal theorists (as opposed, say, to their historical forebears) would be surprised to be told that the continued sustenance of a distinctively liberal political order was their overriding goal. As we saw in our Introduction, when liberals such as Rawls claimed to be neutral between competing conceptions of the good, they could never have meant that they were neutral between liberalism and other forms of politics; and they have never denied that they will proscribe any conception of the good whose pursuit interferes with the equal right of other citizens freely to pursue their own conception of the good. What they distinctively claim is a neutrality of justification which forbids them from invoking any conception of the good in defence of state policies and actions, even if those policies and actions will inevitably have non-neutral effects. In short, it seems that MacIntyre's criticisms of liberal neutrality cannot be taken seriously in the extreme form in which they are stated, since those statements seem to amount to accusing liberals of being liberal.

There may, nonetheless, be a grain or two of truth in the point that he makes. First, it is all very well to say that contemporary liberal political theorists have always known that they are beginning from liberal starting-points; but that fact may not have been so obvious to many people in contemporary society whose primary awareness of liberalism is likely to be precisely its claimed neutrality between competing conceptions of the good. It may not be inconsistent for liberalism to acknowledge the true extent of its neutrality and toleration; but such an acknowledgement might well alter non-academics' views about its attractiveness as a social ideology.

The second grain of truth emerges if we acknowledge that the liberal tradition's distinctive refusal to employ conceptions of the good to justify state actions is of course one that operates only within the realm of politics: individuals are perfectly free to act in accordance with such conceptions in other areas of their lives. In other words, a split between political and non-political matters, between the spheres of public and private morality, is central to liberal thought. But MacIntyre's neo-Aristotelianism rejects that split: it is founded upon a conception of the political community as a fundamental arena within which our understanding and im-plementation of the good life for human beings can be developed, and so integrates politics more closely with considerations that liberalism restricts to the realm of private morality. And MacIntyre's position is not the only one to contest this matter: we might think here of many traditions of religious thought.

What this makes clear is that establishing and maintaining a separation of the political and private spheres is a tradition-specific idea; it is itself a matter of real controversy. And according to MacIntyre, justifying and defending it against its opponents will involve drawing upon specifically liberal conceptions of practical reasoning and of human life more generally; it will involve drawing upon a wide range of other elements in the general liberal moral tradition. If this claim could be justified, it would seem to follow that any attempt to maintain a liberal political order is no less dependent upon the invocation of a general conception of the good life for human beings than is MacIntyre's own position. In short, the neutrality that liberals do typically claim for their conception of politics may be far less significant than it appears.

Of course, whether this criticism, together with the other three criticisms mentioned earlier, should be held to be valid of liberalism in general and of Rawls in particular is a matter that we must leave to later chapters; but it should at least be clearer why MacIntyre thinks that Rawls falls into his target area.

Notes

1 The three volumes that are pertinent to our concerns are: *After Virtue* (hereafter *AV*), *Whose Justice? Which Rationality?* and *Three Rival Versions of Moral Enquiry*.
2 MacIntyre, *Whose Justice?*, p. 366.
3 Ibid., p. 336.
4 Ibid., p. 345.

3

TAYLOR:
the sources of the liberal self

Unlike Sandel and like MacIntyre, Charles Taylor's work in the domain of political theory[1] is integrated into a sweeping analytical account of the development of Western moral and political culture from Plato to post-modernism;[2] and in this account, Rawls appears only fleetingly whilst liberalism has a role primarily as one central strand of modern culture rather than as the sole focus of Taylor's concerns. Moreover, and unlike either Sandel or MacIntyre, Taylor is not inclined to reject liberalism *per se*; on the contrary, he thinks that some of its central claims are worthy of very serious consideration, but only if they can be detached from various erroneous or incoherent ways of elucidating or defending them. Our key question must therefore be whether Rawlsian liberalism counts as one such erroneous defence of liberal values; and this question can be answered only by determining in some detail what sort of errors and incoherences Taylor is concerned to eradicate – errors that relate to the form and scope of moral evaluation in general. In short, before we can determine whether Taylor's work furnishes material for a critique of Rawls, we must follow his exploration of what may seem to be very abstract issues in moral philosophy.

   We can at least, however, state in advance the main aspects of Taylor's framework of thought that have suggested to many of his readers that he has constructed a communitarian critique of liberalism. This suggestion is based upon Taylor's view that human beings are self-interpreting animals, creatures whose identity as persons depends upon their orientation and attachment to conceptions of the good which they derive from the matrix of their linguistic community. If such a communitarian view of human beings is correct, then it would clearly reveal the incoherence of any political theory that embodied a conception of persons as antecedently individuated and/or occluded the necessarily social origin of people's ends – the first and second themes on our original agenda of issues. Another aspect of Taylor's work is his view that moral judgements and intuitions are essentially capable of rational elucidation or articulation, a process that requires the invocation of fundamental and wide-ranging evaluative frameworks, also deriving from the community; these claims imply that Taylor will be hostile to any form of moral subjectivism or scepticism (the fourth theme on our agenda), and deeply suspicious of any political theory that claims not to rely upon anything other than a thin theory of the good (the fifth theme). However, in order to see whether Taylor's views are worthy of respect, we must examine then in more detail.

The status of moral intuitions

According to Taylor, our ordinary and widely shared moral intuitions – for example, a respect for the worth and dignity of others which emerges in instinctive reactions of horror and pity when that dignity is violated – have a dual aspect. On the one hand, they seem fundamental and purely instinctual, like reactions of nausea to certain tastes; on the other, they are articulable in accounts of what elicits them: agents manifesting them are often capable of explaining just what it is about human beings that merits or deserves the reaction. We might, for example, claim that human beings possess a dignity that deserves respect because they are children of God, or rational choosers of ends; in other words, we articulate our intuitions by developing a particular ontology of the human.

It is vital to see that this second aspect of moral intuitions completely distinguishes them from brute reactions such as nausea or delight at certain tastes. In the latter case, we simply do not acknowledge that there is anything to articulate or argue about. If someone is made nauseous by the taste of vodka, there is no question of asking him for an explanation of this or of attempting to persuade him that his reaction is ill-judged; the connection between the substance's properties and the reaction is just a brute fact. In the case of the moral intuition, we also react to a particular property of a given object, but here the property marks the object as one *meriting* the reaction. In this case there is a question as to the fitness of our response to the object; there is room for reasoning and argument about whether our reaction is the correct or most appropriate one, and for charges of inconsistency between our reactions. In short, in those arguments we invoke descriptions of the object whose criteria are independent of our given reactions; we are dealing with an instance of what Taylor has called 'strong evaluation' – discriminations of right and wrong in terms of standards that are independent of our given desires and preferences and that allow us to evaluate their worth.

In effect, then, our moral reactions implicitly acknowledge claims made upon us by their objects, and the various ontological accounts mentioned above are attempts to articulate those claims. Moreover, those accounts cannot simply be regarded as ornamental rhetoric which must be discarded if we are to reach a truly objective understanding of the validity of the reactions themselves; for the account and the reaction are internally related. The terms of the account specify the character or identity of the reaction: in characterizing the property of the object that merits the reaction, they are specifying what the reaction is a reaction *to* and so telling us precisely what reaction it is. If we dispense with the ontological account, there would be no space for an argument at all because the terms of that account are the only possible terms for that argument; in dispensing with it we would thus lose from view precisely what we were arguing about, and transform the reaction into (rather than revealing it to be) something akin to reactions of nausea. Moral growth may require that we repress or alter some of our reactions and develop others, but it could never require us to prescind from our reactions altogether; they are 'our mode of access to the world in which ontological claims are discernible and can be rationally argued about and sifted' (*SS*, p. 8).

Taylor thinks of moral intuitions and moral thinking in general as having three axes. The first has to do with our relations to other human beings – our sense of their worth and dignity, of what we owe them; the second has to do with our conceptions of the good life for human beings in general – our sense of what a full or flourishing human life consists in; and the third has to do with our sense of our own dignity or status – of the characteristics by which we command or fail to command the respect of others. Since all three axes presuppose some conception of the nature or status of human beings, this way of organizing the articulation of moral intuitions emphasizes the point that an ontological account is an essential part of that articulation. It also makes it clear that moral frameworks developed around those three axes will necessarily involve the notion of strong evaluation. For example, people asking themselves what the good life for human beings might be are well aware that their present desires could lead them to answer the question wrongly and waste or otherwise destroy their lives. In other words, any such framework incorporates a crucial set of qualitative distinctions; judging within them involves having the sense that some actions, modes of life or inflections of feeling are incomparably higher than those that might be more readily available to us. Such ends are worthy or desirable in a way that cannot be measured on the same scale as our ordinary desires and ends; they are not just quantitatively more desirable, but rather possess a qualitatively different status, one that commands our respect, admiration and awe.

It is Taylor's claim that no system of moral thinking can avoid engaging in such strong evaluation, even if only implicitly, since if it failed to do so, it would not constitute an ethic at all. In particular, systems such as utilitarianism, which pride themselves on denouncing more traditional moralities such as the honour ethic or the monastic ideal for perversely downgrading or denying the worth of ordinary human satisfactions, are (Taylor argues) themselves committed to distinguishing between different modes of achieving those ordinary satisfactions. An ordinary human life of irrationality, alienation or slavery – in other words, one that ignored or repressed the importance of instrumental reason – could not be regarded by utilitarians as an admirable, worthy or higher life. More generally, the notion that *whatever* we do might be acceptable is untenable simply because that could never be an intelligible basis for a conception of human dignity. In other words, strong evaluation is inescapable in the world shaped by our moral responses.

The self in moral space

So far, Taylor has been arguing that our moral reactions presuppose an ontological account of some sort: we cannot explicate what makes sense of our moral responses without articulating a framework along the three axes outlined above. This already provides strong reasons for rejecting moral subjectivism, where that is understood as the claim that moral intuitions and reactions are no more than the essentially arbitrary expression of preference; for such a claim fails to acknowledge the responsibility we have to articulate the *grounds* of our intuitions insofar as we present those intuitions as moral ones. The next stage of his argument is designed to show that developing, maintaining and articulating such intuitions is not something that human beings could easily or even conceivably dispense with; for the evaluative frameworks whose existence is presupposed by moral argumentation are also presupposed by our concept of personhood. According to Taylor, we cannot make sense of human agency if we dispense with the strong, qualitative discriminations that such frameworks embody.

> Moreover, this is not meant just as a contingently true psychological fact about human beings, which could perhaps turn out one day not to hold for some exceptional individual or new type, some superman of disengaged objectification. Rather the claim is that living within such strongly qualified horizons is constitutive of human agency, that stepping outside these limits would be tantamount to stepping outside what we recognize as integral, that is, undamaged human personhood. (*SS*, p. 27)

Taylor's claim is that a vital part of knowing who I am is knowing where I stand; my identity is defined by the commitments and identifications that provide the horizon within which I can determine from case to case what is valuable, good or worth doing. People who define their identity in terms of their commitment to a church or political party, or their membership of a nation, class or tribe, are not merely claiming that they have a strong feeling of attachment to certain values or views; they mean that such identifications provide an evaluative framework without which they would no longer know what the significance of a wide range of things was for them, without which they would be at sea. Our moral orientation is thus an essential part of our sense of our own identity.

But why should this be so? Taylor's claim is that the question 'Who are you?' is asked to place someone as a potential interlocutor in a society of interlocutors; we answer it by giving our name, our relationships to others ('I'm John's sister'), our social role ('I'm the President'), our commitments ('I'm an anarchist, a Quebecois etc.'). So, someone who qualifies as a potential object of this question is someone with her own standpoint or role amongst others, each of whom has their own standpoint or role – she is someone who can speak for herself. But to be able to answer such a question, to answer for oneself, is to know where one stands – to know what one wants to answer; and that is in part a matter of knowing one's fundamental moral orientation. An agent free of all frameworks would be in the grip of an appalling identity crisis, unable to know where he stood on a variety of fundamental issues, unable to answer for himself on them; and one who did not suffer this absence as a lack would be in the grip of a frightening dissociation, a pathological condition far beyond the range of what we would normally describe as shallowness. Since our identity is what allows us to define what is, and what is not, important to us, it could not be entirely without strong evaluations; so the notion of an identity defined by some mere *de facto*, not strongly valued preference is incoherent.

Thus, the idea that the adoption of a moral framework is optional is fundamentally wrong; a moral orientation is inescapable because the questions to which the framework provides answers are themselves inescapable.

> ... to speak of orientation is to presuppose a space-analogue within which one finds one's way. To understand our predicament in terms of finding or losing orientation in moral space is to take the space which our framework seeks to define as ontologically basic. The issue is, Through what framework-definitions can I find my bearings in it? In other words, we take as basic that the human agent exists in a space of questions. And these are the questions to which our framework-definitions are answers, providing the horizon within which we know where we stand, and what meanings things have for us. (*SS*, p. 29)

Finding my bearings is something I do in a space that exists independently both of me and of my success or failure in orienting myself within it. Taylor's spatial metaphor thus brings out the objective status of the questions to which moral frameworks provide answers, the fact that the space that those questions define is no more a human fiction than physical space itself; we can no more imagine a human life that fails to address the matter of its bearings in moral space than we can imagine one in which developing a sense of up and down, right and left was regarded as an optional human task.

Selves and self-interpretations

One way of summarizing the claims that Taylor makes about the relation between human identity and the possession and deployment of a moral framework would be to say that the identity of the human self is bound up with and partially constituted by that self's sense of the meaning or significance of the objects and situations he encounters in his life. If we rephrase the matter in this way, we can see more clearly that the views Taylor develops in *Sources of the Self* are based upon a fundamental idea which he articulated almost 20 years before, in a paper entitled 'Interpretation and the Sciences of Man'. This idea was that human beings must be thought of as self-interpreting animals, as beings whose nature and identity is not specifiable independently of their self-interpretations; and it is worth looking in more detail at its relation to the later claims we have been examining.

In that early article, Taylor pointed out that a certain notion of meaning had a vital place in any attempt to characterize human behaviour; this is the sense in which we speak of a situation, an action, a demand, a prospect having a certain meaning for a person, for example talking of a terrifying situation or an attractive prospect. Our actions are ordinarily characterized by the purpose sought and explained by reference to desires, thoughts, and emotions; but the language by which we describe those goals and feelings or emotions is also that used to describe the meaning of a situation for an agent. The vocabulary defining such meaning ('terrifying', 'attractive') is closely linked with that describing feeling ('fear', 'desire') and that describing goals ('safety', 'possession').

Moreover, these three sets of terms are so closely related that we can only understand one of them by grasping their relation to the others; as Taylor puts it, they form a hermeneutic circle. For example, an emotion such as shame essentially refers us to a certain sort of situation (a 'shameful' or 'humiliating' one) and to a certain sort of response to it (hiding, covering up and so on); and it is essential to this emotion's being identifiable as shame that it be tied up with situations of this sort and give rise to dispositions of this type. But shameful situations can only be identified as situations that provoke shameful feelings; and the disposition is to a goal that similarly cannot be understood except by reference to the feelings experienced – the hiding in question is one that will cover up my shame, not one that is appropriate to being hunted by an armed enemy.

Just like moral reactions, then, a wide range of human feelings and actions are not brute phenomena (such as nausea), but can be appropriate or inappropriate to their situation: we can feel ashamed of things that another would argue are not genuinely shameful, and fail to respond appropriately to situations that genuinely are shameful ones. More importantly, however, the characterization of human feelings and purposes – and so their specific identity – is inseparable from the vocabulary the agent employs to characterize the meaning or significance of the situations in which he finds himself. And it follows that human behaviour itself (which cannot be understood as action unless related to a background of desire, feeling, emotion and purpose) can only be characterized in terms of the meaning that the situation in which the action occurs possesses for the agent concerned.

At this point, Taylor reminds us that the vocabulary that we employ to characterize the experiential meaning of situations has its particular significance only as part of a semantic field, a set of related but contrasting concepts. Each term in the field derives its meaning from the contrasts that exist between it and other terms in the field. For example, describing a situation as 'fearful' will mean something different according to whether the contrasts available in my vocabulary include such terms as 'terrifying', 'worrying', 'disconcerting', 'threatening', 'disgusting' or not; the wider the field of available contrasts, the finer are the discriminations that can be made by the choice of one term as opposed to another, and the more specific the significance of each term becomes. Thus, the use of the same term as part of two different semantic fields, or its use before and after the introduction of a new term into its semantic field, will result in a change of that term's meaning; and this will in turn effect a change in the experiential meaning of the situations it characterizes, and in the feelings or purposes that are internally related to those situations.

More generally, however, this means that the significance of the situations in which an agent finds himself, and so the import and nature of his emotions and goals, is determined by the range and structure of the vocabulary available to him for their characterization. He cannot feel shame if he lacks a vocabulary in which the circle of situation, feeling and disposition characteristic of shame is absent; and the precise nature of that feeling of shame will alter according to the range of the semantic field in which that vocabulary is embedded (shame as opposed to what?). Of course, the relation between feeling and available vocabulary is not a simple one. It is not just a matter of the vocabulary corresponding more or less adequately to pre-existing feelings, for we often experience how gaining access to a more sophisticated vocabulary makes our emotional life more sophisticated. On the other hand, neither is it a question of thinking making it so, for not any definition can be forced on us, whether by others or by ourselves; and some that we gladly take up can be judged inauthentic, self-deluded and wrong-headed. Nonetheless, however careful we must be in avoiding these opposing errors, it remains true that the relationship between a person's inner life and the vocabulary available to him for characterizing or interpreting it is an intimate one.

Taylor draws the following conclusions from this analysis:

> If this is so, then we have to think of man as a self-interpreting animal. He is necessarily so, for there is no such thing as the structure of meanings for him independently of his interpretation of them; for one is woven into the other. But then the text of our interpretation is not that heterogeneous from what is interpreted; for what is interpreted is itself an interpretation; a self-interpretation of experiential meaning which contributes to the constitution of this meaning. Or to put it another way: that of which we are trying to find the coherence is itself partly constituted by self-interpretation.[3]

This passage makes rather heavy weather of a relatively clear point. Taylor's claim is that to be an agent is to experience one's situation in terms of certain meanings; and this can in a sense be thought of as a sort of proto-interpretation, which is in turn interpreted and shaped by the language in which the agent lives these meanings.

Moreover, if this is true at the fundamental level of feelings and reactions such as shame and fear, it will be even more pertinent at the level of a person's sense of his own character, his conceptions of the good life and his conception of his own nature. In short, a person's identity – both as a specific individual and as a type of agent – is partly (perhaps primarily) constituted by internalized self-interpretations. Or, as Taylor puts it in his most recent writings, the identity of the human self is bound up with that self's sense of the significance and meaning of the objects and situations it encounters in life.

The self and the community

However he puts it, Taylor is clearly opposing any conception of the self that regards human beings as the sorts of entities whose nature and identity is fixed, and so can be studied independently of any descriptions or interpretations offered of it by human beings. In contrast with the objects of scientific study, to ask what a person is in abstraction from his self-interpretations is to ask a fundamentally misguided question.

> We are not selves in the way that we are organisms, or we don't have selves in the way we have hearts and livers. We are living beings with these organs quite independently of our self-understandings or inter-pretations, or the meanings things have for us. But we are only selves insofar as we move in a certain space of questions, as we seek and find an orientation to the good. (*SS*, p. 34)

And for Taylor, this essential relation between selves and self-interpretation entails an equally essential relation between selves and other selves – a relation to the community. We can see this in two ways. First, gaining access to self-interpretations is a matter of gaining access to a vocabulary that embodies them, and according to Taylor a language only exists in a language community. Second, if my self-definitions are thought of as answers to the question 'Who am I?', and this question finds its original sense in the inter-change of speakers, then I can define who I am only by defining my relations to other selves, by establishing where I speak from in the family tree, in social space, in my intimate relations to the ones I love, and so on. Both ways of looking at the matter entail that one is a self only amongst other selves.

Moreover, these two views of the matter are interconnected. On the one hand, Taylor claims that being initiated into a language is a matter of entering into ongoing conversations between those who bring us up; the first meanings of the words I learn are the meanings that they have for me and my conversation partners together. But such talk is primarily talk *about* something, and will serve to characterize the significance of that something for the talkers. So I can only learn what anger, love, anxiety etc. are through my and others' common experience of their significance for us – that is, for people with a particular role or status in the web of relationships that make up our community.

Later, of course, I may innovate, developing an understanding of myself and human life that is in sharp disagreement with my family and background; there is no reactionary exclusion of change or criticism in Taylor's position. But he does want to stress that such innovations can only take place from a base in our common language, and their significance can only be understood if they are placed in relation to (even if only in sharp contrast with) the vision and conceptions of others. The very confidence that we know what we mean depends upon what is in effect a conversation (even if only an imaginary or possible conversation) with human inter-locutors.

> This is the sense in which one cannot be a self on one's own. I am a self only in relation to certain interlocutors: in one way in relation to those conversation partners who were essential to my achieving self-definition; in another in relation to those who are now crucial to my continuing grasp of languages of self-understanding – and, of course, these classes may overlap. A self exists only within what I call 'webs of interlocution'. (*SS*, p. 36)

In short, the full definition of someone's identity usually involves not only his stand on moral and spiritual matters but also some reference to a defining community. This is why any attempt to comprehend the integrity and identity of human beings in what Taylor calls atomistic terms, to regard society as merely an aggregation of such antecedently individuated atoms in the absence of which human beings would still be human, is incoherent. In terms of the two main strands we distinguished under the second heading of our agenda, Taylor's position places him primarily in opposition to philosophical rather than to substantive asocial individualism; if people are self-interpreting animals, they need not give most importance to conceptions of the good whose *content* is strongly communal, but their self-interpretation must be able to acknowledge the necessarily social *origin* of any and all of their conceptions of the good and so of themselves. It was no accident that our earlier answers to the question 'Who am I?' made reference to family relationships and memberships of certain cultures, traditions and nations. Identifying oneself as an Armenian or a Quebecois is an essential part of identifying where one is speaking from and who one is speaking to – it is essential to one's self-interpretations.

Orientation and narration

So far, we have tried to show the strong sense in which Taylor's view of human beings as self-interpreting animals commits him to the view that the individual's relation to his community is constitutive of his identity. What we must demonstrate now is how this generally communitarian framework of thought leads him to other specific conclusions about the nature of human selfhood which we have already seen developed by other communitarian thinkers (in particular by MacIntyre).

As we saw earlier, Taylor's inclination to speak of moral frameworks as means of achieving orientation in a certain space of questions carries the implication that the relevant space exists independently of our ability or inability to find our bearings within it; it is an aspect of human ontology as fundamental as the need to establish our bearings in physical space. Now we must turn to another crucial implication of the metaphor of orientation in space, one that flows from the fact that orientation has two aspects: that there are *two* ways in which we can fail to have it. We can be ignorant of the lie of the land around us, lacking a map of the major landmarks and their relationship to one another; or we can possess a map, and yet not know where to place ourselves upon it. By analogy, our

orientation in relation to the good requires not only some framework that defines the shape of the qualitatively higher but also a
sense of where we stand in relation to this evaluative landmark.
And if it is fundamental to our status as agents that we place
ourselves in a space defined by certain qualitative distinctions, then
where we stand in relation to those distinctions must matter to us:
'Not being able to function without orientation in the space of the
ultimately important means not being able to stop caring where we
sit in it' (*SS*, p. 42). Taylor's point here, with its presumption of the
possibility and importance of constitutive attachments to goods,
has a very Sandelian ring. His claim is that the goods that define
our spiritual orientation are the ones by which we will measure the
worth of our lives (the second of Taylor's axes); and this concern
with the worth or meaningfulness of our lives is best thought of as
a concern with how we are situated or placed in relation to those
goods – whether we are in contact with them or not, whether we
are *rightly* placed with respect to them. And, as the spatial metaphor
further suggests, this issue can arise for us in two different senses.
First, we can ask ourselves how close we are to those goods – to
what degree my life manifests and embodies the domestic harmony or artistic achievement to which I am committed; and second,
we can ask whether we are pointed in the right direction in the
first place – however far away I am from the domestic harmony I
crave, I can at least know that my basic stance and commitment to
that good, my determination to live a life focused upon it, is firmly
set.

In other words, the issue for beings like us is not just where we
are but where we are going: and the direction in which our life is
moving is important to us precisely because our lives are such that
they have direction – they move. Taylor is in effect echoing a central
theme of MacIntyre's work, the notion that my sense of the good,
of qualitative discrimination, has to be woven into my understanding
of my life as an unfolding story. The space of moral questions within
which I must orient myself is part of a larger space of questions
which only a coherent narrative can answer: an answer to the
question 'Who am I?' involves answers to the questions of how I
have become who I am and where I am going. In other words, the
concepts of orientation towards the good and of the narrative unity
or 'quest' structure of a life are mutually implicating and internally
related:

My underlying thesis is that there is a close connection between the different conditions of identity, or of one's life making sense, that I have been discussing. One could put it this way: because we cannot but orient ourselves to the good, and thus determine our place relative to it and hence determine the direction of our lives, we must inescapably understand our lives in narrative form, as a 'quest'. But one could perhaps start from another point: because we have to determine our place in relation to the good, therefore we cannot be without an orientation to it, and hence must see our life in story. From whichever direction, I see these conditions as connected facts of the same reality, inescapable structural requirements of human agency. (*SS*, pp. 51–2)

Hypergoods and practical reasoning

We mentioned at the beginning of the chapter that Taylor was not only hostile to moral subjectivism, to any notion of an unencumbered or antecedently individuated self, and to certain versions of asocial individualism; he was also committed to an attack upon the idea that specific moral or political principles could be defended without invoking anything more than a thin conception of the good for human beings. Having examined his grounds for the first three claims, we can now examine the fourth in more detail, and in particular we must elucidate Taylor's notion of a hypergood.

For, having established the importance of conceptions of the good to the identity of human agents, Taylor goes on to complicate the picture by reminding us that there are many goods in human life, and that they may sometimes (or even very often) come into conflict with one another. What this entails is that any given individual will need to rank the many goods that he recognizes to be worthy of pursuit in his life; and in some cases, this will involve regarding one of them as being of supreme importance relative to the others. Someone may, for example, recognize the value of self-expression, justice, the worship of God and family life, but he may consider one of them – perhaps worship of God – as of overriding importance. Such an individual, whilst recognizing a whole range of qualitative distinctions or moral frameworks, recognizes a qualitative discontinuity between one such framework and all the others; in short,

he imposes a higher-order qualitative distinction in order to seg-
ment goods which are themselves defined in terms of lower-order
distinctions. Taylor calls such higher-order goods *hypergoods*.

Hypergoods are generally a source of conflict, for the obvious
reason that they presuppose an ultimate intolerance of the goods
to which they assign lower rank. More interestingly, however, they
have usually arisen through a historical supersession of earlier, less
adequate views; they present themselves as steps to a higher moral
consciousness. For example, the principle of equal respect is held as
a hypergood by many people today; but those people recognize
that it was not always dominant, that it arose through a process of
conflict and development in which it gradually replaced earlier and
more restricted ethics, and that it continues to find new applications
by challenging other ethics even today (for example with respect
to relations between the sexes). Such transvaluations of values – the
complete rejection of goods previously treated as hypergoods themselves – are inherently conflictual.

Of course, examining such transvaluations raises the question
of practical reason: for, even if a given hypergood establishes its
dominance so that a culture moves away from a previously dominant
ethic towards it, how can we be sure that the transition is a justifiable
or rational one? Why should we accept the judgement that the previously dominant good is more restrictive or less worthy than the
new one, when such judgements are inevitably made from within
the framework of the new hypergood? For Taylor, the very feature
of hypergoods that raises this worry also reveals the way to dissolve
it; for human practical reason is precisely designed to cope with
situations such as these – it is a reasoning in transitions.

Practical reasoning does not aim to establish that some position
is correct absolutely, but rather that some position is superior to
some other position; and it does so by demonstrating the epistemic
gain that flows from making the transition from position A to
position B. We can do this by showing that moving from A to B
resolves a contradiction in A or a confusion that A relied on, or by
acknowledging the importance of some factor that A screens out or
obscures, and so on.

This picture of rationality is strongly reminiscent of MacIntyre's
picture of the ways in which the rationality or validity of a given
moral tradition might be vindicated against the claims of others
by means of its capacity to cope with epistemological crises. It is

therefore unsurprising to discover that Taylor sees this form of argument as having its source in biographical narrative:

> We are convinced that a certain view is superior because we have lived a transition which we understand as error-reducing and hence as epistemic gain. I see that I was confused about the relation of resentment and love, or I see that there is a depth to love conferred by time, which I was quite insensitive to before. But this doesn't mean that we don't and can't argue. Our conviction that we have grown morally can be challenged by another. It may after all be illusion. And then we argue; and arguing here is contesting between interpretations of what I have been living. (*SS*, p. 72)

Taylor's point, then, is not that claims to moral growth (whether at the personal or the cultural level) as a result of the transition from one hypergood to another are incontestable, or guaranteed to convince everyone. The point is that there are, and can be, no criteria for deciding the moral superiority of a given hypergood that do not themselves presuppose some moral framework or other. Any individual's perspective is and must be defined by the moral intuitions she has, the articulations by means of which she grounds them, and the considerations that move her morally; if she abstracts from this, she does not achieve moral objectivity: she becomes incapable of understanding any moral argument at all. A moral agent can be convinced only by changing her reading of her moral experience, and in particular her reading of her life story, of the transitions she has lived through (or refused to live through). Even if my moral framework is grounded in a belief in God, a being who infinitely transcends my moral experience, it is a belief in which I can have rational confidence only if it is itself grounded in considerations that take account of my moral experience.

In effect, then, Taylor's claim that practical reasoning is transitional amounts to the claim that any evaluations of practical reasoning will necessarily involve the invocation of conceptions of the good. Specific moral decisions and positions can be assessed as rational or irrational only by reference to one's own concrete moral experience and intuitions, and the conceptions of the good that they presuppose; and it will also entail the higher-order ranking of competing goods. The rationality of an agent will therefore be judged in *substantive* terms, according to whether his answer is right or not; being rational just *is* getting it right. So, just as one cannot comprehend the nature

of human agency and morality without comprehending their intimate relation to conceptions of the good, so one cannot grasp the
nature of the moral reasoning engaged in by such agents without
appreciating that it is similarly indebted.

However, many modern ethical theories cleave to a procedural
rather than a substantive conception of practical reasoning. For them,
the rationality of the agent is assessed by reference to how he thinks
rather than to the correctness of the answers he reaches; rationality
is a matter of observing the correct procedures. This approach
necessarily involves sidelining conceptions of the good; for re-
defining the value of practical reasoning in terms of its observation
of a certain style or method entails that this value can and must be
assessed entirely independently of the substantive worth of the
conceptions of the good that are thereby chosen. It follows that,
from Taylor's perspective, there are two problems with any such
conception of practical rationality. First, any such doctrine will be
officially committed to denying the existence of a connection (between evaluations of practical rationality and the invocation of values
and goods) which is an inevitable part of making judgements of
rationality in ethics; and second, since the doctrine nonetheless
constitutes one way of making such judgements (of assessing moral
decisions and positions as rational or irrational), it must itself invoke
certain values or goods despite its official commitments.

In the case of procedural conceptions, these values are not hard
to unearth. Emphasizing the style or method of one's reasoning
rather than its conclusions is a way of giving primacy to the agent's
own desires and will; it highlights the importance of free and autonomous choice. Furthermore, it implicitly denies the existence of an
objective order in nature or the universe, for such an order would
determine that some conceptions of the good are right and others
wrong and thus lead us towards a substantive conception of practical
reason. Procedural conceptions of rationality in morals are designed
for a disenchanted universe in which subjects are free to choose not
only their way of life but also the standards in terms of which they
shall measure the worth of those lives. In effect, they are committed
to the hypergoods of modernity, the values identified by Sandel
and MacIntyre as their main targets (although not under that title).

On Taylor's view, however, these substantive commitments are
ones that the proponents of such conceptions are driven by the
demands of their own theory to deny and repress. If they are to

preserve the goods to which they are committed, they must ensure
that the pursuit and achievement of practical rationality is assigned
a certain primacy as against other pursuits; and they can achieve
this only by asserting the priority of the moral domain over other
aspects of human life. At the same time, however, their official
aversion to the invocation of conceptions of the good ensures that
they cannot offer an account of the reasons they have for asserting
this priority, for that would transform their emphasis on procedure
into an ultimate reliance upon arguments of substance. In short,
according to Taylor, the protagonists of procedural reason face a
dilemma. They must segregate the domain of the moral without
being able to explain why; they must defend an absolute boundary
without being able to account for its absoluteness.

> It seems that they are motivated by the strongest moral ideals, such
> as freedom, altruism and universalism. These are amongst the central
> moral aspirations of moral culture, the hypergoods which are dis-
> tinctive to it. And yet what these ideals drive the theorists towards is
> a denial of all such goods. They are caught in a strange pragmatic
> contradiction, whereby the very goods which move them push them
> to deny or denature all such goods. They are constitutionally incapable
> of coming clean about the deeper sources of their own thinking. (SS,
> p. 88)

The priority of right

The pragmatic contradiction in which proponents of procedural
conceptions of practical reasoning find themselves is, in Taylor's
view, also the inevitable fate of those who assign an absolute priority
to the right over the good in their moral and political theorizing.
And this, of course, is the point at which these seemingly abstract
issues in moral philosophy make contact with the concerns of *A
Theory of Justice*. Assigning priority to the right is perfectly justifiable,
and indeed demanded, if this is meant to signify a rejection of
utilitarianism or other consequentialist theories; for then it simply
signifies a first-order substantive insistence that morality ought not
to be conceived simply in terms of outcomes, but should also include
notions of intrinsic worth or duty. But it can also be used to signal
a particular second-order ethical view; in that context, it indicates

not a rejection of the homogeneous good of desire-fulfilment around which utilitarianism is based, but rather a rejection or downgrading of the relevance of any conception of the good. It is in effect an attempt to argue for a moral view without invoking any of the qualitative distinctions that Taylor has argued are inseparable from the elucidation of any moral view whatsoever.

Taylor here takes Rawls as an example. The Rawlsian theory of justice is held to avoid reliance upon any particular conception of the good; for if it did not, then the social institutions that it advocates would effectively impose that conception upon all those who lived their lives within them, and their autonomy would be violated. If, however, we are to assess the principles of justice that emerge from that theory, we must assess them against our moral intuitions – this is what Rawls admits is integral to his method of reflective equilibrium. And if we are to articulate the frameworks and ontological accounts that do and must underlie those intuitions – if, in other words, we are to engage in practical reasoning about them – we would necessarily start spelling out a very substantive theory of the good. Even if we do not spell it out, we are necessarily relying upon a complex and sophisticated sense of the good when we advocate those principles; and the claim, essential to Rawls's understanding of his project, that no such conception is at stake is simply an instance of repression or denial.

Taylor summarizes his point as follows:

> Where 'good' means the primary goal of a consequentialist theory, where the right is decided simply by its instrumental significance for this end, then we ought indeed to insist that the right can be primary to the good. But where we use 'good' in the sense of this discussion, where it means whatever is marked out as higher by a qualitative distinction, then we could say that the reverse is the case, that, in a sense, the good is always primary to the right ... the good is what, in its articulation, gives the point of the rules which define the right. (SS, p. 89)

In other words, Taylor's claim, both with respect to procedural conceptions of practical reasoning and to deontological conceptions of justice, is that their official prohibition on the invocation of anything more than a thin theory of the good is necessarily incoherent. We cannot do without the wide-ranging and fundamental qualitative distinctions which go to make up a thick theory of the good because in their absence we have no way of articulating the moral point of the actions and feelings that our moral intuitions enjoin upon us or present as admirable. They may not always be explicit or clearly articulated in our everyday moral life, but if they were not there to be articulated – or if we are forbidden from drawing upon them – we would be left with nothing that we could recognize as morality. Our moral intuitions would lack the very feature that distinguishes them from brute reactions such as nausea, and that is integral both to the identity of a recognizably human self *and* to the narrative unity of a recognizably human life: they would lack any relation to conceptions of the good.

Taylor and the communitarian critique of Rawls

In his own presentation of the views that we have been examining above, Taylor does not explicitly name Rawls as the target of his critique except when discussing the priority of the right over the good. Rather, he defines his position in opposition to much more general and pervasive strands of cultural thought, such as naturalism and utilitarianism, thus implying that he has bigger fish to fry than a specific contemporary political theorist. Nonetheless, people did regard Taylor as participating in a communitarian critique of liberalism; and it is the purpose of this section to examine the validity of that perception.

In the first place, it is clear that there is a genuine family resemblance between Taylor's work and that of the writers we have examined in previous chapters. More precisely, Taylor's general conclusions and those of Sandel and (more particularly) MacIntyre exhibit a striking degree of convergence. Like both Sandel and MacIntyre, Taylor claims that commitments or orientations towards the good are integral to or constitutive of the identity of the self; moreover, like MacIntyre, he claims that the life of a human being can only be understood in terms of its narrative form – the narrative of that individual's progress towards (or away from) the good. In addition, Taylor argues – just like MacIntyre – that the very notion of morality as a rational enterprise presupposes this view of the person and of a human life, since only they can allow room for a substantive conception of practical reasoning as a reasoning in transitions that must always be rooted in concrete moral experience and a particular moral framework. And of course, Taylor concludes by arguing (again, like MacIntyre) that any moral or political theory that claims to dispense with or to be neutral between conceptions of the good will find itself embroiled in a pragmatic contradiction, forced to rely upon value commitments of a kind, and claiming a degree of generality, that it has officially prohibited.

In addition, underlying and unifying these specific positions we can see in Taylor an essentially communitarian conception of moral frameworks and of the self, but one which more closely resembles MacIntyre's than it does Sandel's. For in Taylor's view, any adequate conception of morality, of the self and its narrative unity, and of practical reasoning must acknowledge the foundational importance of moral frameworks or qualitative distinctions; and all such frameworks are essentially communal in nature: they can be established, maintained and acquired only through membership of a language community. This constitutes a profound attack upon asocial individualism, but an attack upon its philosophical rather than its substantive variants, since it amounts to criticizing moral and political theories for ignoring or repressing the dependence of all conceptions of the good and of the self upon social matrices rather than for ignoring or repressing the importance of conceptions of the good that are strongly communal in content. In this respect, Taylor's affinities are once again with MacIntyre rather than Sandel. And of course, this communitarian inflection in Taylor is in the last resort a consequence of his conception of the self. For if human beings are self-interpreting animals, and the linguistic and experiential resources for such self-interpretations are only to be found in the context of a community of other selves, then Taylor is committed to the view that community is a structural precondition of human agency and selfhood.

What, however, justifies the claim that Taylor's communitarian critique is applicable to Rawlsian liberalism – that Rawls is incapable of acknowledging any of these points? Here, it is worth recalling the way in which we located his criticisms on our original agenda of issues. As we mentioned at the beginning of this chapter, Taylor's conception of human selfhood is such as to generate a critique that is applicable to any political theory committed to an unencumbered or disembodied conception of the self (first theme), to some philosophical versions of asocial individualism (second theme), to certain variants of moral subjectivism (fourth theme) and to any claim to have dispensed with the invocation of a substantial theory of the good (fifth theme). Apart from this fourth and final point, Taylor never explicitly claims that Rawls is propounding a theory that exemplifies these errors. So it seems that Taylor can only be seen as a critic of Rawls under the first three of our headings if Sandel and MacIntyre are right in their belief that Rawls is committed to an unencumbered or emotivist view of the self, one that regards the self as individuated prior to its choice of ends and its participation in communities. The identity of such a self would not depend upon his choice of conceptions of the good, and the course of his life would have no narrative logic; his practical reasoning would be procedural, and his moral frameworks would lack any ultimate rational status. Moreover, anyone committed to such a view of the self would seem to be committed to some form of atomism or asocial individualism, since antecedently individuated selves are logically prior to and so essentially independent of any society of which they might be members. In short, a theory committed to such a conception would be vulnerable to every facet of the argument Taylor has developed under the first three headings of our agenda; and its vulnerability would be a consequence of its fundamentally non-communitarian understanding of the nature of selfhood. But it must be noted that Taylor's work does not, and is not intended to, support the claim that such a conception of the self is one to which Rawls really is or must be committed.

What Taylor's work *does* directly support is the weaker conclusion that Rawls must be committed to *some* particular conception of the self. For according to him, any moral or political theory must rely upon an implicit set of qualitative distinctions and an ontological account of human nature. If that theory is to count as a contribution to moral debate, it will draw upon a sense of the good that must be articulable; and any such articulation will involve an attempt to explain what it is about human beings that entails that they be treated in the way that the theory demands. Taylor's point is thus not the trivial one that any given theory about the just treatment of persons will involve some conception of the person; it is the stronger, dual claim that such a theory can only be defended if the theorist is prepared substantively to endorse a very general conception of the nature of human beings and the worth of their lives. Taylor would thus seem to support the conclusion that Rawls can refuse to engage with his opponents at this fundamental level only on pain of abdicating from the arena of moral debate altogether; there seems to be no half-way house. Rawls's conception of the person may not be what Sandel thinks it is, but he must nonetheless be relying upon some particular ontology of the human.

It might also be thought that Rawls is directly vulnerable to Taylor's critique of procedural conceptions of practical reasoning. For Rawlsian justice as fairness is presented to us as the product of reasoning that takes place in the original position; and in that position, no reliance upon knowledge of a particular conception of the good is permitted. Rather, the observance of certain principles and prohibitions whilst deliberating is held to guarantee the validity of the outcome of that deliberation; in short, a pure procedural conception of justice is at stake. To think that this makes Rawls vulnerable to Taylor's critique would, however, be a mistake; and it is a mistake that Taylor explicitly counsels his reader against making (cf. *SS*, p. 87, n. 60). For, of course, although reasoning *within* the original position is procedural, the reasoning that leads us to *accept* the original position and its constraints as appropriate to questions of social justice is not. On the contrary, restricting reasoning in the original position to a purely procedural form is presented by Rawls as necessary for the maintenance of certain substantive goods – in particular, as reflecting our concern to respect the freedom and equality of all citizens. So Rawls cannot be held to involve himself in a pragmatic contradiction of the sort that Taylor diagnoses in other attempts to defend a procedural conception of justice.

This leaves us with the only direct criticism of Rawls to which Taylor does commit himself – the one that relates to the fifth heading on our agenda. As we saw earlier, Rawls figures explicitly in Taylor's work only as a proponent of the priority of the right over the good, a principle regarded by Taylor as equivalent to the claim that Rawlsian liberalism embodies a view of justice that is not dependent upon anything other than a 'thin' theory of the good. Taylor argues that if the grounds for accepting the priority of the right are fully articulated, they will be found to constitute a very substantive sense of the good, one in which a set of qualitative distinctions hangs together with a particular ontological account of human nature.

What this criticism amounts to is the claim that Rawlsian liberalism cannot be as neutral between competing conceptions of the good as it aspires to be. The absolute priority assigned to the right over the good reflects Rawls's assignment of absolute priority to the value of autonomy; it reflects the fact that autonomy is the Rawlsian hypergood. Reliance upon a hypergood is not in itself a flaw in any moral theory; it is rather *de rigueur*. And Taylor is happy to admit that the liberal hypergood is one that has many attractions. But, according to his arguments about the nature of moral evaluation and debate, it is merely self-delusive for liberals to attempt to defend their values by claiming that they – unlike their opponents – make use of a minimal array of evaluative assumptions about the good life for human beings and about human nature. In effect, Taylor agrees with the main thrust of MacIntyre's argument that, in order to defend its claim about the right way to organize the sphere of political life (that is, separating it from that of ethics or morality more broadly understood by forbidding the invocation of conceptions of the good life for human beings within politics), liberalism must draw upon the conceptions of human good and the general ontology of the human that make up the broad liberal ethical tradition of which this conception of politics is merely a part.

This claim about the wide-ranging roots of liberal political theory has its counterpart with respect to liberal political practice. For Taylor also claims that the goal of developing, protecting and maintaining human beings in their full autonomy as citizens requires a great deal more than the sustenance of a liberal political system; it requires the maintainence of a distinctively liberal society. This follows from his understanding of persons as self-interpreting animals. For such an animal could only *be* an autonomous chooser of ends in a society whose institutions and culture embodied and presupposed a conception of persons as autonomous choosers of ends; it could not otherwise have the conceptual resources to interpret itself in that way and so to be a person of that sort. So the institutions and practices of modern liberal democratic societies (for example negotiations and contracts, public debate on moral and political issues, voting systems, universities) are absolutely vital in ensuring that its members regard themselves as, and so become, people whose interpersonal relations are willed, who have an identity distinct from that of other individuals, who are capable of autonomously choosing and revising their conceptions of the good.

In other words, although it may be a trivial truth that any being recognizable as a human agent must be possessed of a will and be capable of exercising it, it is not a condition of human status that one interpret oneself as being most fundamentally and essentially an autonomous chooser of ends: that will happen (if it happens at all) only in an appropriately liberal social matrix. And two important conclusions follow from this. First, it implies that an individualist political tradition such as liberalism, one that places emphasis upon the right of each human being to a measure of freedom and equality, must not express its concern for the preservation of those rights in ways that ignore or conflict with its need simultaneously to preserve the social structures that underpin them. If, for example, liberals were to present the institutions and procedures that embody its individualist values as purely instrumental affairs, as merely the means by which individuals defend themselves against others, then they may weaken the sense of a common allegiance to those institutions without which they will be unable to carry out their instrumental work, and the society that they help to make up would lose its cohesion. In short, even someone committed to values or goods that are essentially individual in content must also be committed to defending the communal structures underpinning those individualist values.[4]

The second conclusion we can draw depends upon seeing that the communal structures that the liberal is committed to defending are pervasive elements in our social life; universities, modes of negotiation and genres of public debate seem to be 'political' structures only in a rather broad understanding of that term. But then it may be misleading for liberal political theory to present itself as something that could *either* be argued for without drawing upon values that apply far beyond the realm of party politics *or* implemented otherwise than as part of a generally liberal social order. In other words, Rawlsian liberalism in politics may only be defensible as one component in a more general project to establish and maintain a society that embodies a very specific conception of the human good. Taylor thinks that this will involve a significant alteration in the Rawlsian self-interpretation. If Taylor is right, then by adopting this mode of defining itself Rawlsian liberalism will be altering its identity: it will be altering its self. And even if Taylor is wrong about Rawls's self-understanding, it might nonetheless be the case that a wider appreciation of this point about the true degree of liberal neutrality will significantly alter the image of liberalism that occupies the minds of many people in contemporary society.

Notes

1　His most important contributions to that field can be found in the two volumes of his *Philosophical Papers*.
2　An account to be found in his most recent book *Sources of the Self* (hereafter *SS*).
3　Taylor, 'Interpretation and the Sciences of Man', (page reference is to the 1985 collection).
4　This is the point that is central to Taylor's worries about atomism, and to his own analysis of Sandel's critique of Rawlsian liberalism in 'Cross-Purposes'.

4

WALZER:
justice and abstraction

Michael Walzer's critique of Rawlsian liberalism is pitched at a
level significantly different from that of the other three communitarian thinkers we have already examined. Unlike Sandel, Walzer is
not primarily concerned with criticizing the Rawlsian conception of
the person; and unlike MacIntyre and Taylor, he is not interested in
presenting a sweeping historical account of Western culture from
which certain criticisms of liberalism in general and Rawls in particular can be deduced. The position put forward in *Spheres of
Justice* (*SJ*) focuses rather upon the question of what *methodology* is
appropriate to the business of political theory; Walzer wants to
know how one should go about constructing and defending a theory
of justice. More specifically, he concentrates upon how we should
understand the goods for which a theory of justice seeks to articulate distributive principles, and attacks the understanding of this
matter that he identifies in Rawls's theory.

The essence of Walzer's argument may be had from his claim
that 'different social goods ought to be distributed for different
reasons, in accordance with different procedures, by different agents;
and all these differences derive from different understandings of
the social goods themselves – the inevitable product of historical
and cultural particularism' (*SJ*, p. 6). We should note from the outset
that this brief quotation contains two distinct strands of argument.
On the one hand, there is the substantive claim that 'different social
goods ought to be distributed for different reasons', which we will
refer to as the 'differentiated substance' of the theory. This is the

idea, contained in the title of his book, that different goods constitute different distributional spheres within which specific distributive
arrangements are appropriate, and that justice consists in autonomous distributions, whereby the distribution of a good such as,
for example, health care, is in accordance with the principles peculiar
to that good and not corrupted by goods, such as money, that
properly belong to other spheres. On the other hand, there is the
quite distinct point that these differences derive from different
'understandings of the social goods themselves' and that such understandings are 'the inevitable product of historical and cultural
particularism'; we will call this the 'particularistic methodology' of
the theory. This is the idea that the way to see how particular goods
should be distributed is to look at how those goods are understood
in the particular culture in question. As this last sentence suggests,
and as we shall see in this chapter, Walzer is objecting to two distinct
kinds of abstraction, and insisting upon two distinct kinds of particularity or specificity. The political theorist should recognize both
that distributive principles must be good-specific and that good-
specific principles must be culture-specific. Rawls is deemed to be
deficient on both counts.

It is Walzer's particularistic methodology that shows how his
critique of liberalism should be placed on our agenda of issues; for
the idea that the principles of justice must be culture-specific entails
a hostility to any political theory that embodies claims to universality
(the third theme on our agenda). Moreover, like Sandel, Walzer is
careful to offer specific arguments and references to Rawls's theory
that are intended to validate his claim that Rawlsian liberalism is
insufficiently particularistic in its methodology; so we can spell out
the sense in which Walzer's work is intended as a critique of Rawls
simply through our exegetical summary of that work. What may be
less clear is the degree to which Walzer's critique resembles that of
the other writers we have been considering. In particular, his writings
are good- rather than person-oriented; he makes no mention of
a conception of the person underlying those aspects of Rawls's
theorizing to which he objects, and focuses rather upon the meanings
that certain goods have for the persons to whom they are to be
distributed. This might suggest that his approach would better be
regarded as concerned with the distributive aspects of Rawlsian
liberalism than with the emphasis on the freedom of the individual
in relation to her community, which we have claimed to be the

distinctive concern of the communitarian critique. Nonetheless, as we shall see, Walzer's focus on goods and the principles appropriate for their distribution does involve a claim about the importance of the community as the repository of value and thus, implicitly, about the priority of the community over the individual; and the key elements of his critique can be restated in terms that relate them more directly to a conception of the person and of what is in their interests or constitutes their well-being. Moreover, it will also become clear that the presuppositions of Rawls's approach to distributive matters to which Walzer takes exception are in fact a consequence of the distinctive Rawlsian concern for the freedom of the individual – as epitomized in his prohibition on the invocation of conceptions of the good in the sphere of politics.

So much for preliminary orientation. Now we must outline the main elements of Walzer's critique, beginning with his attack on methodological abstraction.

Rawls's methodological abstraction

Walzer is most emphatic in his insistence that the political theorist should not seek to transcend the contexts constituted by cultural particularity and difference. As he puts it:

> My argument is radically particularist. I don't claim to have achieved any great distance from the social world in which I live. One way to begin the philosophical enterprise – perhaps the original way – is to walk out of the cave, leave the city, climb the mountain, fashion for oneself . . . an objective and universal standpoint. Then one describes the terrain of everyday life from far away, so that it loses its particular contours and takes on a general shape. But I mean to stand in the cave, in the city, on the ground. Another way of doing philosophy is to interpret to one's fellow citizens the world of meanings that we share. (*SJ*, p. xiv)

Rather than trying to detach herself from the society in which she lives and assessing it from a vantage-point above the contingencies of culture, the philosopher should seek to articulate those very shared 'meanings' that constitute that culture.

Walzer is explicit that it is theories like Rawls's that are the target here. Referring not only to *A Theory of Justice* but also to works by Habermas and Ackerman[1] which share the structural features to which he objects, he writes that today the system of distributive justice 'is commonly described as the one that ideally rational men and women would choose if they were forced to choose impartially, knowing nothing of their own situation, barred from making particularist claims, confronting an abstract set of goods' (*SJ*, p. 5). In the case of Rawls, this is particularly clear; for the things of which justice demands the principled distribution are 'primary goods'. That is:

> Things which it is supposed a rational man wants whatever else he wants. Regardless of what an individual's rational plans are in detail, it is assumed that there are various things which he would prefer more of rather than less. With more of these goods men can generally be assured of greater success in carrying out their intentions and in advancing their ends, whatever these ends may be. The primary social goods, to give them in broad categories, are rights and liberties, opportunities and powers, income and wealth. (*TJ*, p. 92)

The presentation of Rawls's theory in our introductory chapter should have made clear why he has to invoke some such generalized or abstract conception. The people in the original position are denied knowledge of their particular conceptions of the good and must be motivated rather by 'the thin theory of the good' which defines a person's good in suitably non-committal terms as 'the successful execution of a rational plan of life' (*TJ*, p. 433). With appropriate caveats about the difficulties involved in the term 'neutrality', we might say that the point about primary goods is that they are in some sense neutral between the different conceptions of the good that people might actually choose to frame and pursue. As Rawls puts it:

> I suppose that it is rational to want these goods whatever else is wanted, since they are in general necessary for the framing and execution of a rational plan of life. The persons in the original position are assumed to accept this conception of the good, and therefore they take for granted that they desire greater liberty and opportunity, and more extensive means for achieving their ends. (*TJ*, p. 433)

In short, abstraction from particularity is essential to Rawls's understanding of the goods with which his theory is concerned because it is an integral aspect of the abstraction from particular conceptions of the good that he imposes in order to protect the autonomy of those to whom these goods are to be distributed. Distributive questions here make contact with questions of individual freedom in a way that ensures that Walzer's critique of matters relating to the former can be construed as pertinent to matters relating to the latter. In other words, his goods-based critique of Rawls is by no means as distant from the autonomy-focused critiques of the other three communitarian critics of liberalism as it might appear.

So far, however, we have simply pointed out reasons for thinking that Rawls will be in the target area of Walzer's critique of methodological abstraction. We have not even begun to explore the question of what Walzer thinks is damaging about such abstraction. What is wrong with suggesting that questions of social justice ought to be considered under conditions that minimize the making of particularist claims about the relevant goods?

The problem is not that one will not reach a singular conclusion, for Walzer recognizes that, if they are suitably constrained, rational people will choose a particular distributive system. Nor is the problem that particularism of interest that might lead people to disregard the 'rational' or 'impartial' conclusion because it does not suit them as they actually are in real life. For Walzer, people *can* set aside their own particular interests for the public good. The failure of this approach is rather its lack of attention to a different kind of particularity:

> The problem is with the particularism of history, culture, and membership. Even if they are committed to impartiality, the question most likely to arise in the minds of members of a political community is not, What would rational individuals choose under universalizing conditions of such and such a sort? But rather, What would individuals like us choose, who are situated as we are, who share a culture and are determined to go on sharing it? And this is a question that is readily transformed into, What choices have we already made in the course of our common life? What understandings do we (really) share? (*SJ*, p. 5)

Why should people who necessarily conceive themselves, and the goods that make up the social world in which they live, in 'thick' culture-laden ways disregard that cultural particularity and adopt a 'thin' conception of 'rationality' when thinking about principles to govern the distribution of goods in their society? The abstraction that Rawls's theory requires involves, for Walzer, a disattention to the choices that people have already made and that are embodied in their culture's own particular understandings of the goods that are to be distributed. What we must now examine are Walzer's grounds for condemning such disattention.

Against methodological abstraction: the conceptual argument

The first argument Walzer provides takes a purely conceptual form, in that it follows from his analysis of the very concept of a good. The opening proposition of his 'theory of goods' states that 'all the goods with which distributive justice is concerned are social goods' (*SJ*, p. 7) and it is the various implications of the term 'social' here that underpin his whole approach. Above all, its force is to assert that the meaning and value that goods have are derived from the communities whose goods they are. On the one hand, goods do not have brute 'natural' meanings: they only acquire their significance through a process of interpretation and understanding, of 'conception and creation'. On the other, that process is always and necessarily a social and not an individual one. 'A solitary person could hardly understand the meaning of the goods or figure out the reason for taking them as likable or dislikable' (*SJ*, pp. 7–8). Here we see Walzer giving his own application of the communitarian thought, already observed in Taylor and to some extent in MacIntyre, that points to the inherently social nature of concepts and language. Goods do not come into the world with their meanings attached to them, or if they do, it is only because they have been conceived and created in a manner that is irreducibly social.

And if the meanings of goods are necessarily social, they will have different meanings in different societies. Take an apparently basic pre-interpretive good such as bread; surely here is a good whose 'meaning' is not a matter of social or cultural construction but of biological necessity. Not for Walzer: 'Bread is the staff of life, the body of Christ, the symbol of the Sabbath, the means of hospitality, and so on' (*SJ*, p. 8). While it may be the case that, if it came to the distributive crunch, the first bread-as-the-staff-of-life use would take precedence, even this is not certain. We can easily imagine cultures in which any conflicts that might arise between nutritional uses of bread and religious uses of it could as easily be settled in favour of the latter. We might think perhaps also of those religious sects that understand the meaning of health care, and of the divine will, in such a way that they would rather watch their children die than allow them to receive medical attention. The same 'things' may mean quite different things to different cultures.

What is most important for Walzer about such culture-dependence of meaning is that the meaning of a good and an understanding of the way in which it should be distributed go together, and thus the latter is as inherently social as the former. As he puts it:

> ... it is the meaning of goods that determines their movement. Distributive criteria and arrangements are intrinsic not to the good-in-itself but to the social good. If we understand what it is, what it means to those for whom it is a good, we understand how, by whom, and for what reasons it ought to be distributed. All distributions are just or unjust relative to the social meanings of the goods at stake. (*SJ*, pp. 8–9)

An example may make the force of this point clearer. Take the social good of health care: a Walzerian could argue that, in our society, anyone who understands what health care is (that is, grasps its social meaning) will know that its primary or essential purpose is the treatment of illness and the restoration and maintenance of physical well-being. But it immediately follows from this under-standing that this particular social good should be distributed in a certain way, namely to those who are in need of it, to those who are ill or unhealthy. Anyone who failed to see this would simply have failed to grasp the meaning of this particular good; and although it might be possible to argue that practical political and social con-straints will bring other considerations into the picture when a particular health care system is being set up, the onus of argument is upon those who wish to introduce distributive principles other than those already inherent in the meaning of the good itself.

The difficulty for a Rawlsian approach would seem to be clear: 'There is no single set of primary or basic goods conceivable across all moral and material worlds – or, any such set would have to be considered in terms so abstract that they would be of little use in thinking about particular distributions' (*SJ*, p. 8). Questions of social justice do not arise about primary goods; they arise about specific goods with specific and often radically different meanings in specific societies. But Rawls's principles of justice are intended to apply to the distribution of primary goods, and so will possess a degree of abstractness which will make it impossible for them to be usefully applied to particular goods in particular societies; they will bear as distant and opaque a relation to those goods as does the notion of a primary good itself. If, however, the requisite initial and detailed attention is paid to the social meaning of those specific goods, then they will be found already to contain specific distributive principles. And, given that the meaning of the good is where any theory of justice must begin its analysis and argument, then the distributive principles that are an essential aspect of that meaning must similarly be regarded as the unavoidable starting point and essential bench-mark of deliberations about the just distribution of that good. In short, the particularity of the social meanings of all human goods seems to entail that the methodological abstraction that generates Rawlsian principles of justice will make them either useless or superfluous.

Against methodological abstraction: the democratic argument

Although the conceptual argument against methodological ab-straction is important to Walzer's approach in *Spheres of Justice*, there are grounds for thinking that a more substantive argument is also at work. For example, on the penultimate page of that book Walzer writes that 'There is a certain attitude of mind that underlies the theory of justice . . . : we can think of it as a decent respect for the opinions of mankind' (*SJ*, p. 320). Here, Walzer's worry seems to be that the kind of political philosophy that seeks detachment from social meanings and so from the particular community of which the philosopher is a member will not only result in principles of justice that are impossible to apply to concrete cases; it will also fail to accord proper weight to the opinions of the philosopher's fellow citizens as those are embodied in the present social meanings of specific goods. And in so doing it will reveal the sense in which that kind of political philosophy is undemocratic, or at least prone to undemocratic application.

If we draw on his fuller presentation of this strand of argument in an article that predates *Spheres of Justice* by a couple of years,[2] we can see that for Walzer it is the fact that philosophy aims at truth that gives it its undemocratic implications. For in order to reach 'truth' the philosopher must detach himself from his particular time and circumstances, from the particular ways of thinking prevalent in his culture, rising above such contingency to achieve an objective standpoint. As Walzer puts it, and his terminology makes clear that Rawls and Habermas are again the targets,

> The truths he commonly seeks are universal and eternal, and it is unlikely that they can be found from inside of any real and historic community. Hence the philosopher's withdrawal: he must deny himself the assurances of the commonplace ... To what sort of a place, then, does he withdraw? Most often, today, he constructs for himself ... an ideal commonwealth, inhabited by beings who have none of the particular characteristics and none of the opinions and commitments of his former fellow-citizens. He imagines a perfect meeting in an 'original position' or 'ideal speech situation' ...[3]

For Walzer, taking seriously Wittgenstein's observation that 'the philosopher is not a citizen of any community of ideas',[4] the withdrawal of the philosopher to his original position represents an attempt to leave behind the role of citizen, to achieve the kind of standpoint that gives one's conclusions a status, as 'truths', superior to the mere opinions of the other members of one's political community.

Democracy, however, is not about truth. The justification of democratic government is not that it is likely to yield right decisions, where rightness can be understood as something that could have been arrived at by other means (such as philosophical argument), but that it yields decisions that embody the will of the citizenry. The people's claim to rule rests not upon their knowledge of truth but upon who they are: citizens who can only freely be bound by laws if they themselves make them. 'On the democratic view, it is right that they make the laws even if they make them wrongly.'[5] Since law should be a function of popular will and not of reason, the philosopher's commitment to the latter is likely to be problematic.

Now, even if we accept that understanding of his role that has him seeking heroic detachment from the opinions of his fellow citizens, it does not immediately follow that the truth-seeking philosopher must be aiming to subvert the democratic process. If he presents his arguments in the right spirit, if he simply invites the people to revise their own conclusions in the light of his work, then there is no problem. 'At the moment of publication, at least, he is a proper democrat: his book is a gift to the people.'[6] Nor does Walzer think that the results of philosophical 'objective' thinking are necessarily irrelevant. He does not doubt that the aspiration to realize universal truths is one by means of which particular communities can improve themselves. What worries him is rather that the philosopher will claim for his conclusions a different status from that which he accords to the opinions of his fellow citizens, and, finding that the latter resist some or all of those conclusions, seek to bypass the democratic arena and have them directly instituted in law.

It is here that Walzer's argument becomes clearly aimed at the doctrine of judicial review as that is practised in the United States, where the Constitution accords people certain rights and entrusts the judiciary with the task of interpreting that Constitution and reviewing legislation to ensure that it does not infringe them. The anti-democratic bent of such a procedure should be obvious: indeed it is precisely as a means of protecting individuals against the will of majorities (or, to put it more controversially, the will of the community) that rights may best be understood. Whether or not one can provide a justification of rights that appeals to the same values as those that ground one's commitment to democracy and thus attempt to resolve the tension,[7] it is clear that the basic function of constitutional rights, and of the doctrine of judicial review which serves to protect them, is precisely to act as constraints on the democratic will. Walzer is worried that the philosopher will persuade those judges whose task it is to interpret the Constitution that detached reasoning demonstrates that people have an extensive list of rights. Since 'the more rights the judges award to people as individuals, the less free the people are as a decision-making body',[8] this is subversive of democracy. Indeed, for Walzer this philosophical list of rights invites judicial activity that is radically intrusive on what he calls 'democratic space' as soon as it extends beyond bans on legal discrimination and political repression.

Because the whole point of his detachment is to achieve a stand-point from which he can transcend the particularity of his own community, and because communities will differ in the answers that they reach, it follows that the political success of the philosopher 'would have the effect of enforcing a singular over a pluralist truth',[9] of overriding those cultural differences constituted by citizens' own 'traditions, conventions, and expectations'.[10] Moreover, and more closely connected to the democratic principle:

> It is not only the familiar products of their experience that the people value, but the experience itself, the process through which the products were produced. And they will have some difficulty understanding why the hypothetical experience of abstract men and women should take precedence over their own history . . . They might well choose politics over truth, and that choice, if they make it, will make in turn for pluralism. Any historical community whose members shape their own institutions and laws will necessarily produce a particular and not a universal way of life. That particularity can be overcome only from the outside and only by repressing internal political processes.[11]

Thus the argument for keeping the democratic space free from interference from philosophy is simultaneously an argument for pluralism over singularity and particularity over universality.

Clearly, the substantive issue of the extent to which the rights of individuals should be permitted to constrain the will of the people is too large to be addressed in a satisfactory manner in this context. What is important for our purposes, and what will take us back towards the kind of argument that is central to Walzer's *Spheres of Justice*, is the observation that the case in favour of 'a decent respect for the opinions of mankind' is distinct from that against the incorporation of extensive individual rights in the law. The latter is a particular instance of the much more general former, for clearly the opinions that the philosopher might be urged decently to respect might include ones other than those implying policies that infringe rights.

This distinction is important because it reveals that in this earlier article Walzer is really objecting to two separate aspects of Rawls's theory, which he takes together. On the one hand, what he dislikes is the general failure to attend to cultural particularity, the attempt to transcend his fellow citizens' 'conventions, traditions and expectations'. On the other, the specific focus of his objection is the way in which such disattention leads to a political theory framed in terms of rights which then serve to limit the scope available for popular decision-making. While each of these strands can be formulated in terms of the charge that Rawls fails to recognize the importance of community, the force of such a charge is importantly different in the two cases. In the first case the problem is that Rawls, in seeking a universal standpoint and a single right answer, does not attach proper importance to the values and practices of particular communities. Here it is the pretensions to universality that neglect the importance of community. In the second it is rather that the particular theory that he articulates is one which, in framing itself as a theory of justice and rights, gives priority to the individual over her community. Here it is the liberal framework that is the enemy of community.

It is the first strand rather than the second that feeds into *Spheres of Justice* and that is part of Walzer's distinctive contribution to the communitarian critique. For, as we have said, what is novel about his position is the extent to which it focuses not on the standard problematic of the relation between the individual and her community but on the rather different issue of how we should think about those goods that it is the aim of a theory of justice to distribute. What Walzer is above all concerned to point out is the variety of ways in which different cultures understand the different goods and distributive principles that together make up their social world, and his claim is that a theory of justice must be true to those understandings. We have already seen that the force of this 'must' is partly conceptual in nature: not being true to those understandings condemns one's theory to uselessness. Now we can see that the force of this 'must' is also substantive, that we must be true to those understandings on pain of being undemocratic, of failing to *respect* those whose understandings they are.

What is particularly interesting about Walzer's two-pronged methodological critique is that he is happy, on occasion, to couch it in terms of a general conception of the person. For example, he poses the following rhetorical question:

> By virtue of what characteristics are we one another's equals? One characteristic above all is central to my argument. We are (all of us) culture-producing creatures; we make and inhabit meaningful worlds. Since there is no way to rank and order these worlds with regard to

their understanding of social goods, we do justice to actual men and women by respecting their particular creations. And they claim justice, and resist tyranny, by insisting on the meaning of social goods among themselves. Justice is rooted in the distinct understandings of places, honors, jobs, things of all sorts, that constitute a shared way of life. To override those understandings is (always) to act unjustly. (*SJ*, p. 314)

In other words, what Walzer thinks matters about people is their capacity to 'make and inhabit meaningful worlds', to endow the natural world and brute objects with significance and value – a view that resembles Taylor's vision of human beings as self-interpreting animals. What is communitarian about this claim, and what is signified by the insistence that the world they create is 'social', is the fact that meanings and values are irreducibly communal and cannot be created by individuals acting alone. So, where the liberal identifies people's highest-order interests as being in their capacity as individuals to frame, revise and pursue conceptions of the good, Walzer directs us rather to the point that such processes are necessarily parasitic upon cultural constructions that are essentially communal.

Of course, and as we have already hinted, the pretensions to universality that Walzer identifies in Rawls's theory – and that must be there if his methodological critique of Rawlsian liberalism (in whatever terms it is couched) is to succeed – may be more apparent than real, and this suggestion applies to its understanding of goods as much as to its other aspects. In our chapter on the new Rawls we shall in fact argue that his conception of primary goods is not as abstract or as universal as it seems. For now, having established that two separate lines of argument converge in Walzer's affirmation of methodological particularism in political theory, we can consider some of the objections and difficulties to which this methodological approach seems to be open.

The relativity of social meanings

The fundamental issue raised by Walzer's arguments against methodological abstraction, epitomized in his claim that 'All distributions are just or unjust relative to the social meanings of the goods at stake' (*SJ*, p. 9), is that of relativism. Does it imply that there is no basis upon which we can criticize the social meanings of another culture? No trans-cultural standards to which we can appeal when defending our own and rejecting the distributive practices of other societies? Or that there is no basis upon which we can criticize the understandings of goods conventional in our own society? No place for the political theorist as social critic? Is the political theory that results from the application of such a methodology necessarily conservative, perhaps even failing to see that 'social meanings' are themselves ideological in content, serving to conceal or to justify relations of power and exploitation? If these are the implications, are they acceptable, or should we rather seek a different method-ological approach which might involve less counter-intuitive asser-tions? There are here big questions of interpretation ('What exactly is Walzer's position?') and of argument ('Is it tenable?'), and, in concentrating on the former, we do not aim to do more than indicate the kinds of move that might be made on either side of the relativism debate.[12]

It cannot be doubted that there is a significant relativistic strand in Walzer's position: 'Justice is relative to social meanings . . . There are an infinite number of possible lives, shaped by an infinite number of possible cultures, religions, political arrangements, geographical conditions, and so on. A given society is just if its substantive life is lived in a certain way – that is, in a way faithful to the shared understandings of the members. (*SJ*, pp. 312–13) Consider, to take an extreme example which Walzer himself uses, a society with a well-defined caste system, where a person's position in terms of religious purity, itself a function of one's birth and blood, determines his access to a variety of other goods. As long as the social meanings supportive of that system are genuinely shared, then justice consists in being true to those meanings. However much they may offend against our beliefs about the equal status of all human beings, about the rights of individuals to equality of opportunity, even about the criteria (such as need or ability) relevant to the distribution of particular goods (such as health care or education), we must adopt the relativistic position that says that justice is internal to social meanings, and hence that a grossly unequal distribution of goods, and one that gives little or no weight to the criteria *we* consider relevant, is just. As Walzer says, 'In a society where social meanings are integrated and hierarchical, justice will come to the aid of in-equality' (*SJ*, p. 313).

The example of the caste society makes particularly clear the distinction between Walzer's general methodological injunction to respect social meanings and the more specific claim he makes about our society (which we will examine later), namely that different goods should be distributed for different reasons; for the point about a caste society is that there meanings are not distinct. Rather, '. . . the system is constituted by an extraordinary integration of meanings. Prestige, wealth, knowledge, office, occupation, food, clothing, even the social good of conversation: all are subject to the intellectual as well as to the physical discipline of hierarchy. And the hierarchy is itself determined by the single value of ritual purity . . . Social meanings overlap and cohere' (*SJ*, p. 27). In other words, whilst Walzer's theory implies differentiation of distributive principles for us, this is only because he reads our social meanings as committing us to such differentiation, and in a caste society things will be very different. Of course Walzer is quite able to recognize that in such a society the meanings supportive of pervasive and systematic inequality may not really be shared, and members of the lower caste may actually feel anger and indignation. In that case justice would demand attention to their understandings also, for 'social meanings need not be harmonious' and sometimes 'provide only the intellectual structure within which distributions are debated' (*SJ*, pp. 313–14). But then the basis for criticism would still be 'local', internal to the meanings of the society itself, not an appeal to any external or universal principles; and if the meanings really were endorsed by all members of the society, then there would be no basis for criticism at all.

The extreme relativism apparently espoused in *Spheres of Justice* attracted a great deal of criticism, and in his more recent works *Interpretation and Social Criticism* and *The Company of Critics*, Walzer has been concerned to make clear that his methodological insistence on attention to particularity and to cultural meanings does not commit him to a denial of the possibility of radical social criticism. Properly understood, his argument involves a rejection not so much of social criticism *per se* as of a particular model of the way in which it may appropriately be conceived and presented. What matters is that such criticism be 'internal' or 'connected', recognizing its relation to the culture that it seeks to address and not presenting itself as deriving from an external and universal vantage-point quite detached from that culture. And where our fundamental moral beliefs lead us to reject the practices of another culture, we may be justified in preventing them from being true to their own meanings even if we have to appeal to principles that make little sense to their practitioners.

In terms of one's own culture, political theory as the interpretation of social meanings is not only consistent with the possibility of radical social criticism but in some ways invites it. Even if one grants Marx's claim that social meanings are 'the ideas of the ruling class',[13] those ideas are necessarily such as to leave room for critical manoeuvre. Marx's observation that every ruling class is compelled to present itself as a universal class makes criticism a permanent possibility:

> This self-presentation of the rulers is elaborated by the intellectuals. Their work is apologetic, but the apology is of a sort that gives hostages to future social critics. It sets standards that the rulers will not live up to . . . One might say that these standards themselves embody ruling class interests, but they do so only within a universalist disguise. And they also embody lower-class interests, else the disguise would not be convincing. Ideology strains towards universality as a condition of its success.[14]

The Italian Antonio Gramsci is the Marxist who first articulated this understanding of the social critic as 'connected'. Arguing that in order to establish hegemony – intellectual and moral leadership – over subordinate groups the ruling class must make some sacrifices to those groups, and hence that the ruling ideas will inevitably contain contradictions, he urges the radical critic to initiate 'a process of differentiation and change in the relative weight that the elements of the old ideologies used to possess. What was previously secondary and subordinate . . . is now taken to be primary and becomes the nucleus of a new ideological and theoretical complex.'[15] In contrast to Lenin and the Bolsheviks, whose theoretical framework bore little or no internal relation to that society they used it to shape, the Gramscian social critic can be understood as rearticulating ideas already in the culture, bringing to the fore what was hitherto only latent.

What emerges above all from this strand of Walzer's argument is that he takes 'social meanings' to be loose and interminably subject to interpretation. Any concrete culture will contain a variety of different, even contradictory, conceptual threads which it is the task of the political theorist to articulate into as coherent a whole as possible. Social meanings, it would seem, are by no means closed but yield resources to apologists and critics alike. This in turn suggests that the task of the political theorist is more creative or active than that of merely 'reading off' the meanings of the various goods in her society, and it makes clear a way in which an interpretive meanings-based methodology need not automatically be conservative. While it raises difficult issues, more usually associated with the study of literature, concerning what makes one interpretation better than another – in terms of what criteria are we to choose between the different interpretations offered to us by apologist and critic? – this understanding of the political theorist's task at least involves her in more than merely holding a mirror up to the society and its existing practices. There may, for example, be a pervasive understanding in our society that housework or childcare is a good that is done by women and without pay, but the critic can point to other, equality-based threads in our culture which imply alternative distributive principles, and suggest that we are being truer to our social meanings overall if we change our current practice.

Nor is Walzer committed to a denial of the possibility of criticizing alien cultures by invoking our own values. Already in *Spheres of Justice* he makes it clear that it is perfectly appropriate for us to attempt to convince those who believe them that the doctrines supportive of the caste system are in fact false, and this shows that his relativism is not so extreme as to remove any basis upon which we can assess or judge the social meanings of other cultures. What is prohibited is not the attempt to persuade other cultures to change their understandings but the overriding of those understandings without changing them. We can perhaps identify here readings of Walzer's position that make it weak but plausible. It would seem to be a necessary condition of persuading someone to see things differently that one be intelligible to that person, that one make some sense to her. But in that case it is obviously necessary that one's criticism appeal to the 'social meanings' of her own culture if these are understood to mark the bounds of intelligibility. If one attempts to persuade someone of a value system that in no way maps onto her current beliefs, then one will simply fail to make sense to her, will seem to be talking nonsense. Even if we think that this particular reading renders Walzer's claim too weak to be of interest, for it is reduced now to the idea that one cannot change someone's mind without speaking a language she understands, it is highly plausible to think that one's chances of success will relate closely to the extent to which one is able to appeal to ideas already present in her culture. The critic must 'connect' in a very weak sense in order simply to be intelligible, but it may well be that there is a stronger kind of connection needed if one is actually to change people's minds.

Furthermore, in *Interpretation and Social Criticism* Walzer suggests that there may even be justified grounds for intervening in the practices of another culture even where the attempt at persuasion, and thus at the appeal to understandings latent in the other culture, has failed. For there he posits 'a kind of minimal and universal moral code',[16] one that stands to a thickly constituted moral culture as a hotel room does to a home, constituting a basic framework too thin and spare to provide the detail one might need to know how to live, but nonetheless standing as trans-cultural constraints on shared meanings. Since such a minimal code derives its validity from the fact that it arises, or is discovered, universally, societies that fail to respect it must necessarily be rare exceptions. But when they do, then others may be justified in intervening to prevent its contravention.

> Consider the example of the Spaniards in Central America, who claimed sometimes to speak for Catholicism, sometimes only for natural law. They had, to be sure, a Catholic understanding of natural law, but they may still have been right to oppose human sacrifice, for example, not because it was contrary to orthodox doctrine but because it was 'against nature'. The Aztecs probably did not understand, and yet the argument did not have the same degree of externality as did arguments about the blood and body of Christ (and it may well have connected with the feelings, if not the convictions, of the sacrificial victims).[17]

As the last two clauses suggest, it may well be that some trace of the minimal code was to be found in Aztec culture and that not all members of the society really did share those understandings embodied in the practice of human sacrifice, and to that extent the social critic might regard herself as appealing to currently subordinate strands in the culture. But in this passage that thought is secondary, for Walzer clearly thinks that intervention in the name of the minimal code, here understood as the natural law, would be justified in any case. If we feel that a fundamental value is being violated by members of an alien culture, then we can be morally justified in acting to prevent that violation even when the violaters cannot understand our reasons. Where social meanings run out, where bases for rendering ourselves intelligible are unavailable, we can no longer seek to persuade; but, on some occasions, the seriousness of the issue at stake may nonetheless warrant intervention.

Moreover, there is, implicit within Walzer's approach but not articulated by him, a further possible trans-cultural principle, which he seems not to regard as part of the minimal code but which nonetheless seems to yield a basis upon which we might legitimately criticize another culture even if failing to connect with that culture's own self-understandings. We emphasized above that one principle underlying Walzer's meanings-based methodology was a decent respect for the opinions of mankind. This it is that leads him to advocate social change by persuasion, a process necessarily involving some degree of internality between critique and culture criticized as a prerequisite both of intelligibility and of success, rather than simply by overriding existing social meanings. Recall his rhetorical question: 'By virtue of what characteristics are we one another's equals? One characteristic above all is central to my argument. We are (all of us) culture-producing creatures; we make and inhabit meaningful worlds' (*SJ*, p. 314). Since what grounds the respect for cultural particularity that leads to the relativistic strand in his theory is the principle that we are all equally culture-producing creatures, we might think that our respect for other cultures' ways of doing things need not extend to those cultures which themselves do not recognize this principle. If a society is failing to allow people equally to create the cultural constructions by which they live, then the idea that drives Walzer's argument would seem to justify intervention, not restraint.

This suggestion of course raises a number of difficulties. How are we to know whether a group of people is being excluded from the process of cultural construction? Isn't it a plausible analysis of the caste system that this is just what has happened to the untouchables? Or to women in fundamentalist Muslim communities? We cannot, it would seem, ask people we suspect to be excluded what *they* think, since their acceptance or endorsement of their position might be interpreted either as evidence of their non-exclusion or of the great extent to which they have internalized an identity from the construction of which they have been barred. We might be inclined to think that people accorded equal status in the process of cultural creation would never create cultures that gave them subordinate status, and suspect that those regarded as inferior must have been excluded from the process of creation. But perhaps this is mistakenly and unjustly to apply our own conceptions of what it would be reasonable for people to do in a way that Walzer's anti-universalism and respect for cultural particularity is precisely seeking to avoid.

Although it hardly resolves all the difficulties raised by the question of relativism, it does seem both that Walzer provides at least the suggestion of a trans-cultural critical principle, and, especially interesting given our thematic agenda, that it consists in a conception of the person. We said at the beginning of this chapter that Walzer's contribution to the debate was distinctive in focusing rather on goods than on persons, and this remains valid, but it is worth emphasizing here that his theory can be read as presupposing a particular understanding of what is important about people.

Whatever the merits of this final thought, the evidence of Walzer's later writings suggests that some of the more extreme consequences deduced by his critics from the relativistic strand in *Spheres of Justice* were neither intended nor entailed by his invocation of social meanings. If anything, what emerges is an impeccably liberal emphasis upon the need to respect alien cultures and to give priority to persuasion rather than force when political disputes arise – an attempt to create a space for tolerance without allowing that tolerance to paralyse action on truly fundamental matters. And even given these qualifications, Walzer's original emphasis upon the priority of social meanings remains undiluted; the conceptual argument that Rawlsian methodological abstraction condemns Rawlsian principles of justice to inapplicability, and the substantive argument that it amounts to a failure to respect democratic values, remain.

Complex equality

Now we can turn from the particularistic methodology Walzer espouses to the positive theory of justice (a theory of 'differentiated substance') that emerges when he applies that methodology to contemporary society. This substantive element of Walzer's argument, which we referred to earlier as the 'different goods for different reasons' strand, is relatively straightforward, so our presentation can be correspondingly brief.

According to Walzer's interpretation of the social meanings of the goods produced and distributed in our society, those meanings are distinct; and

> when meanings are distinct, distributions must be autonomous. Every social good or set of goods constitutes, as it were, a distributive sphere within which only certain criteria and arrangements are appropriate. Money is inappropriate in the sphere of ecclesiastical office; it is an intrusion from another sphere. And piety should make for no advantage in the marketplace, as the marketplace has commonly been understood. (*SJ*, p. 10)

What is wrong with the conversion of money into the 'sphere' of ecclesiastical office is that this offends against the social meanings of the two goods in question, and it should be clear how this relates to the methodological considerations that we have been discussing hitherto. Respect for cultural particularity requires attention to the ways in which a community understands its goods, and such understandings carry implications for the way that those goods are distributed. If one good exchanges for another whose meaning is distinct, then this is a violation of the cultural constructions involved.

So, whilst there remains, of course, a concern that goods be distributed in accordance with their own meanings, the thrust of Walzer's theory is such as to focus attention not so much on the distribution of goods considered one by one as on the prevention of exchanges between them. Thus, putting it very crudely, what is unjust about capitalist society is not so much the unequal distribution of money as the fact that money is able to bring its possessor goods, such as health care or education, that properly belong to different distributive spheres. In Walzer's terminology, what is wrong is that money is a 'dominant' good, one that 'tyrannizes' over others. And the mistake in focusing on the more equal distribution of money rather than the prevention of exchanges between it and other goods is that of pursuing 'simple' rather than 'complex' equality.

Let us try to clarify the meanings of these terms, beginning with Walzer's distinction between 'dominance' and 'monopoly':

> I call a good dominant if the individuals who have it, because they have it, can command a wide range of other goods. It is monopolised whenever a single man or woman, a monarch in the world of value – or a group of men and women, oligarchs – successfully hold it against all rivals. Dominance describes a way of using social goods that isn't limited by their intrinsic meanings or that shapes those meanings in its own image. Monopoly describes a way of owning or controlling social goods in order to exploit their dominance. (*SJ*, pp. 10–11)

This distinction allows him to contrast two sorts of demand for justice: first, the claim that the dominant good, whatever it is, should be redistributed so that it can become equally or at least more widely shared (this amounts to saying that monopoly is unjust); and second, the claim that the way should be opened for the autonomous distribution of all social goods (this amounts to saying that dominance is unjust). Walzer's argument is for the latter rather than for the former, that is for the autonomous distribution of goods, distribution in accordance with the good-specific meanings of each, rather than for the more equal distribution of whatever good happens to be dominant.

This distinction between monopoly and dominance leads to another between 'simple' and 'complex' equality: 'Imagine a society in which everything is up for sale and every citizen has as much money as every other. I shall call this the 'regime of simple equality'. Equality is multiplied through the conversion process, until it extends across the full range of social goods' (*SJ*, p. 14). Here one good is dominant – money – but that good is distributed equally. The problem with this, for Walzer, is that it is unstable, for free exchange from an equal starting-point will soon lead to new inequalities, and the only means of sustaining simple equality over time would be a dangerously strong state (that is, a state strong enough to break up incipient monopolies and repress forms of dominance), which would then become the focus of new competitive struggles.

But if simple equality is not viable, does that mean that equality as such is out of the picture? Not at all. We should be thinking rather in terms of complex equality.

> I want to argue that we should focus on the reduction of dominance – not, or not primarily, on the break-up or constraint of monopoly. We should consider what it might mean to narrow the range within which

particular goods are convertible and to vindicate the autonomy of
distributive spheres . . .

Imagine now a society in which different social goods are mono-
polistically held – as they are in fact and as they always will be,
barring continual state intervention – but in which no particular good
is generally convertible . . . This is a complex egalitarian society. Though
there will be many small inequalities, inequality will not be multiplied
through the conversion process. Nor will it be summed across different
goods, because the autonomy of distributions will tend to produce a
variety of local monopolies, held by different groups of men and
women. (*SJ*, p. 17)

From this perspective what's wrong is not inequality as such –
'monopoly is not inappropriate within the spheres' (*SJ*, p. 19) – but
what Walzer call 'tyranny': the disregard of the distinctness of the
principles internal to each distributive sphere. The regime of complex
equality

is the opposite of tyranny. It establishes a set of relationships such that
domination is impossible. In formal terms, complex equality means
that no citizen's standing in one sphere or with regard to one social
good can be undercut by his standing in some other sphere with
regard to some other good. Thus citizen X may be chosen over citizen
Y for political office, and then the two of them will be unequal in the
sphere of politics. But they will not be unequal generally so long as
X's office gives him no advantages over Y in any other sphere – superior
medical care, access to better schools for his children, entrepreneurial
opportunities, and so on. (*SJ*, pp. 19–20)

In short, the way to achieve justice is vigilantly to patrol the barriers
between goods, preventing conversions between goods whose
meanings, and hence principles of just distribution, are distinct.

Since he is methodologically committed to the rejection of general
distributive principles, it is not surprising that the one that Walzer
ends up with is 'open-ended', stating that 'no social good x should
be distributed to men and women who possess some other good y
merely because they possess y and without regard to the meaning
of x' (*SJ*, p. 20). The force of such a principle is to direct our attention
towards the study of the way different goods are indeed understood in different societies, and, if our specific concern is with justice
in our own society, to the interpretation of our own social meanings.
The bulk of *Spheres of Justice* consists of the carrying out of just these

two tasks, and it is by concrete illustration as much as by abstract argument that Walzer makes the case for his particularistic approach to thinking about justice. He richly portrays the sheer variety of ways in which different cultures have conceived the goods they have created and distributed, and argues persuasively that the proper interpretation of our own social meanings of a host of goods, from money and education to hard work, commits us to certain distributive principles. That the strength of his position should lie in its culture- and good-specific detail is of course as Walzer would wish it, but it does not lend itself to summary of the kind required here. If the reader doubts the validity of the approach when presented in its abstract form, she may be more persuaded by its particularistic exemplification and should read the central chapters of the book, for this is certainly how Walzer would wish to persuade her.

Before moving on to consider some of the critical issues raised by Walzer's substantive ideas about justice, it may be helpful to add two further observations on these ideas. First, we should be able to see the connections between them and both aspects of the methodological strand of Walzer's argument. Justice requires that each good be distributed in accordance with its own sphere-specific principles, which are discovered through interpretation of its social meaning. A society is tyrannical if one good dominates others, if it violates those meanings; for in so doing it fails decently to respect the opinions of those who conceive the goods, the process, necessarily social, of cultural creation that endows the goods with meanings in the first place. The open-ended distributive principle and the regime of complex equality which it implies, because they alone give proper weight to social meanings, are thus the only approaches to justice that observe the methodological injunctions discussed above.

Second, it should now be even clearer why Walzer must reject Rawls's conception of primary goods. For it is not only, as we have already seen, that the latter's apparent attempt to come up with a list of 'basic' goods that can be applied cross-culturally fails to respect cultural difference and seeks an abstraction from meaning that renders goods meaningless. It is also that, even with respect to a single culture such as Rawls's own, the apparent lumping together of a range of different goods into a single list neglects the fact that different goods should be distributed for different reasons. The whole idea that people in the original position might think usefully about how to distribute goods whilst neglecting their distinct meanings must, for Walzer, be fundamentally misguided.

The desirability of complex equality

The idea that different goods should be distributed for different reasons, and that we should prevent conversions between goods whose meanings are distinct, has a great deal of intuitive plausibility. There are specific conversions that our society does not permit: we do not, for example, allow people to buy and sell votes, or political offices. Similarly, there are several goods, such as education and medical care, that we tend to regard as so important, so qualitatively different from straightforward commodities, that they should not be distributed in accordance with ability to pay. We may well feel that there is something more unjust about the ability of the wealthy to purchase superior or quicker health care than there is about their ability to purchase superior or quicker cars. Of course, given Walzer's claim to have derived his substantive conclusions via interpretation of the social meanings that we share, it would be surprising if they did not have a certain *prima facie* plausibility. What matters is whether such first appearances survive critical analysis, and we may undertake this, and simultaneously suggest a sense in which Walzer's position might be understood as communitarian, by observing how it relates to those arguments that point rather to the value of the individual's being free to make her own choices about what she does with her resources.

One way to approach this kind of argument is to think about how many of those worries we might have about conversions between different goods would disappear if there were an equal distribution of resources in the first place. Suppose everybody had the same amount of money. Would we still feel that there was something wrong with people using their money to buy health care? Should it not be up to them to decide how to allocate their resources? If they would prefer to take an expensive holiday, or buy a TV satellite dish, than to take out health insurance, it might seem that this is their decision. What makes us think otherwise is not, perhaps, anything about the social meaning of health care that demands that it not be purchased for money. Rather it is a concern that people should equally have access to medical treatment and that the currently unequal distribution of money tells against this; or, putting it another way, that the unequal distribution of purchasing power will mean that the distribution of health care does *not* reflect the free choices of individuals but is distorted in favour of the better off. In a situation of equal resources, the distribution of health care would genuinely reflect the choices of individuals as to how they would like to spend their money, there would be equal access, and in that case there might seem to be nothing wrong in principle with permitting exchanges of this kind.

The argument, which is essentially about the freedom of the individual to choose for herself, can be extended to more extreme cases. We are inclined to think that people should not be permitted to sell their kidneys for money. But if a particular individual would prefer a certain cash sum to the kidney, and another would prefer the kidney to the cash sum, what reason do we have to stop them both doing what they want? Our immediate response is to think that nobody could really freely choose to sell his kidney, that he must be desperate, forced by poverty or analogous circumstance to do something he does not really want to do. Empirically this is doubtless overwhelmingly the case. But we could imagine a situation where someone already comfortably off could, by selling his kidney, earn enough extra to buy himself the Steinway piano he has wanted all his life. If that is his choice, why should he be prevented?

We do not mean to suggest that there are no answers to such questions. The connection between the freedom of the individual and the free market is a very big issue, and those who are suspicious of the latter have many arguments at their disposal. For a choice to be 'free', must the person who makes it have full information? Perhaps we can justify taking health care out of the market on the grounds that individuals are not competent accurately to assess the real likelihood of their falling ill, and so will buy less insurance than would be rational. Does this mean that a choice is only free if it is 'rational'?[18] And who then decides what is and isn't rational? Or might it be the case that lots of choices freely made by individuals aggregate to produce unintended consequences that nobody wants? If so, here again restrictions on individual freedom might be justified. These are just some of the questions central to a full assessment of the case for and against the market, and we cannot pursue them here. All that we hope to have shown is the way in which Walzer's injunction to block exchanges between goods with different meanings involves constraining the individual's freedom to do as she will with what she has.

However we may choose to specify and qualify it, and it is important to recognize that different kinds of liberal accord the market different roles in their political theories, the general shape of the connection between liberalism and the market should be clear. The idea that people should be free to make their own choices about how they live their lives sits neatly with an economic system based upon free exchange. Indeed, there are more sophisticated arguments which claim that the way in which the market determines prices, as a function of supply and demand, has the great virtue of not involving any substantive judgements about the value of particular goods but rather simply reflects the relative value accorded to them by the different people in the economy. In a sense, then, and again on the hypothetical assumption of an equal distribution of resources, the free market can be seen to embody that anti-perfectionist strand, perhaps even that neutrality between conceptions of the good, that we have seen to be central at least to some strands of liberal thought.[19]

The sense in which Walzer's substantive argument might be considered distinctively communitarian can now also be seen. The preventing of free exchanges – of what, echoing Nozick,[20] we might term voluntary acts between consenting adults – in the name of the autonomy of the different distributive spheres, involves the over-riding of individuals' choices in the name of the 'social meanings' of the goods in question. Since the force of that 'social' is to remind us that those meanings are necessarily created and conceived communally, this implies a clear prioritization of the community over the individual. Walzer is explicit that the 'opinions of mankind' that he is exhorting us to respect are 'Not the opinions of this or that individual, which may well deserve a brusque response: I mean those deeper opinions that are the reflections in individual minds, shaped also by individual thought, of the social meanings that constitute our common life'(*SJ*, p. 320). For the liberal, concerned to guarantee the individual's freedom to pursue her own way of life, this may seem unhelpfully vague, especially if she suspects that there is real and significant disagreement within her culture about what the social meanings of goods actually are. Indeed, to hint further at a thought that we shall develop in a later chapter, might not liberalism plausibly be regarded as a response to circumstances characterized precisely by the fact that people do *not* agree about how people should live their lives or how particular goods should be distributed? And might not this be an accurate empirical description of contemporary advanced industrial societies? In such circumstances, the doctrine that people should be free to make up their own minds about how they live their lives and what they do with their resources may look particularly persuasive, and an anti-perfectionist state and a free market might be thought to be the social institutions that embody such a doctrine.

Walzer contra Rawls

Whatever the qualms we might have about certain aspects of Walzer's substantive theory of justice, it is clear that his co-option as a communitarian critic of Rawlsian liberalism depended much more upon his arguments about the methodology that is appropriate to theorizing about social justice in general. In this respect, his critique falls squarely under the third heading on our agenda of issues, for what he identifies in Rawls and condemns in general is any mode of political theorizing that fails to pay attention to the cultural particularity of the contexts within which such theorizing must have application. In brief, it is Rawls's emphasis upon primary goods and the resulting appearance of universal scope attaching to his conclusions that falls foul of Walzer's claim that any theory of justice must base itself upon a careful reading of the particular social meanings of the goods whose distribution is at issue, on pain both of failing to respect democratic values and of failing to be utilizable in any concrete social circumstances. Whether this appearance of Rawlsian anti-particularism accords with reality is a matter we defer to the next chapter.

What gives Walzer's distinctively methodological critique its communitarian bias is the central place it allots to social meanings: the distribution of goods cannot be decided apart from a grasp of the specific meanings of those goods, and those meanings are inherently social – constructed by, derived from and maintained by the community and its practices and institutions rather than by the thoughts and deeds of any individual. Thus, Walzer's work presupposes a conception of the individual's relation to his community, of the importance of communal frameworks and so of the inherent worth of communal practices and institutions, that aligns him very closely with the work of MacIntyre and Taylor. Most strikingly of all, Walzer's vision of human beings as culture-producing creatures is strongly reminiscent of Taylor's claim that human beings are self-interpreting animals.

It may, however, be worth pointing out that Walzer's criticisms of Rawls do not entail that he opposes liberalism *per se*, or at least does not entail that he is hostile to certain central strands of typically liberal political thinking. Walzer is clearly opposed to political theories that give *undue* emphasis to enshrining individual rights in law in a way that seriously encroaches upon the democratic process; and insofar as the Rawlsian emphasis upon primary goods is a manifestation of the general liberal attempt to be maximally neutral between competing conceptions of the good, Walzer is opposed to that attempt. On the other hand, his demand that the political theorist attend to the particularity of social meanings reflects a commitment to the values of tolerance and respect for alien cultures that is impeccably liberal; and insofar as liberal ideas and values have permeated the institutions and practices of our society, then a Walzerian respect for the social meanings that our goods now carry may well result in recognizably liberal conclusions. After all, although his emphasis upon preventing conversions between goods seems to conflict with Rawls's attempt to give absolute priority to individual freedom, the general idea of a separation of spheres has a respectable liberal ancestry. It is, after all, liberals who are keen to insist on the separation, and separability, of church and state, of the economic and the political, and, more generally, of private and public.[21] In this respect, the example of Walzer reinforces the point we made in the previous chapter about Taylor: being a communitarian critic of liberalism by no means entail a wholesale rejection of liberalism and liberal values.

Notes

1 Habermas, *Legitimation Crisis*; Ackerman, *Social Justice and the Liberal State*.

2　Walzer, 'Philosophy and Democracy'.
3　Ibid., pp. 388–9.
4　Wittgenstein, *Zettel*, no. 455.
5　Walzer, 'Philosophy and Democracy', p. 386.
6　Ibid., p. 389.
7　As is argued by Dworkin, 'Rights as Trumps'.
8　Walzer, 'Philosophy and Democracy', p. 391.
9　Ibid., p. 393.
10　Ibid., p. 394.
11　Ibid., p. 395.
12　Dworkin, 'What Justice Isn't', is a clear statement of objections to the relativism of Walzer's theory. This is a reprint of a piece in the *New York Review of Books*, 14 April 1983, pp. 4–6, and the reader may be interested in the subsequent exchange between Walzer and Dworkin in that journal, 21 July 1983, pp. 43–6.
13　Marx, *The German Ideology*, p. 64.
14　Walzer, *Interpretation and Social Criticism*, p. 41.
15　Gramsci, *Selections from the Prison Notebooks*, p. 195.
16　Walzer, *Interpretation and Social Criticism*, p. 24.
17　Ibid., p. 45.
18　A classic essay that considers the different ways in which the concept of liberty has been understood, and in particular its relation to that of rationality, is Berlin, 'Two Concepts of Liberty'.
19　Here, as earlier in our Introduction, we massively simplify the approach of Dworkin, 'What is Equality?'.
20　Cf. Nozick, *Anarchy, State and Utopia*, p. 163.
21　For a fuller discussion on this point see Walzer, 'Liberalism and the Art of Separation'.

Concluding summary

We have now examined each of the writers who have been held to contribute to the communitarian critique of liberalism. But the task of summarizing their views, explaining why they might be thought to conflict with Rawlsian liberalism and elucidating the sense in which each writer might deserve the label 'communitarian' has entailed covering a lot of complex and detailed ground. So it seems advisable to provide a retrospective overview of this material, one which might be thought of as providing an answer to the question 'To what degree do the communitarians form a coherent group?' Since this coherence will be manifest – if at all – on two levels, namely whether their criticisms of liberalism are interrelated, and whether the four are 'communitarian' in the same sense, we will examine them in turn, beginning with the former.

Family resemblances: the criticisms of liberalism

Our treatment of this matter can most helpfully be organized around the agenda of issues with which we began this book, and it will take the following form. Under each of the five headings on that agenda, we shall specify which of the four communitarians develop views that are opposed to the one attributed to Rawls, and which of them explicitly argue that Rawls holds the view they oppose.

The conception of the person

Here, the focus is on a conception of the person as antecedently individuated or unencumbered, a conception that allows no room for the possibility that the attachments that individuals develop to their chosen ends, values, conceptions of the good and communities might become a constitutive part of their identity. Sandel, MacIntyre and Taylor develop views about personhood that attempt to undermine this conception; and Sandel and MacIntyre explicitly argue that Rawls is committed to it.

Asocial individualism

Two separable issues come under this heading: the philosophical error of assuming that any individual's ends, values and identity (regardless of their content) can be thought of as existing independently of the wider communities of which he or she is a member; and the substantive error of failing to acknowledge the true significance of those particular human goods whose content or focus is inherently communal (in particular the good of political community). MacIntyre and Taylor develop arguments that attempt to undermine the philosophical version of asocial individualism, and MacIntyre explicitly argues that Rawls is committed to it; Sandel develops arguments against the substantive version of asocial individualism, and explicitly argues that Rawls is committed to it.

Universalism

Here, the issue is whether Rawls's theory of justice is intended to apply universally and cross-culturally, with no attention paid to the culture-specificity of the subject-matter of such theorizing. Walzer develops a view that attempts to undermine any such conception of political theory; and he also explicitly argues that Rawls is committed to that conception.

Subjectivism/objectivism

The focus of debate here is the view that individuals' choices of ends, values and conceptions of the good are arbitrary expressions of preference, essentially incapable of rational justification. MacIntyre and Taylor develop views that attempt to undermine this position; and Sandel and MacIntyre explicitly argue that Rawls is committed to it.

Anti-perfectionism and neutrality

Under this heading, the accusation is that Rawls's theory of justice is far less neutral between competing conceptions of the good than might appear to be the case. It is argued that the theory, which prohibits the invocation of 'thick' conceptions of the good in the political arena, must itself draw upon just such a conception in its own defence; and that the liberal society that would result from implementing the theory might discriminate against conceptions of the good held by its citizens in ways other than those explicitly sanctioned by the need to protect the autonomy of all citizens. Different versions of this criticism are developed and pressed against Rawls by Sandel, MacIntyre and Taylor.

This way of summarizing the communitarian critique makes two important points very clear. First, as the distribution of names suggests, the third of the communitarian criticisms seems much less tightly connected with the other four than the latter are with one another. Walzer's criticism of the methodological abstraction he identifies with Rawlsian liberalism is not directly supported by the work of the other three critics; and their opposition to the Rawls's conception of the person, his asocial individualism, his moral subjectivism and his claims to neutrality is not paralleled in Walzer's work. The reason for this should by now be evident. As we stressed in the previous chapters, anyone committed to a conception of the person as antecedently individuated is likely to be drawn to defend certain versions of asocial individualism and moral subjectivism, and consequently will be relying upon a strongly non-neutral set of presuppositions in his or her moral and political thinking; but these beliefs neither entail, nor are entailed by, a particular conception of the methodology of political theorizing. To put it crudely, the former beliefs specify the substantive content of a theory and the latter conception specifies its scope; and the question of whether one's theory should have universal application is largely (if not entirely) independent of its content.

Second, within the main group of three critics, it is clear that we are given more reason to oppose the views to which they object than to attribute them to Rawls in particular or to liberalism in general. Whereas Sandel, MacIntyre and Taylor all develop positions that lead them to oppose views that have been attributed to Rawls, Sandel does more to defend the legitimacy of those attributions than MacIntyre, who himself does more in this respect than Taylor. This means that much of the weight of the communitarian attack, understood as an attack upon Rawls, depends upon the textual analysis and interpretations discussed in the first two chapters of this part of the book. If they can be defended, then Rawls is open to a multiplicity of mutually supporting criticisms; but much of the material we have examined is devoted to the general task of undermining the putatively erroneous views than to the more specific one of justifying their attribution to Rawls.

Family resemblances: the communitarianism of the critics

The best way to approach this question is to remind ourselves of the sense in which each critic of liberalism was seen to be a 'communitarian', and then to highlight the similarities and differences between them.

Sandel

Sandel's communitarianism is manifest in his concern to rehabilitate a possibility that a conception of the self as antecedently individuated seems to exclude. Insofar as such a self has an integrity that is given prior to and independently of its choice of ends, it is incapable of developing attachments to those ends that are partly or wholly constitutive of its identity. One such type of constitutive attachment upon which Sandel places great (but not exclusive) emphasis is to the community or communities of which the self is a member, and in particular to the political community.

MacIntyre

On MacIntyre's account of the relationship of the individual to the community, any attempt to give a coherent account of the person and of morality understood as a rational enterprise must make reference to the participation of individuals in essentially social phenomena such as practices and traditions. Here, communal membership is not merely essential to one sort of human good, but is integral to the possibility of attaining any sort of human goods whatever.

Taylor

Taylor argues that any adequate conception of morality, practical reasoning and the person must invoke qualitative frameworks which can be established, maintained and acquired only through membership of a linguistic community. If human beings are self-interpreting animals, and the languages needed for such self-interpretations are essentially social phenomena, then community is a structural precondition of human agency (including moral agency).

Walzer

For Walzer, the meanings – and so the very nature – of the goods for which any theory of justice must establish distributive principles cannot be grasped independently of the specific and widely-varying socio-cultural contexts within which they are produced, encountered and utilised. Since their meanings are social meanings, the goods with which justice is concerned are social goods; and as a consequence, both the practice of political theorising and the very concept of social justice itself must be understood as embedded within and relative to communal frameworks.

If we organize our retrospective overview around these four extremely condensed summaries, then we can see that, at first blush, the four critics of liberalism whose work we have examined utilize the concept of the community in three significantly different ways. MacIntyre and Taylor embody one such way, regarding reference to the community as integral to any account of human selfhood, agency and practical reasoning; but Sandel's claims are much more limited, amounting only to the view that constitutive attachments to the community are *one* important species of human good; and Walzer invokes the community solely in order to give an adequate account of practical reasoning about justice – and about the objects rather than the subjects of justice at that. From this perspective, we might say that MacIntyre and Taylor are the most fully-fledged communitarians, with Sandel and Walzer instantiating two variants of that central type which are different in focus and more restricted in scope.

This initial appearance of diversity is, however, misleading; for it could be argued that all four communitarians are alike in basing their work upon a particular, communally oriented conception of the person. In the case of MacIntyre and Taylor this is clear: Taylor's fundamental view of human beings as self-interpreting animals in linguistic communities is very similar to MacIntyre's neo-Aristotelian view that human beings can only make sense of themselves as persons and moral agents through the concepts and standards bequeathed to them by practices and traditions. As we suggested in chapter 4, much of Walzer's work on the methodology of political theorizing depends in a very similar way upon his view that human beings are essentially culture-producing and culture-inhabiting creatures. And Sandel's concern to rescue and re-emphasize the possibility of constitutive attachments to the community can easily be reinterpreted as a way of highlighting the degree to which the identity of human beings is bound up with their inhabitation of and identification with the smaller and larger communities of which they are members. From this perspective, all four communitarians are united around a conception of human beings as integrally related to the communities of culture and language that they create, maintain and inhabit.

This way of characterizing their communitarianism has the added advantage of relating it very closely to their criticisms of Rawls; for, as we have already noted, a large part of the case for accusing Rawls of asocial individualism, moral subjectivism and insufficient neutrality between conceptions of the good depends upon attributing to his work a conception of the person as antecedently individuated. Such a conception of the person is clearly fundamentally opposed to the one that we have claimed underlies the work of the communitarians: for if selves are antecedently individuated, then the possibility of developing constitutive attachments to the community is excluded and the idea that the creation, inhabitation and maintenance of communal frameworks might be integral to one's personhood cannot be adequately acknowledged. And of course, seeing the fundamental opposition between liberals and communitarians in terms of competing conceptions of the person underlines the central role in this debate of the charge that Rawls is committed to one such conception; for if this charge does not stick, then many of the other putative criticisms of Rawls will not stick either.

If, however, we wish to characterize the dispute between liberals and communitarians in a more abstract or value-oriented way, then we might venture the following formulation. Sandel's most fundamental reason for thinking that Rawls is committed to a metaphysical conception of the person as antecedently individuated is that it would account for the absolute priority that Rawls attaches to protecting the autonomy of the individual; in this sense, therefore, the role Sandel attributes to that conception of the person reflects his perception of the primacy of autonomy in the liberal framework. And of course, one of the key consequences of developing a conception of the person as culture-creating and culture-inhabiting is that emphasis falls upon capacities that the individual can only exercise by acting in concert with other human beings. Culture and society are the creations of human communities: they cannot be produced or maintained on an individual basis, and the resources they provide which are so essential to human selfhood and agency are bequeathed to the person by his or her community. Thus, the communitarian conception of the person opposes the classic liberal emphasis upon individual autonomy by stressing the degree and extent of that individual's necessary dependence upon the community.

What this formulation suggests is that there need not be a flat opposition or contradiction between these differing liberal and communitarian emphases. More specifically, the communitarian stress upon the ways in which an individual should not be thought of as autonomous of his or her community does not entail that individual autonomy should be altogether scrapped or entirely downgraded as a human good. It is rather designed to question the absoluteness of the priority and the universality of the scope that liberals are prone to assign to that good; it serves to suggest that both the priority and the scope should be modified or restricted. This is why, of all the communitarians, only MacIntyre is explicitly and almost unqualifiedly hostile to liberalism as a general moral tradition; Taylor is explicitly concerned to attack certain ways of defending liberalism rather than to attack the tradition as a whole, many of Walzer's methodological recommendations have a strongly liberal ring to them, and Sandel is explicitly concerned merely to suggest that liberalism has limits. In this sense, the communitarian critique of liberalism might be thought of in Sandelian terms: it is an attempt to identify the limits of the attractiveness and worth of autonomy, not an attempt to deny that attractiveness and worth altogether.

PART II

RAWLS'S RESPONSE

5

Rawls's political liberalism

Rawls's liberalism, the conception of justice as fairness and its purported theoretical presuppositions and implications, has, we have seen, been the target of a variety of distinct but interrelated communitarian criticisms. The questions that we must now address are twofold, and, while we do not observe a strict division of labour, our chapters in this part of the book essentially deal with each in turn. First, and the basic exegetical task of this chapter, we must ask whether Rawls is really committed to views of which the communitarians are critical; this will involve us in the business of presenting our best understanding of Rawls's actual position. Second, we must consider in detail the responses to the communitarian critique that this position makes available to him and assess whether the core ideas that underlie those responses are cogent; this is the matter of chapter 6. Summarizing in very broad terms the discussion that is to follow, we shall argue that Rawls's theory, as he would now have us understand it, is on the whole not susceptible to the communitarian critique, as that critique was originally formulated. This leaves open the possibility both that justice as fairness as presented in *A Theory of Justice*, or at least some formulations of some aspects of it, was a proper target, and, as we shall argue in chapter 6, that the theory in its current incarnation can only avoid communitarian objections by relying on claims that are themselves doubtful.

Leaving such issues until later, in this chapter we ask the apparently straightforward question of whether the communitarians have correctly perceived their target. Does Rawls believe what the communitarians attack? Can a Rawlsian liberal disown those features of her position to which they object, claiming that their attribution to Rawls's theory of justice depends upon misreading and misunderstanding? Is Rawls really committed to a conception of the person as unencumbered and antecedently individuated, to a view of the individual as prior to society, or to the belief that moral commitments are no more than subjective expressions of preference? In methodological terms, is he seeking an inappropriately universal or abstract conception of justice? Does his liberalism rely upon a conception of the good rather thicker than that claimed? In fact, as we shall see, each of these issues is complex and requires careful consideration, partly because there is much disagreement over what exactly Rawls's position now is; much of this chapter will be devoted to the presentation and justification of a particular reading of Rawls's political liberalism in the context of such disagreement.

Two introductory questions remain. We refer in the title of this chapter to 'the new Rawls' but, while there is no doubt that some elements of the presentation of his theory in Rawls's articles published since 1971 constitute significant changes in the way we are to understand that theory, it is far from clear quite how much is new. How much of Rawls's subsequent writings has been simply restatement and clarification of the original argument and how much is real change? When does a shift in emphasis or in presentation become a change in position? Whatever our answer we should be clear that the ideas at the heart of the theory, the original position and the principles of justice derived therefrom, are not at issue; that is why we were able to present them in our introductory chapter without prejudice to the question under discussion here. What may or may not have changed is not the conception of justice as fairness itself but the way we should understand that conception: its status, what other views it relies upon, the shape of the argument for it; in sum, what kind of theory it is.

A full answer to this question would require detailed textual analysis of a kind that is inappropriate given our general purpose in this book. In this context, it is sufficient to make the point that Rawls himself clearly regards the significant change as that which now makes the theory a specifically *political* conception of justice, or a specifically *political* brand of liberalism. As he says: 'The distinction between a comprehensive doctrine and a political conception is absent from *Theory*, and while I believe nearly all the structure and substantive content of justice as fairness . . . is unchanged when it is seen as a political conception, the understanding of the view as a whole is very significantly shifted.'[1] We shall explain what he means by this distinction between a comprehensive doctrine and a political conception shortly; here the point is just that this is where Rawls himself locates the major change in the way he would have his theory understood. Since, however, the sense in which the theory is 'political' has itself been subject to a variety of interpretations, this is far from the end of the matter. Some theorists attracted to the conception of justice as fairness have understood Rawls's move to the political to involve claims that they wish to deny, and this has sometimes resulted in a situation whereby liberal theorists sympathetic to justice as fairness have sought to defend the old Rawls against the new. We shall consider a variety of possible interpretations of the move to political liberalism below, defending Rawls's own view that, while it does indeed involve a significant shift in the way the theory is to be understood, this is not of the kind that should worry those who fear that it is political in the wrong way.

As well as asking how much is really new about the new Rawls, we must also consider the senses in which Rawls's writings subsequent to *A Theory of Justice* can be understood as a response to the communitarian critique that we have been discussing in our previous chapters. As we said in our Introduction, the structure of this book reflects our judgement that it is illuminating to read the new Rawls in the light of that critique, but we recognize that this formulation masks variety of difficulties. To the extent that Rawls has shifted position, can we think of this as a deliberate response to points made by communitarians against the original theory? Even if not at the level of conscious deliberation, might it not be that those points played some role in leading Rawls to a new understanding of the kind of theory that justice as fairness is? Where there has been no change in position, but merely shifts of emphasis or presentation, might not these have been motivated, consciously or not, by the communitarian critique? Again these are complicated questions, properly addressed only by detailed scholarship of a kind inappropriate here.

A number of points are nonetheless worth making. On the one hand, even where Rawls is not changing his position but is genuinely clarifying what he was saying all along, this might well be presented or formulated in such a way as deliberately to bring out the sense in which he is not asserting what communitarians have taken him to assert. That an aspect of Rawls's more recent writings be presented, whether explicitly or implicitly, as a response to communitarian criticism is of course not sufficient to show that it involves a real change in position, since it is perfectly possible for Rawls simply to be pointing out the ways in which his critics have misinterpreted him. On the other hand, there are occasions where Rawls presents an aspect of his theory that clearly does relate to its new 'political' features in ways that make explicit reference to communitarian criticisms. While this does not establish that the 'political' move was motivated by the communitarian critique, it does show that it is that move which allows Rawls to respond to criticisms from that quarter in a way that would not otherwise be available to him. An important consideration weighing against the idea that we can understand Rawls's more recent (re)statements as responses to the communitarian critique in any important sense is the fact that a great deal of the shift in presentation or position was already there in the Dewey Lectures of 1980,[2] which predate the publication of any of the communitarian criticisms. However, while it is true that those communitarians explicitly taking Rawls as their target should have paid more attention to those lectures and might have avoided some of their more egregious misinterpretations if they had done so, these dates are not in themselves decisive, since ideas can be around, unpublished and perhaps not even systematically committed to paper, for a long time before they appear in books or articles.

In a sense, of course, both the causal relations involved and the question of the extent to which they operate through conscious intentionality are of only tangential interest. Whatever the truth of these matters, we would stand by our claim that it is fruitful to read the new Rawls in the light of the communitarian critique of liberalism in general and his *A Theory of Justice* in particular, and this holds whether he is restating and reformulating his original position or changing it.

Justice as fairness as political

Granting that, from its presentation in *A Theory of Justice*, justice as fairness might seem to be embedded in a comprehensive moral doctrine, Rawls is keen to insist that it is not, that it is intended rather as a political conception, and, as we have seen, he acknowledges that this makes a significant difference to the way that his theory should be understood. Clearly, then, our initial task must be to see what he means by calling it 'political', and how this is distinct from the reading that his original book encouraged.

At their most succinct, the distinguishing features of a political conception of justice are:

> first, that it is a moral conception worked out for a specific subject, namely, the basic structure of a constitutional democratic regime; second, that accepting the political conception does not presuppose accepting any particular comprehensive religious, philosophical, or moral doctrine; rather, the political conception presents itself as a reasonable conception for the basic structure alone; and third, that it is formulated not in terms of any comprehensive doctrine but in terms of certain fundamental ideas viewed as latent in the public political culture of a democratic society.[3]

In this section we shall unpack these three features in turn, leaving until later the crucial issue of why Rawls should want a conception that is 'political' in these senses. While the two questions are intimately related, it is rather more straightforward to see what makes a conception political for Rawls than it is to see why he should seek such a conception, and we shall begin with the easy bit.

First, then, is the point that the theory is intended to apply to a specific subject, what Rawls calls 'the basic structure', and spells out as 'a society's main political, social, and economic institutions, and how they fit together into one unified system of social co-operation'.[4] The essential point here is that the conception of justice as fairness is not intended to be general in its scope: it is not supposed to tell us what justice requires in all situations, nor how all institutions must be organized if they are to be just. The two principles apply quite specifically to the basic political, social, and economic institutions of society; how churches, universities, firms, families, hospitals, institutions not belonging to the basic structure, are justly to distribute the goods with which they are concerned are questions on which justice as fairness is silent. While these other forms of association must be bound by the constraints that arise from the principles of justice, so that, for example, liberty of conscience demands that religions cannot burn heretics, only excommunicate

them, the special aims and purposes of these different forms mean
that quite different principles of justice may apply within them.

The first respect in which the conception is political, then, is in its
subject; it applies specifically to the political sphere, as long as this
is understood broadly, as it is in ordinary usage, to include not only
political but also major social and economic institutions. The second
concerns rather what we might call its *status*. The idea that 'accepting
the political conception does not presuppose accepting any particular
comprehensive religious, philosophical, or moral doctrine' takes us
to the heart of the new Rawls.

His point here is that the various claims built into his conception
of justice as fairness, those ideas embodied in the thought experiment
of the original position and the principles of justice that are derived
from it, do not rely upon any full-blown theories about how people
should lead their lives in general, in private as well as in their
political conduct. In contrast to utilitarianism, for example, which,
as a comprehensive moral doctrine, is usually taken to indicate to
its adherents what they ought to do in all aspects of their lives,
Rawls's specifically political conception is intended to stand independently of, and not to presuppose, any such expansive understanding of moral, religious or philosophical values or ideals. We
have already noted that this is the shift from the presentation of the
theory in *A Theory of Justice* that Rawls is most ready to acknowledge; in that work 'it is assumed that the members of the well-
ordered society . . . accept the same conception of justice and also,
it seems, the same comprehensive doctrine of which that conception
is a part, or from which it can be derived'.[5] It is crucial for Rawls,
for reasons we shall address shortly, that justice as fairness does not
in fact rely upon any such comprehensive doctrine but stands independently as a specifically political conception. According to him,
one does not have to be committed to any particular comprehensive
moral ideal in order to accept the moral claims, including the
identification of people's highest-order interests, that are built into
the characterization of the original position.

The third respect in which the conception is political, which we
may think of as concerning its *method* or *source*, is that it is formulated
'in terms of certain fundamental ideas viewed as latent in the public
political culture of a democratic society'. Justice as fairness should
be understood not as the elaboration of a particular comprehensive
ideal but rather as the systematic articulation, the 'working up' into

a coherent pattern, of intuitive ideas that, because they are embedded in our society's main institutions and the historical traditions of their interpretation, can be regarded as implicitly shared. Whether the conception can be extended to other societies, with quite different political cultures, is a separate question. The conception applies only to the basic structure, it presupposes no particular comprehensive ideals, and it builds upon only those ideas that are to be found within the shared public political culture of a constitutional democracy. These are the three senses in which the conception is political.

Society as a fair system of cooperation between free and equal citizens

Before addressing the crucial and controversial question of why Rawls should want his conception of justice to be 'political' in the ways sketched out above, it is necessary first to spell out in greater detail exactly how the various features of justice as fairness do indeed fit this characterization. In order to understand the force of the claim that it is a political conception, we need to be clear about the ways in which its various elements can be regarded as satisfying the constraints that Rawls claims that they do satisfy. How does the content of the conception, as that was outlined in the first part of our introductory chapter, avoid invoking any comprehensive ideals? What does it mean to say that it applies only to the basic structure of society? How can it be understood as the articulation of ideas that are latent in the public political culture of a constitutional democracy?

The key points here, and those in terms of which these three features of the political will be seen to interrelate, can be expressed in two stages. First, that the original position, which, as we have seen, can be regarded as the embodiment of the various substantive normative claims that lie at the heart of justice as fairness, is intended to model the idea that society should be regarded as a fair scheme of cooperation between citizens conceived as free and equal. Second, that that very idea, that understanding of how we should regard society and its members, is itself taken to be implicit in our public political culture. The original position, then, models the normative claims not of a comprehensive moral, religious, or philosophical doctrine but of a conception of society that is political both in the sense of applying specifically to the organization of society's political institutions and in the sense of being derived from the public political culture.

We have already, in our introductory chapter, indicated the ways in which the original position represents people as free and equal, and it is not difficult to see how it involves the idea that society should be a fair scheme of cooperation. The understanding of principles of justice as the result of a contract, as the outcome of a process of bargaining between people seeking their own rational advantage, implies a model of society as something in which people cooperate with one another because it makes sense for them as individuals to do so, with the veil of ignorance ensuring that the scheme of cooperation will be fair. What is new about the move to the 'political' is the idea that the original position is intended to model our culture's understanding of people *as citizens*. It is this location of the conception of justice as one for people specifically *qua* citizens, as involving claims only about the way people understand themselves for the purposes of politics and not necessarily in their private lives, that provides the resources for responses to various strands in the communitarian critique, as well as raising further problems of its own.

Response to Sandel: person qua citizen Thus we are now in a position to see how Rawls might seek to reply both to Sandel's worries about the conception of the person and to Walzer's objections to two distinct kinds of abstraction from particularity that he identifies in the original position. While we shall later suggest that Rawls does not in fact make all the moves that we outline here, so that the reader needs to read our whole chapter to get our considered view of his actual position, it is important to realize that this claim about the political character of his liberalism was read in different ways by different people, and it is useful, precisely in order more clearly to identify what he *does* say, to outline what he might seem to be saying, and was taken by some to have been saying, on the evidence so far presented.

Taking the conception of the person first, the reader will recall that Sandel's charge was that justice as fairness presupposed an incoherent metaphysics – that we could not be detached from our ends, values, and our community in the way that the liberal supposed and the original position represented. Rawls's response might seem to be twofold. On the one hand, he appears to deny that the conception of the person that lies at the heart of the theory is there because it is 'true'; it is there because it is a fundamental intuitive idea latent in our public political culture. On the other, he seems to deny that it is a conception of people as such, as if it were intended to capture something about people all the way down; it is a conception of people *qua* citizens, explicitly limited to the sphere of politics.

The apparent claim that the conception of the person modelled in the original position enters the theory not because it is true but because it is latent in our public political culture immediately raises the question of why exactly Rawls should think it appropriate to pursue the method he does. Surely the political philosopher's job is to tell us what is really important about people, how society really ought to be, not merely to present in as coherent a way as possible whatever ideas he happens to find in his culture? This is obviously an aspect of the question of why Rawls should want to 'go political' in the first place – why he should want his theory to have the subject, status and method outlined above – and this is a question we wish to defer to the next section. For now it is pertinent only to note that it looks as if Rawls could reply to Sandel that he is not really interested in whether the conception of the person at the centre of the theory is coherent or not, since its coherence or otherwise is irrelevant. Communitarian objections to the liberal conception of the person are misplaced if these are understood as critical of Rawls's own theory, since what matters for him is not the 'truth' of that conception so much as the fact that it is latent in the public political culture.

The second aspect of his move on this issue is the idea that this is a political conception of the person, a conception of the person as citizen. As he puts it:

> ... we adopt a conception of the person framed as part of, and restricted to, an explicitly political conception of justice ... persons can accept this conception of themselves as citizens and use it when discussing questions of political justice without being committed in other parts of their life to comprehensive moral ideals often associated with liberalism, for example, the ideals of autonomy and individuality.[6]

What Rawls is saying here is that people can understand themselves in a certain way when it comes to thinking about politics, can regard themselves as having particular interests as citizens, whilst having quite different self-understandings, and quite different interests, in other, private or non-political, areas of their lives. One does not have to think that autonomy is what is important in all spheres of existence, one does not have to regard autonomy as a comprehensive moral or philosophical ideal, in order to think that it is important in politics, or, we might say, relevant to the purposes of political justice. *Qua* citizen, people can think that what matters is that they are able to frame, revise and pursue conceptions of the good, whilst *qua* private individual – *qua* father, Catholic, aesthete – they may have quite different understandings of their identity and interests.

We should now be able to see the significance of the denial that justice as fairness presupposes any comprehensive moral, religious or philosophical doctrine, as well as the significance of the acknowledgement that in *A Theory of Justice* it might look as if it does so. The conception of the person represented by the original position is a conception that people can affirm of themselves as citizens whatever their more comprehensive conceptions of the good. While in the initial presentation of the theory it looked as if you had to be committed to a liberal understanding of what is important about people all the way down, as it were, or to a claim about the metaphysical essence of people, Rawls now seems to be saying that one can hold a liberal conception of people as citizens, one that regards people as free and equal in the senses represented by the original position, without being liberals in a fuller or more comprehensive sense.

It goes without saying that each of these moves is controversial and raises difficult issues. We have already suggested that a proper understanding of the first requires an appreciation of the reasons why Rawls should want to pursue the distinctively political method that he does, and discussion of this point will have to wait until the next section. One reason why we have attempted so clearly to distinguish between the two moves identified here is precisely that one might want to endorse one and not the other. Most importantly, it seems plausible to support the claim that the conception of the person should be understood as one appropriate specifically to politics, but reject the suggestion that it should derive its place in the theory from the fact that it is latent in the public political culture of a democratic society, arguing rather that, though limited in its sphere of application, it must be affirmed as true in its own right.

Whatever the merits of this halfway house position, it is necessary here just to say a little more about this idea that a conception of the person as citizen need not presuppose the validity of any metaphysical or comprehensive doctrine.

First, it might be helpful to distinguish between the metaphysical and the comprehensive, and here it is noteworthy that Rawls has changed his terminology: in 1985 he was arguing that justice as fairness is 'political not metaphysical', but later he abandoned this formulation in favour of the distinction between the political and the comprehensive. The point here is that it is possible that even if the conception of the person involved were not merely that of the person as citizen but did indeed involve a comprehensive moral, philosophical or religious doctrine, such as a fundamental commitment to autonomy in all areas of life, still this might not commit the advocate of the theory to any genuinely *metaphysical* claim, where the term 'metaphysical' refers to an ontological claim about the essence of human beings. To Sandel's charge that the original position shows the way in which liberalism presupposes an unencumbered subject, a shadowy self detachable and detached from all its ends, the liberal might reply directly that it does no such thing: the original position simply models the claim that what is important about people is their capacity to reflect upon and revise the particular attachments that they happen to have, and one can think this important without holding that people can detach themselves from all their values at the same time. Of course, the process of reflection and revision goes on against a background of other values or commitments; it is true that we cannot detach ourselves from everything at the same time for then there would indeed be no basis upon which to make a judgement. But the original position does not embody the claim that we can so detach ourselves; Sandel misreads the original position, since, in taking it to embody (incoherent) metaphysical commitments, he fails to see that it is intended only as a 'device of representation', as a means of presenting a certain understanding of people's interests and capacities. The liberal response to the charge of incoherent metaphysics could simply be to disown any metaphysical claim, and this response could be made even by those who assert the conception of the self as part of a comprehensive doctrine and not merely as a political conception.

This position will of course be particularly attractive to those who, whilst wanting to rebut Sandel, are nonetheless uneasy about

Rawls's claim that the conception of the person as citizen pre-supposes no comprehensive claims, and, while we address this issue in greater detail below, it is appropriate here to signal the kinds of worries one might have about it. The problem really is whether it is plausible to think that people who are deeply committed to particular values or ways of life, perhaps to particular religious doctrines, which do not themselves accord highest priority to the value of individual freedom or autonomy, can nonetheless hold an understanding of themselves as citizens that does. While we can well see that the comprehensive liberal will have this conception, for it will be no more than the particular application of his comprehensive doctrine to the sphere of the political, it would seem to involve those committed to other comprehensive doctrines in a degree of schizophrenia. When it comes to thinking about politics and about what justice demands, we are to suspend or bracket our beliefs – beliefs that perhaps give our life its meaning and make up our very identities as individuals – in favour of a particular understanding of citizenship and society. And it is important to recognize that, for Rawls, it is always the political conception that wins: it is not just that there is a hint of schizophrenia here, there is the further claim that in cases of conflict it is always the political conception that must have priority. The demands of justice, the requirements of the political, must come first, before the claims of those comprehensive doctrines with which they must simultaneously and schizophrenically be held. Putting this worry another way, it seems that Rawls wants to allow those affirming the political conception of the person as citizen to believe in comprehensive doctrines involving other, non-liberal, values and commitments, but, in asserting the priority of the political conception, he requires that those comprehensive doctrines be held in a rather less than whole-hearted, one might say a rather liberal, way.

Response to Walzer: good-specific and culture-specific With respect to the critique of justice as fairness from Walzer, it will be recalled that we identified two distinct objections, both of which could be formulated in terms of Rawls's failure to attend to particularity. On the one hand, his use of primary goods was criticized for neglecting the fact that different goods must be distributed for different reasons, that principles of distribution must be good-specific. On the other, his supposed attempt to construct a universal vantage-point from which to derive principles of justice was attacked for failing to recognize the importance of 'social meanings', of a culture's own particular understandings of its goods. Taking seriously the senses in which Rawls's conception of justice is 'political', we shall argue, indicates the way in which both of these objections are misplaced.

In the first place, primary goods are by no means as abstract as they look. Far from being an undifferentiated mass of things that people might want, they are actually rather carefully related to the principles proposed for their distribution in just the way that Walzer demands. To see this we need to recognize their internal relation to the specifically political ideas of the basic structure and the conception of the person as citizen. In an article published the year before *Spheres of Justice*, Rawls asserted that 'Primary goods are not . . . to be used in making comparisons in all situations, but only in questions of justice which arise in regard to the basic structure. It is another matter entirely whether primary goods are an appropriate basis in other kinds of cases.'[7] He was similarly explicit on the relation between primary goods and the conception of the person as citizen:

> Note that by relying on primary goods, justice as fairness asserts that for questions of justice only certain kinds of consideration are relevant . . . The idea of restricting appropriate claims to claims to primary goods is analogous to taking certain needs alone as relevant in questions of justice. The explanation is that primary goods are things generally required, or needed, by citizens as free and equal moral persons who seek to advance . . . conceptions of the good. It is the conception of citizens as such persons, and as normal cooperating members of society over a complete life, which determines what they require. Since the notion of need is always relative to some conception of persons, and of their role and status, the requirements or needs of citizens as free and equal moral persons are different from the needs of (e.g.) patients and students . . .[8]

This last sentence indicates that in fact Rawls and Walzer have rather similar views about the need to relate principles of justice to the particular goods that they are to distribute. The difference is only that where Walzer talks of principles being good-specific, Rawls puts the point rather in terms of their being 'role-specific' or 'conception of the person-specific'. If we think of primary goods as 'citizen goods', of health care as 'patient goods' and education as 'student goods', and acknowledge Rawls's point that different

principles may be appropriate in these different contexts, then the
similarity becomes rather striking.

If it is the internal relation of justice as fairness to the basic
structure and the conception of the person as citizen that enables a
specifically political understanding of Rawls's theory to avoid the
first Walzerian challenge, it is its derivation from the public political
culture, the fact that that conception of the person enters the theory
as a fundamental intuitive idea latent in the public political culture
of a constitutional democracy, that renders it immune to the second
charge of seeking universality and abstracting from cultural particularity. Whilst we would wish to defer discussion of whether
Rawls is committed to a methodological position that is the same as
Walzer's apparently relativistic one, for this relates to the question
of why he should make the move to the political, it is clear that
Rawls pursues a method that attends to the social meanings of a
particular culture in a way that seems to obey Walzer's claims about
the methodology appropriate to political philosophy.

Nothing could be more in line with Walzer's injunctions to respect
social meanings than the claim that 'since justice as fairness is intended as a political conception of justice for a democratic society,
it tries to draw solely upon basic intuitive ideas that are embedded
in the political institutions of a constitutional democratic regime
and the public traditions of their interpretation'.[9] Far from representing an attempt to transcend cultural particularity and to reach
a perspective from which one can construct a theory of justice that
applies universally, the original position represents, is a device for
the representation of, an understanding that is explicitly culture-
specific: the understanding of society as a fair scheme of cooperation
between free and equal citizens. For Rawls, 'We look . . . to our public
political culture itself, including its main institutions and the
historical traditions of their interpretation, as the shared fund of
implicitly recognised basic ideas and principles.'[10] What we find
when we do so is a particular understanding of society and its
members, and the original position is nothing other than an attempt to portray that understanding. Here too, in his methodological
attention to what in Walzer's terms we would call 'shared social
meanings', we see that Rawls avoids the Walzerian charge of failure
to attend to particularity. Rather than seeking distance from the
political community, Rawls does precisely what Walzer would have
him do: he articulates our shared social meanings.

Why political?

Although we have gone some way towards understanding the sense in which Rawls would have us read his conception of justice as political, and have been able to outline the sorts of responses to particular communitarian criticisms made available to him by that reading, we have still not broached the question of what it is that leads Rawls to insist upon the specifically political aspects of his theory. To understand what he really means in claiming that his conception is political we need above all to see what *motivates* the search for a conception with the three features that we have discussed, and this issue, which takes us into yet deeper waters, can no longer be avoided.

We observed at the beginning of this chapter that there has been a deal of disagreement over what exactly the 'political' nature of Rawls's liberalism amounts to, and indeed Rawls himself has found it necessary to devote an article ('The Domain of the Political and Overlapping Consensus') to the correction of the view that it is political 'in the wrong way'. In this context, it is important to proceed cautiously and by clearly defined steps. First, we shall show that what motivates Rawls's concern for a political conception of justice is the importance of its being publicly justifiable to the members of a society characterized by what he calls 'the fact of pluralism'. Second, we shall go on to consider and reject two reasons why one might seek public justifiability: scepticism and pragmatism. Here we shall find it necessary to identify two distinct sources of confusion that have led to a great deal of misinterpretation. On the one hand, we shall clearly distinguish between the idea of public justifiability and the claim that his conception of justice stands (or can stand) as the kernel of an overlapping consensus; it is important to see that the point about consensus arises only as a secondary issue, to do with the stability of justice as fairness rather than with its primary justification. On the other, the idea of an overlapping consensus itself has been subject to misunderstanding; we shall emphasize both that the claim is not intended as a sociological description of the here and now and that the kind of stability with which Rawls is concerned is itself of a particularly moral and not merely a pragmatic kind. We shall then go on to identify what we take to be the real reason for Rawls's concern for public justifiability, emphasizing the sense in which it is not only wholeheartedly moral but also thoroughgoingly liberal.

The essential reason why Rawls seeks a conception of justice that is political in the three senses identified is that he wants something that can be publicly justified to all members of a pluralist society. As he puts it:

> Now one reason for focusing directly on a political conception for the basic structure is that, as a practical political matter, no general and comprehensive view can provide a publicly acceptable basis for a political conception of justice. The social and historical conditions of modern democratic regimes have their origins in the Wars of Religion following the Reformation and the subsequent development of the principle of toleration, and in the growth of constitutional government and of large industrial market economies. These conditions profoundly affect the requirements of a workable conception of justice: among other things, such a conception must allow for a diversity of general and comprehensive doctrines, and for the plurality of conflicting, and indeed incommensurable, conceptions of the meaning, value and purpose of human life (or what I shall call for short 'conceptions of the good') affirmed by the citizens of democratic societies.[11]

Leaving aside for the moment the references to practicality and workability, which we shall pursue shortly, what's crucial here is the thought that modern societies contain a diversity and plurality of conceptions of the good. Nor, for Rawls, is this a mere historical condition that is likely to pass away. Rather, the 'fact of pluralism' is a permanent feature of modern democracies.

Given the aim of finding a conception of justice that can be publicly justifiable to all citizens, it is clear why it is crucial that his theory does not presuppose the validity of any comprehensive religious, philosophical or moral doctrine. For the fact is that people disagree about these latter; any conception that presupposed one comprehensive doctrine would necessarily conflict with some other, precluding the possibility of agreement between citizens committed to these alternative views. We should also be able to see how the other two features of the political fit in: the method of looking to intuitive ideas latent in the public political culture makes sense because those ideas can be regarded as implicitly shared, at least as available to all citizens whatever their own particular conceptions of the good; and the restriction to the basic structure comes in because that is the sphere of life on which, for reasons to do with the content of the public political culture, public reasons are most likely to be available. The understanding of society as a fair scheme of cooperation between free and equal citizens, an idea latent in the public political culture and with implications only for the just organization of the basic structure, is something that can be justified to all members of society despite the fact of pluralism; despite the fact that they will be committed to conflicting and incommensurable conceptions of the good.

We can also see the relation between the wish to avoid controversial claims, claims that presuppose the validity of a particular comprehensive conception, and the exclusion of reasons that is represented by the veil of ignorance and the original position. In denying the people in the original position knowledge of their particular conceptions of the good, Rawls is modelling the idea that appeals to those conceptions are inappropriate when it comes to thinking about justice, and this is an aspect of his liberalism that we have already talked about. What can distinctively be remarked upon here is the connection between this exclusion of reasons and the desire for a conception of justice that can be publicly justified, that can be mutually acceptable to citizens committed in their private non-political lives to quite different moral, religious and philosophical beliefs.

Eliminating two reasons: not scepticism or pragmatism

Why is Rawls so committed to coming up with a conception that can be publicly justified in this way, that does not appeal to controversial truths? Two reasons may suggest themselves and, since each is in a different way central to the liberal tradition yet neither is Rawls's reason, it may be helpful to proceed by indicating how and why he seeks to distance himself from them. The first reason is scepticism about the status or 'truth' of controversial truths; the second reason is an overriding pragmatic commitment to stability and workability. When we have eliminated these two possible reasons we can go on to consider the one that motivates Rawls himself.

The first reason to seek a conception that does not appeal to

controversial truths, then, might be a scepticism either that there
are such truths or that we can know them. Since, in our judgement,
a great deal of support for liberalism derives from views such as
these, and since it is this strand in the liberal tradition to which
some of the communitarian critics were objecting, it is important to
be clear that Rawls explicitly rejects the idea that his concern for
public justifiability presupposes a scepticism or indifference as to
the truth of particular comprehensive doctrines. Indeed, he points
out that since such scepticism or indifference itself amounts to a
controversial claim that conflicts with many comprehensive doctrines, it would be self-defeating if the motivation to avoid controversy was itself grounded in such a position. Rather, the idea is
simply to avoid taking a position of any kind:

> Properly understood . . . a political conception of justice need be no
> more indifferent, say, to truth in morals than the principle of toleration,
> suitably understood, need be indifferent to truth in religion. We sim-
> ply apply the principle of toleration to philosophy itself. In this way
> we hope to avoid philosophy's long-standing controversies, among
> them controversies about the nature of truth and the status of values
> as expressed by realism and subjectivism. Since we seek an agreed
> basis of public justification in matters of justice, and since no political
> agreement on those disputed questions can reasonably be expected,
> we turn instead to the fundamental intuitive ideas we seem to share
> through the public political culture.[12]

One can believe in the truth of a particular conception of the good
and still hold that its truth is irrelevant or inappropriate to questions
of justice. The Rawlsian liberal can argue for an anti-perfectionist
state, can endorse the exclusion from politics of reasons arising
from comprehensive doctrines, whilst being committed *qua* private
individual to the truth of any such doctrine. What matters is that
she should recognize the supreme importance of achieving a state
that is mutually acceptable or publicly justifiable.

Nevertheless, it is worth observing that there does seem to be a
kind of scepticism involved in Rawls's position and this relates to
his claim that the fact of pluralism is a permanent condition: even
if acceptance of Rawls's conception of justice does not require us to
disown the truth of those comprehensive doctrines to which we are
committed as private individuals, it does, as he presents it, require
us to hold two quasi-sceptical beliefs: first, that there will, in a

democratic society, always be a diversity or plurality of such doctrines, so that common affirmation of a single one could only be
achieved by the oppressive use of state power; and, second, which
explains the first, that such disagreement is reasonable, that the
difficulties in arriving at agreement – what Rawls calls the 'burdens
of reason' – are such as to make disagreement reasonable and not
necessarily the product of prejudice or blindness. If the first seems
best read almost as an empirical sociological claim, that a variety of
doctrines are likely to find adherents in a democratic regime, the
second, in seeking to explain it by reference to what is 'reasonable',
would appear to be more philosophical. However we characterize
them, the point here is that they both to some extent represent
sceptical views: they require the individual committed to the truth
of her particular comprehensive doctrine to accept not only that she
will not be able to persuade everybody else of its truth but also that
their failure to see it may be reasonable.

If the reason to go for public justifiability is not any fundamental
scepticism or indifference about the truth of comprehensive doctrines, is it rather an essentially pragmatic concern with agreement
as the precondition of a stable political society? In his recent writings,
Rawls has emphasized the sense in which the aim of his theory
is practical, and it is this emphasis that has led some to see it as
pragmatic in a way that might seem inappropriate to a proper
defence of liberalism as a moral doctrine. At times it has looked as
if Rawls is presenting his conception of justice as practical rather
than moral, as if the aim of the political philosopher were to eschew
moral matters altogether in favour of coming up with whatever can
serve, as a practical political matter, as a basis of agreement.

It is in order to correct this misunderstanding that it is necessary
to be clear both on the distinction between public justifiability and
overlapping consensus and on the precise nature of the latter. Rawls's
claim that his conception of justice is stable, in that it is something
that can serve as an overlapping consensus between people committed to quite different conceptions of the good, has led some to
read his project as simply that of conflict-avoidance, identifying
whatever it is that people can agree to despite their differences,
which would seem to imply a role for the political theorist as at
once pragmatist and sociologist. On this reading, the conception of
society as a fair scheme of cooperation between citizens conceived
as free and equal, enters the theory for no reason other than that it

is that on which there is consensus in our pluralistic societies. This immediately raises two problems. First, why should the political theorist see her task as the empirical one of identifying that to which people committed to different conceptions of the good agree? Second, if it is supposed to be an empirical claim that the conceptions of the good held by citizens in contemporary democratic societies overlap on this conception of the person as citizen, is it not highly implausible? At least when we add that Rawls requires people to give priority to this conception in any conflict with their comprehensive doctrines?

In fact, as is now clear, these questions are to some extent misplaced. Rawls does not proceed by pragmatically looking for an underlying consensus which can serve to prevent conflicts arising between the various comprehensive doctrines around; the question of the stability of justice as fairness arises only as a secondary question, to be considered after it has been justified on other grounds. As he puts it:

> Justice as fairness is best presented in two stages. In the first case it is worked out as a free-standing political (but of course moral) conception for the basic structure of society. Only when this is done and its content – its principles of justice and ideals – is provisionally on hand do we take up, in the second stage, the problem of stability and introduce the idea of an overlapping consensus: a consensus in which a diversity of conflicting comprehensive doctrines endorse the same political conception . . .[13]

Although the question of the stability of his conception of justice is indeed of great importance to Rawls, it would be a mistake to see it as his primary concern. The conception is worked out in the first instance as the articulation of a particular set of (very great, political) values, and only after this has been done, when consideration turns to the issue of whether it is stable, does the idea of an overlapping consensus begin to be relevant.

It is not hard to see why there has been misunderstanding, for the idea that his conception can serve as the basis of an overlapping consensus would seem very similar to the search for public justifiability or mutual acceptability which we have argued plays a central and primary role in the justification of the conception. Nonetheless, it is important to distinguish between the two: Rawls seeks to avoid presupposing the validity of any particular comprehensive doctrine, he goes to the public political culture, not because his overriding aim is to identify an existing overlapping consensus but because he wants a conception that is justifiable using only ideas that are available to everyone. Whether the conception that he comes up with can actually serve as a stable basis of agreement is a separate question. Of course, as he acknowledges, the fact that the conception has not presupposed the validity of any particular comprehensive doctrine, but has rather been derived from the public culture, significantly increases the likelihood of its forming the kernel of an overlapping consensus, but the two are in principle quite different issues.

Having recognized that a concern with stability is only of secondary importance, so that justice as fairness gets its primary justification from the fact that it articulates the very great values of the political and not from any mere claim that it can be made to work, it is important also to understand the kind of stability in which Rawls is interested. Here there are two points to keep in mind. First, the stability in question is a stability over time. As Rawls puts it, 'The second stage consists of an account of the stability of justice as fairness, that is, its capacity to generate its own support, in view of the content of its principles and ideals as formulated in the first stage.'[14] The issue is not whether the range of opinions current in contemporary democratic societies overlap sufficiently to render justice as fairness stable here and now, it is whether that conception of justice, if realized, has the capacity to generate its own support.

The second point concerns the nature of the support generated. Rawls's claim that his conception of justice can serve as an overlapping consensus is not the claim that individuals or groups will find it in their interests to abide by its principles, as if the overlapping consensus were a mere *modus vivendi*, an agreed way of living together based upon negotiation and compromise: 'An overlapping consensus . . . is not merely a consensus on accepting certain authorities, or on complying with certain institutional arrangements, founded on a convergence of self- or group-interests.'[15] Rather, if his political conception of justice will serve as an object of consensus it will be as a moral conception affirmed on moral grounds, and, unlike a *modus vivendi* that must be understood as reflecting a particular balance of power, its stability does not depend upon any particular distribution of power between those espousing different comprehensive views.

All Rawls's talk about the idea of an overlapping consensus relates specifically to the issue of whether a conception of justice that has been justified on other grounds can be thought able to develop and sustain its own support in the future, where the kind of support in question is not that grounded in self-interest but rather a moral support, a willing endorsement of the values articulated by the conception. Rawls is not interested in whether there currently exists a consensus on the conception of society as a fair scheme of co-operation between free and equal citizens, nor in whether the balance of power between those committed to different conceptions of the good is such as to make it rational for them to agree to tolerate one another's differences. He is interested in whether that conception of society and its citizens is something to which people *can*, in the future, come to agree despite their commitment to different and conflicting conceptions of the good, and the kind of agreement he is interested in is that which derives from the moral endorsement of those values, not from any self-interested convergence on a *modus vivendi*. There are, then, various senses in which Rawls's approach is not pragmatic: questions of stability are secondary and enter the picture only when justice as fairness has been justified on independent grounds, as the articulation of the very great values of the political; the claim that justice as fairness can serve as the kernel of an overlapping consensus is a claim not that it builds upon already existing agreement but that it is such that it can generate its own support; and the kind of support that it can generate is not a merely pragmatic acceptance but a genuinely moral endorsement.

As in the case of the relation between liberalism and scepticism, what makes it is especially important to insist upon the point that Rawls's theory is not merely pragmatic is the fact that reasons of this kind have played a significant role in the liberal tradition, and perhaps underlie some of the support for liberalism that one finds in our contemporary culture. Rawls's conception of justice represents a development in the contract approach to political theory and of course one important strand of thought within the contract tradition is the Hobbesian idea of the state as something to which people agree out of self-interest, because they wish to avoid the nasty, brutish and short life characteristic of the state of nature that would result from the lack of contractual agreement. Once Rawls places the fact of pluralism at the heart of his argument for political liberalism, it can easily look as if he is a liberal of the Hobbesian brand, with willingness to tolerate differences simply being the necessary condition of social stability. Although Rawls's concern with the practicality of his theory is real and distinctive, his insistence on the way in which his political liberalism differs from a *modus vivendi* is crucial to a proper understanding of his position. It matters to him not just that justice as fairness be stable but that it be so in a particularly moral way, gaining the genuine allegiance of its citizens who will come to accept it for the values that it embodies rather than because they can do no better. This is in sharp contrast to those Hobbesian strands of liberalism that would see it as the outcome of a process of negotiation between self-interested parties.

Rawls is not, then, a liberal for either of two reasons which, we suggest, commonly underlie a commitment to liberal politics. Many think that people should be free to choose for themselves how they live their lives, or that the state should be anti-perfectionist, because they think either that all ways of life are equally good and any judgements as to their relative merits are merely subjective or that even if some ways of life are better than others we have no way of knowing which are which. While Rawls's political liberalism indeed seeks to avoid judgements of this kind, it is important to see that it does so for quite different reasons. Nor does his liberalism result from an overriding commitment to stability and workability, as if the reason to tolerate each other's differences, to exclude contro-versial matters from politics, were simply that their inclusion would necessarily lead to conflict and social disorder. While some may regard a liberal political framework, requiring, for example, the toleration of mistaken or worthless conceptions of the good, as the price that has to be paid for a quiet life in a society characterized by the fact of pluralism, this is not how Rawls regards it.

Public justifiability and political values

Having eliminated two plausible answers to the question of why Rawls is so concerned about public justifiability, we are at last in a position to turn to the real reason. The justification for excluding controversial truths from the original position, for going to funda-mental intuitive ideas latent in the public political culture, lies in the social role of justice, which is 'to enable all members of society

to make mutually acceptable to one another their shared institutions
and basic arrangements, by citing what are publicly recognised as
sufficient reasons'.[16] The concern for public justifiability derives from
the straightforward and substantive moral claim that a good political
society is one which all of its citizens can reasonably be expected to
endorse. The fundamental reason to seek a conception of justice
with the three features of the political outlined above is the supreme
moral value of a society transparent to all of its members. Given the
fact of pluralism, the permanent existence of diverging and conflicting comprehensive doctrines or conceptions of the good, such
a conception must not presuppose the validity, or invalidity, of
any particular ones. Rather, if public justifiability is to be achieved,
it is important that the conception presuppose only ideas that are
latent in the public political culture. The twin ideas of society as
a fair scheme of cooperation between free and equal citizens are
such.

Two related features of this line of argument are especially worthy
of comment, since these, when combined, are the features that have
tended to lead to confusion with respect to what is actually a
reasonably straightforward position. The first is the extent to which
it is wholeheartedly or thoroughgoingly liberal; the goal of public
justifiability itself presupposes a distinctively liberal understanding
of the nature of politics and the proper relation between the
individual and the state. The second is the fact that the conception
of the person as free and equal thus plays something of a dual role;
it is both what leads Rawls to seek a conception of justice that is
publicly justifiable and what he finds when he goes to the public
political culture in order to do just that.

To see that Rawls's position is grounded in thoroughly liberal
premises, we need only ask why one should care that the basic
structure of society be regulated by principles that are publicly
justifiable. What is so great about a society that is transparent to its
members? His answer is in terms of what he calls 'the liberal political
ideal': namely that 'since political power is the coercive power of
free and equal citizens as a corporate body, this power should be
exercised, when constitutional essentials are at stake, only in ways
that all citizens can reasonably be expected to endorse publicly
in the light of their own common, human reason'.[17] Here is the
undeniably liberal essence of Rawls's theory. At the heart of his
approach is an avowedly liberal conception of the political relation-

ship and of what makes a regime legitimate: political power is coercive, and its exercise must, if it is to respect citizens as free and equal, be publicly justifiable to them. What leads Rawls to espouse a methodology constraining him to the working up of ideas latent in the public political culture is a distinctively liberal understanding of the proper relation between the individual and the state, and one that he himself formulates in terms of the claim that as citizens we are free and equal. His theory is thus liberal from the very bottom up.

The reason why it is necessary to emphasize this point is that it has looked to some as if Rawls were attempting to deny that his theory is liberal in any respect other than that it is a theory articulating the ideas to be found in a public political culture that happens to be liberal. This appearance results from the dual role played by the liberal conception of the citizen as free and equal. On the one hand, as we have just seen, it is what leads him to seek public justifiability in the first place. On the other, it is also part of the content of the public political culture to which he restricts himself in seeking a conception that is publicly justifiable. Indeed, it was in this second way that we first introduced the idea of people as free and equal citizens earlier in this chapter; it entered the theory because it was latent in the public political culture. It is not surprising, then, that there has been misunderstanding, for an understanding of people as free and equal citizens is both what leads you to seek public justifiability and what is publicly justifiable. In insisting, partly in response to critics such as Sandel, that you can get to justice as fairness without presupposing the validity of any comprehensive doctrines, Rawls has been at great pain to stress the latter, that the conception of the person as free and equal citizen can be derived from the public culture alone, and, as we saw above, this can give the impression that it enters the theory solely because it is publicly justifiable and not at all because Rawls is committed to it. Once we see that the reason to accord weight to what is publicly justifiable, to the content of our public political culture, is that this follows from our fundamental commitment to the liberal political ideal, we will no longer be tempted to read Rawls's theory as liberal only because our political culture is liberal. Far from indicating the disowning of essentially liberal premises, Rawls's stress on public justifiability is actually a manifestation of them.

There is a sense, then, in which the viability of Rawls's political liberalism rests upon a fortunate coincidence and the conditions of its success are rather stringent. If the liberal political ideal, which presupposes an understanding of people as free and equal citizens, is to fulfil its commitment to the public justifiability of principles to govern the political domain, then it is essential that that understanding of people itself be a component of the public political culture rather than relying on any particular, and reasonably disputable, comprehensive views. The criteria for moral legitimacy imposed by such an understanding can only be met if that understanding is itself public. To see the serendipity involved we need only think about those societies in which what is publicly justifiable is something other than the liberal conception of the person that leads Rawls to seek public justifiability. There political institutions cannot fully satisfy the ideals of Rawls's liberalism since they cannot meet the criteria of justification that it lays down for them.

It is important to see that these considerations stand quite independently of, and indeed prior to, any concern with overlapping consensus and stability. Since, as we have seen, the kind of stability with which Rawls is concerned is a peculiarly moral kind of stability, a particular mode of compliance and not at all the fact of compliance as such, the boundary between the two stages of justification may seem rather blurred. Nevertheless, the distinction can be maintained. In the first stage, justice as fairness is presented as an articulation of certain very great values appropriate to the domain of the political. Since these values include the idea of society as a fair scheme of cooperation between free and equal citizens and the associated ideal of public justifiability, it is fortunate that, in being latent in our public political culture and not presupposing any controversial views, they meet the empirical conditions laid down by their own criteria of justifiability. What matters here is that justice as fairness is publicly justifiable. In the second stage, we think about whether the conception that we have worked out will be stable in the sense of being able to generate its own support, to serve as the basis of an overlapping consensus between people committed to different and conflicting conceptions of the good. In arguing that it can, Rawls is claiming that the values of the political, the value of having a society that can be publicly justified and to which all reasonable citizens can agree, will, given certain facts about moral psychology, normally be such as to outweigh the other elements of those comprehensive conceptions. People can be expected to accept that it is

inappropriate to use political power to enforce their own comprehensive views, even though they regard them as true, because
they accept the overriding value of a society that is publicly justifiable, of a society in which the coercive power of the state is not
used against those who are equal in status and reasonably disagree
about comprehensive views. It would seem, then, that the claim
that justice as fairness is stable is nothing other than the claim that
the political values that it expresses will be recognized to be so
important as to lead people to bracket as inappropriate the differences that they hold as private individuals. This would seem to be
a sociological claim about the likely perceived merits of liberalism
which is itself grounded in a normative claim about its moral value.
If the theory avoids requiring schizophrenic citizens, it does so only
by assuming that people will see the merits of liberal values in the
sphere of politics.

Responses to Sandel and Walzer (again) Let us consider briefly the
implications of the reading of Rawls's current position that we have
offered for the kinds of response that he can give to Sandel and
Walzer. Earlier in this chapter we suggested that Rawls's recent
writings indicated a position that enabled him to deny that his
theory had (some of) the features to which these communitarian
critics object and, before we go on in our last section to consider
Rawls's more offensive moves against the communitarian critique,
it may be helpful to get clear on how things stand with respect to
the responses already outlined. The general shape of the move
proposed above was that Rawls's insistence that his theory is
political, that it builds solely upon a conception of the person as
citizen and represents an articulation of ideas latent in the public
political culture, rendered his theory immune to certain criticisms;
namely that it presupposed an incoherent conception of the self
and that it was abstract in method or universal in aspiration in a
way that neglected an attention to social meanings appropriate to
a political philosopher. Now that we are clearer on what motivates
the move to the political, we can be more careful in our assessment.

In relation to Sandel, we suggested that there were two kinds of
response apparently available to Rawls. On the one hand, he could
seek to dissociate himself from a commitment to the validity of the
conception of the person, claiming that it enters the theory only
because it is an idea latent in our public political culture. On the
other, he could claim that it is a conception of how people should

understand themselves only for the purposes of politics and without any of the more general metaphysical or moral implications that Sandel seeks to pin on it.

The reading of Rawls's position offered in the previous section would seem to tell against the first response. If, as we have argued, the move to the public political culture and a concern with public justifiability – the liberal ideal of political legitimacy – themselves presuppose the validity of a conception of people as free and equal, then Rawls can hardly seek to disown his own commitment to that conception. While it may also be the case that the conception is public, and while this may be a necessary condition of the success of justice as fairness as a political conception, its publicness is only relevant for Rawls because of a prior commitment to public justifiability which itself presupposes something like the idea that people as citizens are free and equal. If this is right, then it clearly lets Sandel's worries about the validity of that conception back in again. If, that is, Rawls's first premises are indeed liberal, then he cannot hide behind the claim that our public political culture is liberal also. Rather, he must argue directly for those premises, for the moral value of a society justifiable to all of its citizens. His liberalism must stand up and be counted, not, as it sometimes seems, lie concealed behind a quasi-sociological claim about the content of the political culture of a constitutional democracy.

The second response, on the other hand, the insistence that the conception is only of the person *qua* citizen, would seem to remain intact. Provided we can make sense of the idea that people will, in the name of public justifiability, give priority to a certain set of (liberal) political values whenever those values come into conflict with the particular comprehensive doctrines that they affirm as true, then we can see how Rawls's conception of justice might claim to build solely upon a purely political concept of the person.

We also identified two possible responses to Walzer's critique. On the one hand, Rawls could argue that his distributive principles were intimately related to the (primary) goods that they were to distribute; on the other, his methodology seemed to involve precisely the kind of articulation of shared social meanings that Walzer was advocating. Combining these two points, we might say that Rawls could present himself as articulating the distributive principles internal to the sphere of citizenship in a constitutional democracy.

Here again, as in the case of Sandel, it seems that one of these responses, the claim to be presenting a theory specific to the political domain, remains appropriate, while the other requires emendation.

For although it is indeed the case that Rawls presents his theory as the working up of ideas latent in our public political culture, and to that extent can be regarded as Walzerian in his methodology, we have seen that what grounds this methodology is a prior commitment to the value of public justifiability, itself an implication of a certain understanding of citizens and their proper relationship in political society. There is, then, a crucial respect in which Rawls's approach differs from Walzer's: it is not at all that Rawls is committed to the idea that justice is the articulation of shared meanings *whatever they may be*. On the contrary, it seems to us that he is only able to present his theory as the working up of the public culture, and thus independent of any controversial or comprehensive doctrines, because it happens that the content of that culture coincides with the foundational values with which he begins. While it is indeed important that his conception of justice be publicly justifiable to the citizens whom he seeks to address, and in this respect he would endorse Walzer's concern with the world of meanings that we share, this interest in public justifiability follows from a commitment to a liberal conception of people as free and equal and does not require Rawls to accept the relativistic aspects of Walzer's position. In societies where the shared political culture is itself illiberal, Rawls need not regard justice as truth to that culture.

Response to Taylor   We are now also in a position to make some brief remarks about how Rawls might respond to an aspect of the critique of liberalism presented by Taylor, that which accuses it of an inappropriately atomistic understanding of the relation between the individual and society. Although we were careful to point out that Taylor does not directly attribute to Rawls the view that he criticizes, it is nonetheless worth making explicit the sense in which Rawls's political liberalism does not make the error of neglecting the way in which society is prior to the individual. It will be recalled that Taylor's emphasis on the fact that persons are self-interpreting animals leads him to hold that the liberal conception of the person is parasitic upon a social matrix supportive of such a conception. The liberal tendency to give priority to the individual over her community neglects, for Taylor, the extent to which it is the community in which people live that, by providing the conceptual resources in terms of which they come to understand who they are, shapes who they are and the values that they have. We shall see here that Rawls is not only well aware of this but regards it as integrally related to the question of public justifiability which we have seen to be so important to him.

Although, for the sake of clarity, we have only sketched the bare outline of Rawls's notion of public justifiability, the idea that society should be transparent to its members and the reasons for requiring such transparency are spelled out by him in some detail in terms of what he calls the full publicity condition. Justice as fairness must be public not only in the sense that it builds upon ideas latent in the public political culture and so its principles can be mutually acknowledged by all citizens, but also in the sense that its very justification can be mutually recognized. The theory must be fully public where this means that the whole justificatory background, everything that we have talked about in this chapter (and the great deal more that we have omitted), must itself be publicly available to citizens. What is relevant in our current context is the point that some of the argument for why his theory should be public in these ways involves recognition of precisely the processes that Taylor emphasizes as important.

We can identify two stages of argument here, the first of which is contained in the following rather lengthy quotation:

> ... the principles of justice apply to the political constitution and the basic institutions of society, which normally include, even under favourable conditions, some machinery of legal coercion ... Moreover these institutions can have decisive long-term social effects and importantly shape the character and aims of the members of society, the kinds of person they are and want to be. It seems fitting, then, that the fundamental terms of social cooperation between free and equal moral persons should answer to the requirements of full publicity. For if institutions rely on coercive sanctions ... and influence people's deepest aspirations, the grounds and tendency of these institutions should stand up to public scrutiny. ... Publicity ensures ... that free and equal persons are in a position to know and to accept the background social influences that shape their conception of themselves as persons, as well as their character and conception of their good. Being in this position is a precondition of freedom; it means that nothing is or need be hidden.[18]

Only if 'social institutions' and 'background social influences' are transparent, if nothing is or need be hidden, can the fact that such arrangements 'influence people's deepest aspirations' and 'shape their conception of themselves as persons' be rendered compatible with freedom. This is an implication of the idea, traceable back to Kant, that if the individual is to be free she must be aware of all those processes influencing her. It is precisely because Taylor is right, because our social matrix does affect our self-understandings and, in that sense, the community precede the individual, that freedom requires that the matrix or the community be publicly justifiable to the individuals who live in it.

The second stage of argument linking public justifiability to recognition of the importance of the social matrix is the idea that, if public, justice as fairness fosters that very conception of the person upon which it builds. For Rawls, once a moral conception is public, it

> assumes a wide role as part of public culture. Not only are its first principles embodied in public and social institutions and public traditions of their interpretation, but the derivation of citizens' rights, liberties and opportunities invokes a certain conception of the person. In this way citizens are made aware of and educated to this conception. They are presented with a way of regarding themselves that otherwise they would most likely never have been able to entertain. Thus the realization of the full publicity condition provides the social milieu within which the notion of full autonomy can be understood and within which its ideal of the person can elicit an effective desire to be that kind of person.[19]

Justice as fairness itself plays an educative role in helping people to see themselves as free and equal, as having the capacity to frame, revise and pursue conceptions of the good. This strand of the argument for publicity again recognizes that people will to a great extent form their understanding of themselves as citizens from their public culture and from the conceptions of the person and society implicit in it. Rawls's observations on the importance of a particular social milieu to the ideal of individual autonomy meet perfectly Taylor's communitarian emphasis on the way in which the liberal individual necessarily depends upon a particularly liberal social matrix.

Rawls the communitarian

The general thrust of our discussion in the previous section was to emphasize that the *primum mobile* behind Rawls's theory, what gets the whole thing going, is a commitment to a specifically liberal ideal of political society – a certain understanding of how people should be regarded from the point of view of politics, of the political relationship, and of what makes a political regime legitimate. While Rawls can accommodate some of the communitarian criticisms by emphasizing the sense in which his theory applies particularly to politics and does not claim to be true to or valid for our moral experience more generally, he cannot avoid others by distancing himself from the liberal understanding of politics that underpins the theory and by claiming merely to articulate the values that he finds in our community. If this suggests that Rawls's approach is more wholeheartedly liberal than it sometimes appears, it is our purpose in this final part of our discussion to bring out the senses in which it is more communitarian.

It is true that Rawls's political liberalism begins precisely from the denial that community of the kind after which communitarians seem to hanker is possible or desirable at the level of political society. As he says:

> justice as fairness does indeed abandon the ideal of political commu-
> nity if by that ideal is meant a political society united on one (partially
> or fully) comprehensive religious, philosophical or moral doctrine.
> That conception of social unity is excluded by the fact of pluralism; it
> is no longer a political possibility for those who accept the constraints
> of liberty and toleration embodied in democratic institutions.[20]

What motivates Rawls's concern that his liberalism be distinctively political, having the three features that we outlined near the beginning of this chapter, is precisely the claim that democratic societies are inevitably and permanently characterized by a plurality of different and conflicting conceptions of the good and that the only way to ensure agreement on any conception would be by the oppressive use of state power. Liberalism, on this understanding, is a response to the lack of any morally acceptable possibility of any more substantive or specific form of political community. Rawls's position, then, is a direct rejection of (the morally acceptable possibility of) communitarian demands for a political society built around a shared comprehensive conception of the good.

While this is the essence of Rawls's response to the communitarian critique, it is important to see that it leaves room for two senses in which he can claim his conception to recognize values that we may think of as distinctively communitarian and that have been emphasized by communitarian critics of liberalism. On the one hand, a variant on the compatibilist move that we have already come across, it is quite acceptable to the political liberal that communities in the full sense exist at the non-political level. On the other, his political conception of liberalism does indeed involve a commitment to shared values, to the idea of a common good of the kind that communitarians emphasize; the point is simply that they are not those of any comprehensive doctrine. While the first of these points is essentially concessionary, the second can be presented as rather more positive: if Rawls is right in his analysis of our contemporary political culture, then his political liberalism can be regarded as truer to our community than the vision of politics to which the communitarians subscribe.

Non-political community and identity

The reader will recall that Sandel's critique rejected the disembodied or unencumbered self, antecedent and standing in a purely voluntary relation to its ends, which he claimed lay at the heart of liberalism and found its clearest expression in Rawls's original position. Such a conception of the self manifested, for Sandel, an inadequate or even incoherent understanding of the way in which people relate to their values and purposes; we are constituted as the people we are by those ends that give our life its meaning; our very identity is bound up with our commitments and attachments in such a way that we could not, at least in some cases, think of ourselves as revising our ends and remaining the same person. On his account the voluntarist liberal picture, in positing a shadowy detached self behind the particular ends that we happen to have, is untrue to our moral experience and misses the way in which we are constituted as the individuals we are by the social context, the community, in which we live.

Rawls's response is that Sandel's concerns are entirely appropriate in spheres other than the political:

> Note that what is impracticable is not *all* values of community (recall that a community is understood as an association of society whose unity rests on a comprehensive conception of the good) but only *political community* and its values. Justice as fairness assumes, as other liberal political views do also, that the values of community are not only essential but realizable, first in the various associations that carry on their life within the framework of the basic structure, and second in those associations that extend across the boundaries of nation-states, such as churches and scientific societies.[21]

What distinguishes the associational from the political, for Rawls, is precisely the fact that the former is voluntary where the latter is not. Where people have voluntarily chosen to enter associations, he seems to be saying, there they may realize the values of community.

While this may not seem much of a concession to the communitarian whose precise worry about liberalism may be its misguided insistence on voluntarism and who may, in response, query whether people really do experience their membership of, for example, churches as acts of voluntary association, Rawls is more explicitly conciliatory when he makes clear that his conception of justice has room for the validity of Sandel's claim about the phenomenology of our moral experience, about how it seems to us that we relate to our ends:

> It is essential to stress that citizens in their personal affairs, or in the internal life of associations to which they belong, may regard their final ends and attachments in a way very different from the way the political conception involves. Citizens may have, and normally do have at any given time, affections, devotions and loyalties that they believe they would not and indeed could not and should not, stand apart from and objectively evaluate from the point of view of their purely rational good. They may regard it as simply unthinkable to view themselves apart from certain religious, philosophical, and moral convictions, or from certain enduring attachments and loyalties. These convictions and attachments form part of what we may call their 'nonpublic identity' ... We think that if we were suddenly without these particular convictions and attachments we would be disoriented and unable to carry on.[22]

But, for Rawls, it is crucial to see that this is not how we regard ourselves for the purposes of politics. Our public identity, our identity as citizens, remains the same whatever changes we may undergo in our personal commitments, and, as citizens, we regard ourselves as independent from, and capable of revising on reasonable grounds, our conception of the good. Here again we may remark upon the tinge of schizophrenia involved in this insistence on the split between the public and the private; Rawls's claim is that Sandel's objections to the liberal subject would be well taken if that were intended to model our self-understandings in non-political spheres, but are misplaced when we see that it is only as citizens that we regard ourselves as free from our ends.

Political liberalism as communitarianism

The concessionary aspect of Rawls's position, then, is that values of community are realizable in spheres other than the political and that we can indeed regard our non-public identities as constituted by our ends rather than as preceding them by an act of choice. We can present him in rather more positive fashion, however, by noting two senses in which his political liberalism itself constitutes a communitarian doctrine. The first sense is the Walzerian one: if the communitarian claim is methodological – that justice consists in fidelity to a community's shared meanings – then Rawls's justice as fairness is a better communitarian theory than is Walzer's. The second sense is the more substantive one that Rawls's political liberalism itself embodies a particular understanding of community, that what motivates the exclusion from politics of reasons appropriate to people's non-public lives is precisely a shared aim, a conception of community and a recognition of the value of goods that can only be realized communally. Rawls's conception of justice as fairness is communitarian both in terms of its source – it articulates the shared values of the community which it addresses – and in terms of its content – those shared values themselves involve a commitment to an understanding of politics that is distinctively communitarian.

We have already argued that Rawls's theory represents not an attempt to transcend cultural particularity, as Walzer suggests, but rather an attempt to be true to our culture, and this claim stands despite Rawls not being committed to Walzer's more sweeping relativism. Even though Rawls does not regard the task of the political theorist as that of articulating shared meanings whatever they may be, he does see something close to that as the proper method for a political theorist in a constitutional democracy, where those shared meanings have a particular content. We would further maintain that, with respect to societies of that kind, Rawls's method is not only consistent with Walzer's approach but more successful: Rawls is truer to our shared meanings than is Walzer.

For Rawls recognizes how little we do share. What motivates his search for a specifically political conception of justice is a recognition of the fact of pluralism, of the fact that there are and will continue to be, without oppressive use of state power, a diversity of conceptions of the good. Given this fact, all that we can agree to, and what gets embodied in the original position, is an understanding of politics, a conception of political society and of the person as citizen, which leaves people free to frame, revise and pursue whatever conceptions of the good they choose. Where Walzer seems to suppose that beneath our apparent differences of opinion we all actually share an understanding of the way in which particular goods should be distributed, Rawls's liberalism starts from the acknowledgement that we do not, that the citizens of a democratic society will espouse quite different understandings of how people should live their lives and how goods should be distributed. If it is Walzer who insists that different cultures will understand their goods in different ways, it is Rawls who recognizes that different members of our culture will do so.

Rawls abstracts not from our culture, as Walzer supposes, but from those particular comprehensive conceptions of the good espoused in it, and he does so because that is the way to be true to our particular culture and those meanings that we do indeed share. This is what makes his understanding of primary goods not only sphere-specific, as we have already argued, but also more faithful to our shared meanings than is Walzer's view that we agree in our more specific judgements. Primary goods, as we have seen, are goods internally related to our understanding of what it is to be a citizen in our society: they are goods that people need *qua* citizens and that can thus serve as a publicly justifiable metric of advantage. The abstraction involved in the conception of primary goods, of which Walzer is so critical, represents not, then, an abstraction *from* our particular culture and social meanings but rather a careful attention to the abstraction from particular conceptions of the good that precisely characterizes that culture and those meanings. Political liberalism *must* abstract from particular comprehensive conceptions of the good because that abstraction is itself demanded by our shared meanings.

In a (significantly) parenthetic remark in *Spheres of Justice* Walzer makes the following observation on what should happen if there is disagreement on social meanings:

> A given society is just if its substantive life is lived in a certain way – that is, in a way faithful to the shared understandings of its members. (When people disagree about the meaning of social goods, when understandings are controversial, then justice requires that the society be faithful to the disagreements, providing institutional channels for their expression, adjudicative mechanisms, and alternative distributions). (*SJ*, p. 313)

'Being faithful to the disagreements' seems to us a remarkably accurate analysis of Rawls's political liberalism. If he is right in thinking that the meanings that we share are those of society as a fair scheme of cooperation between free and equal citizens, whilst we disagree about comprehensive conceptions of the good, then it is Rawls who is the true communitarian.

The second sense in which Rawls's theory is communitarian is that which concerns its content rather than its source or method. Beginning with the claim that his political liberalism involves a commitment to a common aim, and one that can be an important part of a person's identity in just the way that communitarians emphasize, we shall, building on the previous remarks, go on to see that what motivates the conception of the person of which communitarians have been so critical is precisely a commitment to a certain conception of community: the very reason to exclude from politics conceptions of the good that may indeed be constitutive of our non-public identities is a belief in the value of a certain sort of (political) community.

Responding to those who charge liberalism with being excessively individualistic and instrumental in its understanding of politics, who claim that it regards society as nothing more than the outcome of an agreement between individuals or associations cooperating solely to pursue their pre-social individual or associational advantage, Rawls emphasizes both that his political conception of justice does involve a commitment to a shared goal and that this goal can become an important part of an individual's identity. As he says:

> ... in the well-ordered society of justice as fairness citizens share a common aim, and one that has a high priority: namely, the aim of political justice, that is, the aim of ensuring that political and social institutions are just, and of giving justice to persons generally, as what citizens need for themselves and want for one another. It is not true, then, that on a liberal view citizens have no fundamental common aims. Nor is it true that the aim of political justice is not an important part of their identity (using the term 'identity', as is now often done, to include the basic aims and projects by reference to which we characterize the kind of person we very much want to be). But this common aim of political justice must not be mistaken for (what I have called) a conception of the good.[23]

A society well ordered by justice as fairness is not a private society, in which individuals or associations cooperate to pursue their private advantage, it is one that recognizes a common aim and indeed gives that aim priority over the private interests that people may have, for these latter can only be pursued within the constraints of a just framework.

But even this way of putting the point fails to bring out the sense in which political liberalism embodies a concern for community. To do this we need to consider not just the fact of a common aim but its content, for one could formulate even the Hobbesian position in terms that see the common aim of stability and security as sufficient to outweigh an individual's or association's sectional interests. In contrast to this, the common aim that underlies Rawls's position is that of a society that can be publicly justified to all its members. It is this conception of political community that motivates us to exclude from consideration when thinking about justice reasons that depend upon those comprehensive conceptions of the good about which we disagree. It is the value of a society that can be publicly justified, that can be willingly endorsed by all of its members despite their holding conflicting comprehensive conceptions of the good, that gives us reason to exclude reasons emanating from those conceptions. For Rawls this value is social not just in the instrumental sense that it can only be realized by individuals in cooperation with others but also intrinsically; the goods of political society are intrinsically valuable, and their value is sufficiently great to lead us to give priority to their achievement over the other values to which we are committed in our personal lives. Where Sandel thinks that the liberal separation of the self from her particular ends involves a neglect of the value of community, for Rawls such a separation, such a willingness to distinguish the citizen from her comprehensive conceptions of the good, is required precisely for the achievement of the intrinsically valuable good of a political society that is publicly justifiable.

Notes

1 Rawls, 'The Priority of Right', p. 254 n. 2.
2 Rawls, 'Kantian Constructivism in Moral Theory'.
3 Rawls, 'The Priority of Right', p. 252.
4 Rawls, 'Justice as Fairness', pp. 224–5.
5 Rawls, 'The Domain of the Political', p. 248.
6 Rawls, 'Justice as Fairness', p. 245.
7 Rawls, 'Social Unity and Primary Goods', p. 163.
8 Ibid., p. 172.
9 Rawls, 'Justice as Fairness', p. 225.
10 Ibid., p. 228.
11 Rawls, The Idea of an Overlapping Consensus', p. 4.
12 Ibid., p. 13.
13 Rawls, 'The Domain of the Political', pp. 245–6.
14 Ibid., p. 234.
15 Rawls, 'The Idea of an Overlapping Consensus', p. 11.
16 Rawls, 'Kantian Constructivism in Moral Theory', p. 561.
17 Rawls, 'The Domain of the Political', p. 244.
18 Rawls, 'Kantian Constructivism in Moral Theory', pp. 538–9.
19 Ibid., p. 553.
20 Rawls, 'The Priority of Right', p. 269.
21 Rawls, 'Justice as Fairness', p. 241.
22 Ibid., p. 241.
23 Rawls, 'The Idea of an Overlapping Consensus', p. 10 n. 17.

6

Political liberalism: for and against

Now that we have offered a general interpretation of the position Rawls has developed in his more recent writings, we can go on to spell out in more detail the ways in which he might utilize it in responding to his communitarian critics. We will then be able to determine whether the perceived disagreement between them really exists, and, if it does, which party to the dispute is right. So, we will begin this chapter by reminding ourselves of the state of the argument with respect to each of the five thematic headings we established at the outset, in each case attempting to answer on Rawls's behalf the array of interrelated questions that we posed under those headings in our Introduction. We will then suggest some reasons for thinking that the theoretical assumptions that ground those Rawlsian answers may not be as reliable as they seem.

Respecting the limits of the political

The conception of the person

Under this heading, we declared at the outset that Rawls would never deny that his theory of justice as fairness was built around some particular conception of the person. For that theory explicitly embodies the claim that, when it comes to matters of justice, people should be regarded as distinct from their particular natural endowments, social position and ends, but possessed of a highest-order interest in their capacity to frame, revise and rationally pursue their conceptions of the good – and such a claim amounts to an assessment of what is important about people, what constitutes their well-being. What is controversial about Rawls's conception of the person is not its existence or relevance, but rather its scope, its source or origin, its status, its validity and coherence, and its desirability. We shall examine each of these five questions in turn.

As Rawls's more recent writings have made clear, he takes his conception of the person to be a political conception. This means that it is a conception of the person *qua* citizen, one that is latent in the public political culture of constitutional democracies but that does not form part of a comprehensive moral or philosophical doctrine – where 'comprehensive' means 'inclusive of conceptions of what is of value in human life, ideals of personal virtue and character, and the like, that are to inform much of our non-political conduct'.[1] On this understanding of the conception of the person, we can quickly summarize its scope: it applies only to the person insofar as she is an inhabitant of the public political realm and not to any other aspect of her life. Its source also seems clear: it derives from the shared resources of the public political culture. The question of its status is more difficult to determine; but the answer lies in establishing why Rawls's conception of the person has the source it does. The reason is not that Rawls believes that only theories relying upon such shared conceptions could provide social blueprints whose implementation was practically feasible, and not that Rawls has a Walzerian respect for shared social meanings as the ultimate foundation of any political theorizing. It is rather that he attaches great importance to the public justifiability of a political theory; for him, a society whose political arrangements can be justified to all its citizens is one possessed of great moral value, and his political theory can only provide such a justification if it restricts itself to public and shared political conceptions and values. This restriction means that Rawls's theory cannot depend upon the truth of a philosophical doctrine of the self, or upon any moral or political doctrines that have application beyond, or invoke values or conceptions that are not available in, the public political realm (what Rawls calls general and comprehensive moral conceptions); for any such doctrines would, by definition, be controversial, and his theory could not then be publicly justifiable.

However, this conception of the person does not enter Rawls's theory *solely* because it is publically justifiable: it enters because Rawls substantively endorses it as the way one *ought* to conceive of the person as citizen. Indeed, his view that the public justifiability of his theory is a good thing depends upon his having a respect for citizens as free and equal (as deserving of political arrangements that they can all freely endorse regardless of their particular conceptions of the good), and this respect amounts to a substantive commitment to the very conception of the person as citizen that he claims to find in our public political culture. So, although Rawls's conception of the person derives from the public political culture, and although its capacity so to be derived is something that this conception demands of itself, its real source or ultimate justification – and so its true status – is not sociological but moral. It could not form part of any *comprehensive* moral doctrine, since it would then fail the test of public justifiability, but it remains a substantive doctrine for all that. In short, Rawls is not merely building with whatever materials are at hand; he is endorsing his political edifice and its constituent values and conceptions from top to bottom.

On this understanding of the scope, source and status of Rawls's conception of the person, the communitarian attacks upon it will seem clearly misplaced. For they focus upon its validity as a general account of our moral experience and its coherence as a philosophical account of human nature. But if Rawls's claim that persons ought to be regarded as detached from their particular natural and social endowments and conceptions of the good is restricted to the domain of politics, then it does not imply that we can generally step back from each and every one of our value commitments, or that we are metaphysically detached from them; and so the invalidity or incoherence of such ideas – even if it could be established – would not reflect upon the tenability of Rawls's theory of justice as fairness. *Pace* Sandel and others, the fact (assuming it is a fact) that our commitments to certain values and communities partly constitute our identity as individuals is not something that Rawls even needs to address, let alone something he is committed to denying.

Nonetheless, one further question about Rawls's conception of the person remains – the issue of its desirability. For even if we accept that it involves no incoherent metaphysical or philosophical presuppositions, it is still open to us to question its attractiveness as a substantive moral conception of persons as citizens. For example, Rawls's anti-perfectionism entails a sharp separation between the political and the personal in the lives of every citizen; it is a requirement of citizenship in a Rawlsian society that each individual, when thinking about justice, should suspend or bracket the moral or religious beliefs that may give her life its integrity and meaning, in favour of a restricted and distinct understanding of herself as citizen. This split between public and private will of course be entirely acceptable to anyone cleaving to a comprehensive moral doctrine which embodies a commitment to an anti-perfectionist state; for according to such a doctrine, what is of worth in human life *per se* is understood to entail just such an exclusionary conception of the conduct of human life in the political sphere. But this split or exclusion will involve those committed to other comprehensive doctrines in a greater or lesser degree of schizophrenia; and this painful internal cleavage will be exacerbated by Rawls's further belief that, insofar as one's non-political commitments come into conflict with the publicly available political conception, the latter always wins. The demands of justice, the requirements of the conception of the person as citizen, must come before the claims of those comprehensive perfectionist doctrines with which they must simultaneously and schizophrenically be held.

To sum up: if the communitarians are to renew their attack upon the Rawlsian conception of the person, they seem to have two options. First, they can contest Rawls's claims about the true scope, source and status of that conception: for if it is not restricted to the domain of the political in the ways Rawls claims, then the communitarians' original criticisms of its validity and coherence might retain some of their force. Second, they can attack the desirability of the conception, even given its restricted status; for it posits a split between the political and the personal which seems to require that those holding comprehensive perfectionist doctrines hold them in a rather half-hearted (perhaps even liberal) way, and it accords an absolute priority to the political over the personal which gives the value of autonomy a primacy that it may not fully deserve. We shall examine these two possible avenues in more detail when we turn to our fifth heading – the question of the neutrality of Rawlsian liberalism.

Asocial Individualism

Under this heading, the communitarian critics focused upon Rawls's contractual approach to political theory, arguing that this approach (as exemplified in the original position) embodies the belief that people's ends are formed independently of or prior to society, which is regarded as the outcome of negotiation between individuals whose ends are already given. For the communitarians, such an asocial individualist view embodies two different sorts of mistake: it denies the important philosophical truth that people's conceptions of the good and of themselves are dependent upon a social matrix; and it ignores or represses the importance of human goods whose content is communal, in particular the significance of the good of political community – for by regarding politics merely as an arena within which people cooperate with others solely in order to pursue their private advantage, Rawls ignores the possibility that the bonds of fellow citizenship can function as a (or as the most) significant constitutive attachment in people's lives.

Rawls's response to these two criticisms is to stress the fact that the original position is a device of representation whose function is to dramatize and articulate a particular substantive conception of the person as citizen. It embodies no sociological or philosophical claims about the relative priority of the individual to society, but rather forms part of an argument for the development and maintainence of a type of society within which citizens accord a particular moral status to one another. It is precisely because Rawls recognizes that the social matrix influences the ways in which people see themselves that he requires that his conception of justice be fully public, for only then can such influence be compatible with the individual freedom that the conception is concerned to protect. And of course, this emphasis upon public justifiability is morally driven, as is the conception of the person that is to be justified; so the vision of society that this entails, a society in which each citizen acknowledges the freedom and equality of all other citizens and is committed to maintaining the institutions and practices that preserve it, does not reduce the social to an arena for the extraction of egoistic benefit. If anything, it pictures society as the domain in which individuals can achieve a good in common which they could not achieve alone – a view that is clearly in some sense communitarian.

In this respect, Rawls himself has admitted that his use of rational choice machinery in *A Theory of Justice* was misleading, since it suggested that justice as fairness was a theory for individualistic egoists.

> ... it was an error in *Theory* (and a very misleading one) to describe a theory of justice as part of a theory of rational choice. What I should have said is that the conception of justice as fairness uses an account of rational choice subject to reasonable conditions to characterize the deliberations of the parties as representatives of free and equal persons; and all of this within a political conception of justice, which is, of course, a moral conception.[2]

Rawls's 'reasonable constraints' form the framework within which rational choice is exercised: the Rational is a specification of how the people in the original position are motivated, but the Reasonable is a specification of how the original position is set up in the first place. Since this means that the Reasonable is prior to the Rational, and embodies a variety of moral concerns, including claims about what sort of political community is worthy of allegiance, then we have no grounds for regarding Rawls's use of rational choice machinery as a sign that he is an asocial individualist in the substantive sense.

Nonetheless, the common good that Rawls seeks in politics is undeniably an individualistic good; the highest-order interests that we possess as citizens are interests that we have as individuals, and for Rawls it would be unacceptable for our community to deprive us of them. In particular, it would be unjust for a political community to be founded on a comprehensive conception of the good, whether liberal or otherwise; so in this sense, Rawls is deliberately setting his face against certain strong readings of the good of political community. This is an issue to which we will return under the fifth heading of our agenda, when we examine Rawls's attribution of priority to the right over the good; and any further discussion of the issues it raises must wait until then. But we can at least say that this would seem to be one point upon which any renewal of the communitarian critique under this heading could focus.

And other possible lines of attack in a communitarian vein also remain open. They must, of course, dispense with the language of metaphysics and sociology, and refrain from conflating Rawls's commitment to individualism with a commitment to egoism; but they might nonetheless attempt to argue that a political community founded upon (even a non-egoistic) individualism is in some way inadequate or undesirable. Two obvious criticisms along these lines spring to mind, according to both of which such a community turns out to be inadequate or undesirable by the lights of individualism itself. First, it might be argued that the very capacities and self-understandings that the Rawlsian individualist values can only be fostered by a state that intervened to support and encourage them in ways that seem to violate the very neutrality between conceptions of the good that the Rawlsian individualist demands of the state. Second, it might be argued that a society that is neutral in the requisite sense will be one in which some at least of the valuable (but not necessarily individualist) ways of life between which citizens choose will wither away; and since the value of that capacity to choose depends upon the value of the choices that can be made, this will lessen the value of the very capacity to which the Rawlsian individualist gives an absolute priority.

The theorist who has developed these lines of criticism with most force is a defender of liberalism – Joseph Raz. As we will see in chapter 8, his conclusion is that a truly liberal state must be much more interventionist than that prescribed by Rawls; what is needed is a much more communitarian form of liberalism, a liberalism based upon a more comprehensive commitment to, and a more per-fectionist interpretation of, the specific value of autonomy, and so to a more non-neutral or sectarian liberal state than Rawls is pre-pared to countenance. We shall touch upon these issues again when we discuss Rawls's anti-perfectionism and neutrality under the fifth heading of our agenda.

Universalism

Under this heading, the communitarian critique (primarily mounted by Walzer) argued that Rawls's theory of justice was designed to apply universally and cross-culturally, and thus failed to attend to the ways in which different cultures embody different values and practices, a fact that has significant consequences for the intelli-gibility and/or justifiability of claims about social justice. The new

Rawls's response to this criticism is clear: by emphasizing that his conception of the person is derived from the public political culture of constitutional democracies, he shows that his general theory of justice as fairness is importantly culture-specific. The abstraction from people's particular natural and social endowments and from their particular conceptions of the good that is embodied in the original position is an expression of our particular culture's conception of the person as citizen; it is therefore an abstraction that results from Rawls's close attention to cultural particularity rather than from his failure to do so.

Here, however, we must recall the relative importance that Rawls assigns to public justifiability and to the political conception of the person. Rawls is substantively committed to the conception of the person as citizen that he claims to find in our public political culture, and the respect for public justifiability that drives his turn towards that culture is itself motivated by that same commitment (by his belief that citizens deserve to have political arrangements they can all freely endorse); so his commitment to public justifiability is only one aspect of his wider substantive view that a society arranged in accord with his theory of justice is the best sort of society for human beings to inhabit. But this implies that, if he were to find himself in (or, more generally, to find himself considering) a non-liberal society whose public political culture did *not* embody his conception of the person, then the impossibility of providing a public justification of liberalism would not in itself *oblige* him to refrain from advocating and working towards the liberal reconstruction of that society in other ways. In other words, if the course of action dictated by his commitment to public justifiability and that dictated by his commitment to the conception of the person as citizen ever diverged, then Rawls could perfectly consistently sacrifice the former value to the latter; he could argue that his primary commitment was not to whatever ideas happen to be publicly justifiable, but to the ideas embodied in his political conception of the person.

To sum up: Rawls's conception of the person is an elaboration of resources latent in the public political culture of liberal democracies, and is designed to apply solely to the sphere of politics; but it is not necessarily designed to apply solely to the sphere of politics in societies whose public political culture contains that conception of the person, that is to the politics of liberal democracies. Rawls's commitment to public justifiability is not the consequence of a

Walzerian belief that social justice is nothing other than truth to the social meanings prevalent in the given society; it is a further expression of his belief that the conception of the person prevalent in the public political culture of liberal democracies embodies the right understanding of social justice. This does not mean that Rawls *must* regard his theory of justice as having universal cross-cultural validity and application; but neither does it mean that Rawls *must* restrict its validity and application to those cultures in which the resources for elaborating that theory are publicly available. As far as can be judged from his recent writings, he has not definitively committed himself either way on this issue.

Subjectivism/objectivism

The communitarian critique under this heading accused Rawls of a commitment to a philosophical scepticism about the rationality and objectivity of value judgements. Rawls's fundamental concern for a neutral state and his specific invocation of a veil of ignorance in the original position were held to derive from a belief that either moral judgements in general or judgements about conceptions of the good in particular were arbitrary expressions of preference, inherently incapable of being rationally justified.

The new Rawls makes it clear that his real reason for excluding considerations about conceptions of the good from the sphere of politics is that the value of a political community that can be publicly justified to all its citizens is so great as to give us a strong moral reason to exclude such considerations even if we believe them to be objectively valid. He is not therefore committed to philosophical scepticism of the more specific kind just mentioned: as we saw earlier, that would have amounted to a reliance upon a controversial philosophical doctrine and so to the violation of his commitment to public justifiability. He neither accepts nor rejects the view advanced by more objectivist liberals, the view that some conceptions of the good, some ways of life, are objectively better than others, and a framework of liberal rights is required if people are to be able to make informed and rational judgements about which is which. And of course, although he is agnostic on the question of whether or not some conceptions of the good are objectively better than others, he is not and cannot be agnostic about the values that underlie his commitment to anti-perfectionist liberalism – he takes them to embody the right way of thinking about politics.

Nonetheless, there remains an element of what might be called quasi-scepticism in Rawls's most recent writings; for if his defence of his exclusionary principle in political debates relies upon his commitment to public justifiability, then the main reason for excluding conceptions of the good from the realm of politics must be that such questions are extremely controversial and so not available as a freely agreed basis for moral judgements between citizens. But this in turn implies that if agreement upon all or at least a significant part of the answers to such questions *were* ever reached, then there would be no basis for excluding reference to such matters in the realm of politics, and Rawls's objections to a non-neutral, sectarian state would disappear.

Rawls has not explicitly addressed this hypothetical question; and his reason for doing so seems to be a deep scepticism about the likelihood of the question ever becoming a real one. In his recent writings he has laid great stress upon pluralism as a permanent feature of modern culture, one that is unlikely to change because it is *reasonable* for people to disagree about conceptions of the good. So, in order to assess the nature and import of this scepticism, we must examine more closely what Rawls's notion of reasonable disagreement actually means; but this is a task that we can best perform after addressing the question of Rawl's anti-perfectionist neutrality under the fifth heading of our agenda.

Anti-perfectionism and neutrality

The fifth and final heading under which the communitarians attacked Rawls has to do with the latter's anti-perfectionism. From the outset, Rawls has argued that, rather than seeking to act on those perfectionist ideals that often guide people when they live their individual lives and pursue their own conceptions of the good, the state should deliberately refrain from acting on any such ideals and seek only to provide a neutral framework within which people can make their own individual choices. Rawls has typically given expression to this political anti-perfectionism by claiming that his political theory makes the right prior to the good: the liberal state must act to protect the rights that people have to pursue and revise their conceptions of the good, and so must rule out any conceptions of the good whose pursuit would violate those rights; but beyond this the state must always refrain from acting on the basis that one conception of the good is more valuable than another. The communitarian attack has been devoted to suggesting that this claim to neutrality is an illusion; such a liberal state, by upholding a framework of rights and refraining from any further action, is in effect presupposing the validity of a distinctively liberal conception of the good. Rawls can only justify the assignment of priority to the right over the good by invoking a distinctively liberal understanding of how people should live; the exclusion of conceptions of the good from the domain of politics itself presupposes a particular conception of the good.

In his recent writings, Rawls has dealt explicitly with this issue. In 'The Priority of Right and Ideas of the Good', he makes it clear that his idea of the priority of the right is such that it is compatible with the utilization of no less than five different ideas of the good in the overall theory of justice as fairness. The relevant sense in which justice as fairness is nonetheless significantly neutral between conceptions of the good is that its anti-perfectionism does not presuppose any particular *comprehensive* religious, philosophical or moral doctrine; justice as fairness applies only to the sphere of politics and is elaborated from ideas latent in the shared public political culture, and so does not form part of, or depend upon the truth of, a conception of what human life as a whole – outside as well as inside the realm of politics – ought to be. These claims clearly require more detailed examination.

The five ideas of goodness in the theory of justice and fairness are: the idea of goodness as rationality, the idea of primary goods, the idea of permissible comprehensive conceptions of the good, the idea of political virtues, and the idea of the good of a well-ordered political community. The first two ideas together form what Rawls earlier called his 'thin' theory of the good. The first amounts to the assumption that all participants in discussions about justice will acknowledge certain values such as the fulfilment of basic human needs and purposes and the possession of a rational plan in terms of which individuals order and organize their lives; the second, as we saw when discussing Walzer's critique of primary goods, constitutes a minimal specification of what resources persons understood as citizens (and so as free and equal persons) can be presumed to require regardless of which particular life-plan or conception of the good they may adopt. Taken together, these two ideas provide content for the deliberations that take place in the original position; they give those deliberating behind the veil of ignorance something to deliberate about.

The third idea, that of permissible conceptions of the good, simply underlines the priority Rawls attaches to the right: his liberal state will obviously and necessarily discriminate between those conceptions of the good whose pursuit is compatible with a respect for the rights of all citizens to do likewise, and those whose pursuit violates those rights – and it will prohibit the latter. In this sense, an anti-perfectionist state is not neutral between all possible conceptions of the good – it could hardly do otherwise and still be a recognizably liberal state; but it is nonetheless neutral in another important sense, for its prohibition of certain conceptions of the good is not itself based upon considerations that derive from any particular conception of the good. As Rawls would now put it, the grounds for these prohibitions are not derived from a comprehensive religious or moral doctrine, but from a purely political one. In addition, of course, a Rawlsian state will be neutral in the sense that it will secure equal opportunity to advance any *permissible* conception of the good; as we saw in our Introduction, liberal state institutions must not be intended to favour any particular permissible comprehensive doctrine, although it is not sociologically possible for them to have neutral effects, for example upon which permissible comprehensive doctrines secure, and which lose, adherents over time.

It is the final two ideas of the good that bring out an element in Rawls's thinking not so evident in his earlier writings. His concept of the political virtues is a way of characterizing those forms of judgement and conduct that are essential to sustain fair social co-operation over time between citizens regarded as free and equal; they are the character traits that specify the ideal of a good citizen of a democratic liberal state. As such, the state is perfectly within its rights to foster and strengthen these virtues in its citizens; for example, it can legitimately act in such a way as to encourage the virtues of toleration and mutual trust (for example, by discouraging certain sorts of racial and religious discrimination) without thereby becoming a sectarian state, because such virtues are not ones that characterize ways of life belonging to comprehensive religious and philosophical doctrines.

Connected with this is the fifth idea of the good in political liberalism: the good of a well-ordered political society – the good that citizens realize both as persons and as a corporate body in maintaining (partly by the exercise of the political virtues) a just constitutional regime and in conducting its affairs justly. Emphasizing this point reveals that, although political liberalism abandons the idea of a political community based on a comprehensive religious or philosophical doctrine, it does not abandon the idea of political community *per se* in favour of a conception of society as a private society, one in which individuals and groups cooperate solely for their own personal advantage without any common ends. For in a well-ordered liberal society, citizens do have ends in common: they affirm the same political conception of justice, and so share the substantive and valuable end of supporting just institutions and giving one another justice accordingly. Such a society is of course good for the individuals within it, since it allows them to develop and exercise their two moral powers; but it is also a genuinely social good – only realizable through joint activity based on a shared final end. And no such goods fall foul of the state's duty to remain neutral because they remain goods specified solely from within a political conception of justice.

The importance of these last two ideas of the good in political liberalism is, of course, that they reveal Rawls to be committed to the idea that a political society can itself be an intrinsic rather than a merely instrumental good for citizens both as individuals and as a corporate body; they show that Rawls has a significant conception of a political community and of goods to be achieved in common that cannot be achieved alone. At the same time, however, he is clearly hostile to any conception of the good of political community that founds it upon a comprehensive doctrine: for even if such a community could be seen to have benefits for those capable of sharing it (for example, further heightening their sense of fellowship with other citizens, or extending the realization of deeply valued principles), it would entail violating the value of public justifiability by introducing controversial issues into the political domain. Rawls defines the extent of his political communitarianism by drawing a distinction between classical republicanism and civic humanism. Both are conceptions of the good of political community, but the former embodies the view that the preservation of democratic liberties requires the active participation of citizens possessed of those virtues needed to maintain a constitutional regime, whereas the latter advocates political participation on the grounds that this is the privileged locus of the good life for human beings. Rawlsian justice as fairness is entirely compatible with classical republicanism, and it is happy to permit individuals to seek the good life in political activity; but it is opposed to civic humanism in just the way that it is opposed to the use of any comprehensive conception of the good in politics. If it is to a civic humanist conception of politics that communitarians such as Sandel and MacIntyre are inclined, then they are right to think that Rawls excludes it, but wrong to imagine that he does so by oversight; rather, he explicitly rejects such a strong conception as a threat to the rights of citizens in a context of moral and political pluralism. In short, if this is what is meant by their accusation that Rawls propounds a substantive asocial individualism, that he fails sufficiently to emphasize the importance of constitutive attachments to the political community, then he will be happy to plead guilty to the charge.

Nonetheless, even if Rawls is hostile to civic humanism, he is happy to embrace classical republicanism; and this makes his anti-perfectionist liberalism communitarian in a significant sense, but a sense that Rawls takes to be compatible with it being purely political, and so that allows him to regard as entirely misdirected any accusations that his claims to neutrality are delusive. To be sure, his political liberalism is substantively liberal: its anti-perfectionism is based on such values as public justifiability and the conception of the citizen as a free and equal person, and prohibits any conceptions of the good whose pursuit would violate the rights of citizens so conceived; but neither these prohibitions nor these values presuppose any comprehensive moral or philosophical doctrines, because they do no more than elucidate ideas that are latent in the public political culture and applicable only to the sphere of politics. So, on Rawls's own most recent understanding of his theory, a purely political anti-perfectionist liberalism is entirely compatible with a strong (if not the strongest) conception of political society as a community; indeed, justice as fairness can be thought of as exemplifying a non-comprehensive variant of political communitarianism.

Defending the limits of the political

Clearly, if Rawls's own depiction of justice as fairness is accurate, then it would seem that the debate between communitarians and his brand of anti-perfectionist liberalism is likely to result in a large measure of synthesis, although it will not satisfy advocates of neo-Aristotelianism in politics. But Rawls's ability to claim that the communitarian fire is largely misdirected – that he is not pre-supposing a comprehensive doctrine of the person, that he is not presupposing that the individual is sociologically or logically prior to society, that he is not conceiving of political society as a private society but that he is nonetheless genuinely anti-perfectionist – depends solely upon the distinction that he draws between purely political liberalism and liberalism understood as a comprehensive moral doctrine, and his corresponding claim to be restricting himself to the resources provided by a purely political conception. So, if he can demonstrate the feasibility of making that distinction and of restricting himself to the political rather than the comprehensive side of it when defending the central elements of his theory of justice, his escape from the main communitarian criticisms seems assured. But if he cannot – if, for example, he cannot justify the anti-perfectionist distinction between the political and the non-political spheres of life that is central to justice as fairness without invoking aspects of a comprehensive liberal moral doctrine – then his escape route may be blocked. It is to this question that we must now turn.

We mentioned earlier in this chapter, under the first heading on our agenda, that the separation between the sphere of the political and that of the non-political, which Rawls's liberalism imposes, in effect calls for a rather schizophrenic attitude on the part of those citizens whose comprehensive conception of the good is not one that embodies such a commitment to anti-perfectionism in politics. The idea of such a separation is of course integral to some comprehensive moral doctrines, and so its implementation would contribute to the unity and integrity of the lives of those cleaving to such doctrines; but those whose life is given its shape and meaning by comprehensive doctrines that do not contain such an idea are in effect being asked to bracket off these fundamental beliefs, to treat them as if they were mere preferences, in the political domain. Of course, Rawls can and does argue that this bracketing off is imposed for the sake of substantial and genuine goods, both individual and corporate; conforming to the anti-perfectionist liberal conception of the person as citizen confers real and lasting moral gains, and most of those in contemporary liberal democracies who do cleave to comprehensive perfectionist doctrines are likely to recognize the value of the goods upon which Rawls has placed such emphasis. But Rawlsian liberalism does not simply require that perfectionists recognize the goods of a well-ordered anti-perfectionist liberal polity to be something whose attractions ought to be acknowledged in calculations about how to live one's life within such a polity; it further requires that, when these political goods conflict with other goods drawn from more comprehensive moral and religious conceptions, all citizens must allow the political goods to triumph over – to trump – those other goods.

The fundamental question that Rawls must face is how he can and should respond to someone who acknowledges that the goods of an anti-perfectionist liberal polity are goods, but believes that in some important cases they can be trumped by the goods that form part of the comprehensive perfectionist doctrines to which she is committed. How, in short, can he defend the inviolability of the separation of the political sphere from that of the rest of citizens' personal lives when it is put in question by someone who is committed to a comprehensive moral doctrine that does not itself embody such an anti-perfectionist view of politics?

Rawls's position on this question is unclear. In 'The Idea of an Overlapping Consensus', he considers such a challenge (from a religious believer who argues that the salvation of citizens' souls requires that the limits of anti-perfectionism be breached), and responds as follows:

> At this point we may have no alternative but to deny this, and to assert the kind of thing we had hoped to avoid. But the aspects of our view that we assert should not go beyond what is necessary for the political aim of consensus. Thus, for example, we may assert in some form the doctrine of free religious faith that supports equal liberty of conscience; and given the existence of a just constitutional regime, we deny that the concern for salvation requires anything incompatible with that liberty. We do not state more of our comprehensive views than we think would advance the quest for consensus.[3]

In fact, this last sentence requires qualification; for in a remark immediately preceding this passage, Rawls deploys a distinction between a partially and a fully comprehensive doctrine, and suggests that in dealing with such challenges he needs only to invoke a partially comprehensive liberalism. In his terms, a fully comprehensive doctrine is one that covers all recognized values and virtues within one rather precisely articulated scheme, whereas a partially comprehensive doctrine comprises at least some non-political values and virtues and is rather loosely articulated. But even if we accept this qualification, the fundamental concession has nonetheless been made; for regardless of whether the comprehensive liberalism Rawls invokes is precisely articulated or not, it is undeniably comprehensive: it involves going beyond the resources of purely political liberalism. And this means that, in order to defend his supposedly purely political distinction between the political and the non-political spheres, Rawls must in fact draw upon a comprehensive liberal moral doctrine and contradict the opposing non-liberal one (for example, by denying that salvation requires anything more than liberty of conscience). In other words, according to this passage, the Rawlsian distinction between the political and the non-political which encapsulates his anti-perfectionism presupposes a comprehensive doctrine or conception of the good, and so cannot itself be justified without violating the neutrality of the liberal state.

However, in 'The Domain of the Political and Overlapping Consensus' (a later article), Rawls offers a significantly different outline of the response he would make to a perfectionist's questioning of the boundary between the political and the non-political spheres. Once again, his imagined interlocutor is a religious believer:

> If it is said that outside the church there is no salvation, and that hence a constitutional regime, with its guarantees of freedom of religion, cannot be accepted unless it is unavoidable, we must make some reply. From the point of view of political liberalism, the appropriate reply is to say that the conclusion is unreasonable: it propose to use the public's political power – a power in which citizens have an equal share – to enforce a view affecting constitutional essentials about which citizens as reasonable persons, given the burdens of reason, are bound to differ uncompromisingly in judgement.[4]

Here we re-encounter the notion of reasonable disagreement that we first met when noting Rawls's quasi-scepticism under the fourth heading on our agenda; and now we can examine it in more detail. What Rawls calls 'the burdens of reason' in this domain of human deliberation are such factors as the following: when reasoning about comprehensive conceptions of the good, the evidence is complex and conflicting, the weight to be attached to any given piece of evidence is contestable, our concepts are vague and subject to hard cases, and our judgements are imponderably but decisively and differently influenced by the distinctive texture of our individual moral experience. What he takes this to show is that there are sources of disagreement over conceptions of the good that (unlike such factors as prejudice, self-interest and wilfulness) are compatible with the full reasonableness of all parties to the disagreement. And given these ineradicable burdens of reason, we must expect to encounter substantial, perhaps intractable but entirely reasonable disagreements over such questions.

Rawls's second type of response to the critic of anti-perfectionism is therefore simply to remind him of these burdens of reason; he points out that those who disagree with the critic's comprehensive religious doctrine may well be doing so reasonably, and suggests that it would as a consequence be unreasonable to impose that doctrine upon them. Such a response is clearly much more suited to Rawls's desire to avoid the invocation of a comprehensive doctrine; for by attempting to rebut the non-liberal position as unreasonable, he is not necessarily rejecting as incorrect the comprehensive doctrine upon which it is based, and neither does he seem to be invoking part of a comprehensive doctrine himself. He seems simply to be invoking an uncontroversial fact.

Even in the case of this more modest strategy, however, a critic of Rawlsian liberalism may have qualms. In the first place, some of Rawls's phraseology in the quoted passage suggests that he might be taking the burdens of reason to be more burdensome than they are. When, for example, he says that 'citizens as reasonable persons, given the burdens of reason, are *bound* to differ uncompromisingly in judgement' (our italics), it sounds as if he takes reasonable disagreement on such matters to be inevitable – as if the goal of establishing rational agreement on comprehensive doctrines is *necessarily* chimerical. But the points he adduces as comprising the burdens of reasons do not license this conclusion. They amount to the claim that disagreement about conceptions of the good can be (and perhaps is often likely to be) reasonable; but this is not equivalent to the claim that such disagreement could never be overcome, that there could never be such a thing as reasonable agreement about such matters: to say that disagreement is to be expected is not to say that it is inevitable. So even if a critic of Rawlsian liberalism accepts that it would be unreasonable to urge that the state act according to the tenets of a comprehensive doctrine upon which there is no society-wide rational agreement, he need not accept that such urging is bound to be unreasonable, because he need not accept that such rational agreement is bound to be lacking.

This may seem to be a quibble, but in fact it reveals that Rawls's point about the burdens of reason is a sociological rather than a conceptual or logical one; his quasi-scepticism is really founded upon an empirical belief that the fact of pluralism is permanent rather than upon an irrefutable demonstration that it is intrinsically impossible to establish reasonable agreement on comprehensive doctrines. But then there is scope for Rawls's critic to question whether this sceptical conclusion is as unavoidable as Rawls seems to think. And here, Rawls's use of a believer in the doctrine that there is no salvation outside the church to stand as representative of his perfectionist critics seems to stack the deck against those who incline towards optimism rather than pessimism; for it is a lot more plausible to claim that rational social agreement will never be established on the question of God's existence and nature than to claim that such agreement could never be established on such matters as the value of heterosexual marriage or the immorality of abortion, pornography and sado-masochism. It does not, for example, seem wildly implausible to imagine a society that acknowledges the goods of a well-ordered anti-perfectionist liberal polity, but that comes to an agreement, based upon rational but perfectionist considerations, on the immorality of sado-masochistic practices, and resolves to sacrifice the autonomy of its citizens in this specific respect for the sake of discouraging people from choosing such a way of life; indeed, this might even be a description of contemporary British society. So Rawls's sociological scepticism may be less firmly based than it looks.

But the most important issue that such (possibly hypothetical) considerations highlight is a fundamental question about the internal consistency of Rawls's defence of anti-perfectionism on the grounds that it is the only reasonable policy to adopt in the face of social disagreement on comprehensive doctrines. For such a defence implies that anti-perfectionism is required only when such disagreement exists; so that if it were ever removed or its scope restricted by the exercise of reason, there would be a corresponding diminution of the need to maintain an anti-perfectionist state. But the establishment of, and state action designed to reflect, reasonable social agreement upon some aspect of a perfectionist comprehensive doctrine could result in a localized but definite encroachment upon the autonomy of citizens as Rawls understands it; and how could someone substantively committed to an anti-perfectionist liberal polity regard such a consequence as permissible or just?

Rawls's talk of pluralism as a *fact* (however permanent), together with his explicit commitment to public justifiability, would seem to push him in the direction of regarding the anti-perfectionist neutrality of the state as a circumstance-dependent requirement of justice; for a fact can always be otherwise, and any state action based upon a reasonable social agreement would be one that could be publicly justified. But his substantive commitment to the political conception of the person, his belief in the great values of an anti-perfectionist liberal polity, would seem to push him in the direction of making the anti-perfectionism of the state inviolable; for state action based on reasonable social agreements might well encroach upon what he understands as the autonomy of its citizens. In short, Rawls's defence of anti-perfectionism as required in the face of reasonable social disagreement seems to be inconsistent with a whole-hearted commitment to the very anti-perfectionist conception of politics for which it is supposed to provide a justification. So, if he really is committed to the inviolability of the requirement that the liberal state be anti-perfectionist, his defence against those who wish that requirement to be violated cannot simply be to invoke the burdens of reason; but the only other defensive strategy that he has deployed involves the invocation of elements of a comprehensive liberal doctrine, which violates the requirement that his theory of justice be a purely political conception.

It may be helpful to sum up the course of this discussion. At the centre of Rawls's theory of justice as fairness is the requirement that citizens maintain an anti-perfectionist state, drawing a sharp distinction between their understanding of themselves as members of the political sphere and their self-understandings in the personal sphere. In order to defend that requirement whilst observing it himself (thereby also avoiding the attacks of the communitarians in particular and the arena of controversial issues in general), Rawls must restrict himself to the resources provided by a purely political rather than a comprehensive liberalism. He offers two different justifications. The first involves arguing that violating the requirement would be wrong; but such an argument explicitly invokes elements of a comprehensive (even if only partially comprehensive) liberal moral doctrine and so fails to observe the limits of the purely political. The second involves arguing more modestly that violating the requirement would be unreasonable; but the grounds for this claim would seem to legitimate violations of the requirement in certain circumstances, and so themselves put in question the inviolability of Rawls's own commitment to anti-perfectionism.

What this suggests is that Rawls, in his efforts to provide a purely political defence of anti-perfectionist liberalism, faces a painful dilemma. He can either observe the requirement that his theory of justice restrict itself to the domain of the political, but only at the cost of regarding his commitment to anti-perfectionism as circumstance-dependent; or he can maintain the inviolability of his anti-perfectionism, but only at the cost of invoking elements of a more comprehensive liberal doctrine. If he chooses the first option, he makes a substantial and substantive concession to his perfectionist critics by ceding the absoluteness of his anti-perfectionism; but if, as seems most likely, he chooses the second option, he is forced to admit that the supposedly purely political Rawlsian state is in fact based upon a comprehensive moral doctrine, and so fails to live up to its own claims to neutrality.

Notes

1 Cf. Rawls, 'The Idea of an Overlapping Consensus', n. 4.
2 Rawls, 'Justice as Fairness', n. 20.
3 Rawls, 'The Idea of an Overlapping Consensus', p. 14.
4 Rawls, 'The Domain of the Political', p. 243.

PART III

LIBERALISM, POLITICS AND PERFECTION

Introduction

In this part of the book, we widen the focus of our investigation: after spending a great deal of time examining Rawls's theory of justice as fairness, we now turn to two other contemporary variants of liberal political thought which differ significantly from it – those advanced by Richard Rorty and Joseph Raz. However, this widening of focus does not, we hope, amount to a dissolution of our book's unity of theme. In the first place, since the communitarian attack is as much directed at the liberal tradition as a whole as at one representative of it, and since other liberal theorists might have resources for neutralizing their communitarian opponents that Rawls is not in a position to deploy, cultivating our awareness of the real variety of positions that are subsumed under the label of 'liberalism' is vital to an understanding of the true state of the argument in the liberal–communitarian debates. And in addition, the respects in which Rorty and Raz differ from, and resemble, Rawls are ones that allow us to improve our grasp of the nature and the validity of two key aspects of Rawls's own thought; so Rawls's disappearance from centre stage does not mean that our investigations will not continue to illuminate the distinctive nature of his theorizing. It might help to orient the reader in this part of the book if we develop this second claim in a little more detail.

In chapter 5, we saw that the species of liberalism that Rawls now propounds is both anti-perfectionist and purely political: it advocates a split between the sphere of politics and that of private morality, and attempts to justify that idea without drawing upon any comprehensive moral doctrines. In chapter 6, we spelt out in some detail the ways in which a faithful observation of the limits of the political would allow Rawls to avoid most of the communitarian criticisms; but we ended by arguing that his attempts to defend the anti-perfectionist split against its opponents only succeeded in observing those limits at the cost of reducing anti-perfectionism to a circumstance-dependent requirement of justice. This suggests that, if Rawls wishes to maintain a full-blooded commitment to a split between political and private morality, he must confront his communitarian critics on the terrain that they seemed to assume that he occupied from the outset – that of competing comprehensive conceptions of the good; he must be prepared to defend the value of autonomy, not just as a primary concern in politics, but as a central value in human life.

The liberal might make two responses to this chain of reasoning. One would be to urge Rawls to develop another way of defending his anti-perfectionism whilst observing the limits of the purely political: our arguments were directed against the two types of justification that Rawls has hitherto offered, but there may be other ways of articulating a purely political liberalism which avoid the difficulties we detected in Rawls's own version. This is where Rorty comes in: for in recent years, he has been applying his general philosophical anti-foundationalism to the sphere of political theory, and propounding a form of liberalism that – in his own words – stays on the surface, eschewing controversial and fruitless philosophical, metaphysical and religious arguments without abandoning the value of autonomy in politics. Rorty's liberalism without foundations seems to have captured the imagination of many political theorists, and so would merit some consideration in its own right; since, however, it might also provide Rawls with a new and more defensible way of observing the limits of the purely political, and since Rorty himself has presented his political liberalism not only as an interpretation of Rawls's new position but as a riposte to Rawls's communitarian critics, we have more immediate reasons for exploring Rorty's views in greater depth. That will be our task in chapter 7.

But the difficulties in which Rawls finds himself embroiled as a result of cleaving whole-heartedly to an anti-perfectionist view of politics might lead to a second, very different response; they might give liberals reason to doubt whether anti-perfectionism is the best way of understanding what a commitment to individual autonomy demands in the sphere of politics. For not all strands of recognizably liberal thought hold that one must exclude from politics considerations that quite properly apply to us as individuals in the private sphere; indeed, some liberals argue that individual autonomy is so important a part of human well-being that the liberal state must be a perfectionist state, drawing upon its comprehensive conception of the good and embodying the resulting judgements about the relative value of different ways of life in its laws. The most able and sophisticated advocate of this sort of perfectionist liberalism in recent years has been Joseph Raz; and in chapter 8, we will examine in some detail the challenge that his work poses to Rawls's anti-perfectionism.

7

RORTY:
liberalism without foundations

In a paper entitled 'The Priority of Democracy to Philosophy' and a book entitled *Contingency, Irony and Solidarity* Rorty develops a form of anti-foundationalist liberalism, attributes it to the new Rawls and defends it against the communitarians. Attributing such anti-foundationalism to Rawls is, in our view, a complete misreading of the import of the latter's political liberalism. As we attempted to demonstrate in the second part of this book, Rawls's decision to restrict himself in his theorizing to the ideas and values that are latent in the shared public political culture of contemporary Western liberal democracies is motivated by a substantive commitment to the value of public justifiability; it manifests his recognition of the value of a society in which the state's use of coercive power over free and equal citizens is capable of being justified to each and every one of those citizens in terms of values they all accept. Rorty heartily agrees with Rawls's conclusion, but he is driven to it by fundamentally philosophical arguments against the possibility of pursuing any other strategy; for on his view, anyone who believes that the liberal values and ideas latent in our public political culture might require or could conceivably be furnished with independent support is guilty of certain philosophical confusions. In short, where Rawls's turn to the public political culture is a self-denying ordinance fuelled by a specifically liberal value commitment, Rorty's is the political manifestation of a general philosophical hostility to any attempt to provide rational foundations for systems of values and concepts.

However, the very fact that Rorty overestimates his kinship with the new Rawls means that (as we mentioned in our Introduction to this part of the book) he may be able to buttress Rawls's commitment to a purely political liberalism by providing a version of it that avoids the difficulties that we identified in chapter 6. Certainly, it would be imprudent to draw the conclusion that the general strategy of articulating a political theory that stays on the surface is doomed to failure before investigating the nature and viability of the most prominent and provocative contemporary representative of that school of thought. And regardless of the true nature of Rorty's relation to Rawls, his critique of the communitarians is very relevant to our purposes in this book; indeed, his distinctive and controversial reasons for restricting political theorizing to the realm of public culture are made manifest in that critique, so we shall devote most of our attention in this chapter to it.

In effect, Rorty attempts to justify his proposed restriction on political theorizing by attacking three commonly held reasons for thinking that it cannot or should not be observed. Those considerations are:

1 The belief that all political theories have philosophical or metaphysical foundations that raise issues and ideas not to be found in the public political culture.
2 The belief that justifying a political system merely by invoking the public values that grow up around it simply begs the question against those who reject both the system and its supporting culture.
3 The belief that proving the validity of certain values and ideas present in the public political culture involves determining whether or not they (as well any philosophical doctrines that they might presuppose) correspond to a reality external to that culture.

Rorty's view is that the communitarian critique of Rawls's theory of justice embodies a version of all three claims. This view seems initially plausible: for as we have seen, much of the communitarian attack has understood its focus to be not so much on Rawls's substantive theory but rather on the purportedly more value-neutral conception of the person upon which that theory is based, and so seems to take it for granted that political theories are and must be possessed of metaphysical foundations, and that they must accordingly be committed to defending this foundational conception as *the* correct or valid conception of personhood.

According to Rorty, however, no version of these three claims is coherent. Theories of the self are not value-neutral foundations for political theories but rather another way of articulating (in a different mode of discourse) the very same value commitments with which the political theory is imbued; accordingly, since their invocation can add nothing to the rational credentials or the plausibility of that political doctrine, we need not (*qua* political theorists) go beyond the confines of the public political culture in order to address the issues that such philosophical discourses might raise. Moreover, the notion that the values and conception of the person embodied in such a theory must be justifiable in terms that do not beg the question against those who do not share those values and conceptions is a philosophical confusion; and so is the notion that they must be justifiable in terms of their correspondence to a reality that is external to them. Not one of these three assumptions therefore provides any reason for liberals to think that, in order to justify their doctrine, system and culture, they must utilize resources that go beyond the values and conceptions that make it up. On the contrary: the resources latent in the public political culture of the liberal democracies seem to be all that is available, and so must be all that is required, to justify the liberal political system. As Rorty puts it: '. . . it is not evident that [liberal democratic institutions] are to be measured by anything more specific than the moral intuitions of the particular historical community that has created those institutions'.[1] In effect, then, liberals are free to ignore any critics of liberalism whose criticisms are so radical as to put in question the moral intuitions of Western liberal democracies; or, as Rorty prefers to phrase it, it is right that '. . . we heirs of the Enlightenment think of enemies of liberal democracy like Nietzsche or Loyola as, to use Rawls's word, "mad"'.[2]

In the remainder of this chapter, we will attempt to assess the cogency of this philosophically motivated turn to the public political culture by asking whether Rorty's arguments really do give him the licence to ignore Nietzschean, Loyolan (or communitarian) criticisms of liberalism.

Foundational theories of the person

Rorty's first claim is that theories of the person should not be viewed as indispensable and value-neutral foundations upon which any blueprint for society must be erected. In order to convince us of this, he offers the following characterization of Rawls's references to the nature of the person in his political theory:

> He does not *want* a 'complete deontological vision', one that would explain *why* we should give justice priority over our conception of the good. He is filling out the consequences of the claim that it is prior, not its presuppositions. Rawls is not interested in conditions for the identity of the self, but only in conditions for citizenship in a liberal society ... Rawls is not attempting a transcendental deduction of American liberalism or supplying philosophical foundations for democratic institutions, but simply trying to systematize the principles and intuitions typical of American liberals.[3]

This claim seems very plausible. There is of course much talk about the nature of personhood in the context of moral and political arguments; but its focus and purpose seems very different from such talk in the context of philosophical metaphysics. In the latter case, we might for example want an account of the criteria we have for judging the identity of a person over time, an answer to the question 'What makes person A at time X the same person as person B at time Y?' In the former case, we want to know what it is about human beings that means that they should be treated in certain ways, for example, to know why their autonomy should be respected. To provide a political theory of the person is thus not a matter of straying into metaphysics; but neither is it a matter of providing a foundation for one's theory of society that was in any sense lacking hitherto. It is rather an attempt to articulate under a new aspect the specific vision of life and the concomitant set of values that must already be implicit in any blueprint for the basic structures of society. After all, given that such blueprints have to do with the organization of the communal life of human beings, it would be extremely surprising if they were not to embody a view of what matters about them as persons, and the same point holds in reverse; but there seems no obvious *a priori* order of priority between the two ways of articulating that underlying vision.

To this extent, Rorty's claim is compatible with that of communitarians such as Charles Taylor. However, whereas Taylor also argues that resort to such a theory is not dispensible, Rorty concludes that it is: since it adds nothing to the content or credentials of the original blueprint, that entire mode of discourse can if necessary be avoided without rational penalty; and since participating in it opens the liberal to complex and tortuous controversies, discretion would seem to be the better part of valour. (Rorty also happens to think that if the liberal *did* wish to advance a theory of the person, the most appropriate one would not be that which the communitarians attribute to Rawls but rather the one they offer as their own best account of the matter. But that further twist in Rorty's argument is fundamentally marginal to it, since – by his own lights – the liberal should eschew any such wish.)

But the conclusion that such theories are dispensable is not warranted. It may follow from what has been said that a defender of a given political theory might eschew *articulating* her vision of society in terms of a theory of the person; but it does not follow (as Rorty claims) that she is free to ignore criticisms of her political blueprint that are couched in terms relating to the nature of the people that blueprint would create.

Someone who responds to Rawls's blueprint by saying 'But this is not the way people ought to live!' or 'This society would cripple and distort its citizens!' may or may not be employing a vocabulary that Rawls himself might have wished to avoid; but since talk of the nature of the person is one alternative arena for articulating and arguing about a set of values that also underlies talk of the structure of one's ideal society, then an attack upon liberalism couched in terms of the person is *ipso facto* an attack upon liberal social blueprints. Such forms of critique are focused upon values that are central to the liberal position irrespective of the aspect under which it is presented; accordingly, they cannot simply be ignored by the defender of liberalism. In short, even if a liberal theory of the person is an optional adjunct to the Rawlsian project, insofar as that theory of the person does genuinely accord with or give expression to the values underlying liberalism, then anyone committed to the Rawlsian blueprint is thereby committed to the theory of the person. *Pace* Rorty, he is also thereby committed to the task of responding to criticisms of that theory of the person, and so of venturing beyond the terrain of the public political culture.

Alien vocabularies

Rorty continues his anti-foundationalist critique of the communitarians by attacking an assumption that he takes to be ubiquitous in
political theorizing, namely that a given social blueprint can only
be regarded as superior to its competitors if it is possible to produce
justifications of it that any interlocutor must be able to acknowledge
as valid regardless of his value commitments. Given this assumption,
then invoking a philosophical or metaphysical theory of the person
to justify one's political theory will appear to provide precisely the
abstract, value-neutral terrain that the project of rational justification
requires; such a move would, for example, allow the liberal and the
anti-liberal to confront one another in terms that will make sense to,
that do not beg the question against, either vocabulary. But Rorty
rejects the assumption that the liberal is obliged to make any such
move:

> We have to insist that not every argument needs to be met in the
> terms in which it is presented. Accommodation and tolerance must
> stop short of a willingness to work within any vocabulary that one's
> interlocutor wishes to use, to take seriously any topic that he puts
> forward for discussion . . . there may not be enough overlap between
> two such networks to make possible agreement about political topics,
> or even profitable discussion of such topics.[4]

It is important to note at once that Rorty offers no reason to
accept that this assumption of tolerance is what motivates the communitarian focus on philosophical theories of the person; even if
cleaving to such an assumption would be *one* explanation of their
turn to philosophy, there are many other equally plausible
explanations, and Rorty gives us no grounds for excluding them.
However, even if this particular speculative diagnosis of Rorty's
were right, it remains very unclear whether that assumption of tolerance is incoherent in the way he suggests.

There is, of course, a kernel of truth in his remarks: for if the
vocabularies of two political thinkers are incommensurable to a
degree that hinders the articulation of their views in terms com-
prehensible to both, then a failure to reach agreement does not
invalidate the position of either. Moreover, even if the two disputants
comprehend one another and yet still fail to agree, this does not in

itself condemn either party's view; indeed, the issue over which they are disputing may be so fundamental to the outlook of one that a failure to prevent the other party from acting upon his own views would constitute a failure of commitment: for example, as we saw when discussing Walzer in chapter 4, a failure to convince an Aztec society that human sacrifice was wrong does not in itself make intervention to prevent such sacrifice immoral or unjustifiable. In short, eliciting the agreement of all those we might encounter in political debate is not in itself a criterion for the correctness of our position in that debate.

However, this valid point does not entail that we might simply dismiss or ignore all anti-liberal critiques on the grounds that they are ineradicably alien; for it is the process of attempting to comprehend, evaluate and change the opinions of a given interlocutor that alone can determine whether his views make sense, his agreement constitutes something we should value and his criticism something we should heed. For an interlocutor to be an interlocutor, his remarks must indeed be intelligible to 'we' liberals; and liberals need not *necessarily* worry if their arguments fail to elicit agreement from all non-liberal interlocutors. It does not, however, follow that liberals need only justify themselves to liberals; for being alien in the relevant sense is not determined by whether the interlocutor is or is not a liberal. It is determined by the process of argument.

On occasion, Rorty seems to recognize this banal truth: 'We do not conclude that Nietzsche and Loyola are crazy because they hold unusual views on certain 'fundamental' topics; rather, we conclude this only after extensive attempts at an exchange of political views have made us realize that we are not going to get anywhere.'[5] Moreover, there are even points in his article when he hints at the routes he would take in such political exchanges: 'The liberal response . . . must be, therefore, that even if the typical character types of liberal democracies *are* bland, calculating, petty, and unheroic, the prevalence of such people may be a reasonable price to pay for political freedom.'[6] Such sketches of an argument may reap dividends if they were to be filled out in ways that the article simply leaves to our imagination; but it is clear that this is where Rorty's real work against the anti-liberals must be done. And if this *is* the true site of the conflict, then Rorty's suggestion that the criticisms of such anti-liberals must be beyond the bounds of intelligibility simply because they reject the constituent ideas of liberal political cultures is no more than wishful thinking. The fact that the notion of universal agreement is a chimera in political theory (as well as elsewhere in philosophy) gives Rorty no basis for ignoring or dismissing all anti-liberal critiques in advance, and so no basis for restricting political discourse to the resources of the dominant contemporary culture.

Concepts, truth and reality

So, if Rorty's rejection of the first two assumptions we listed earlier was the sole basis for his suggested revisions of methodology in political theory, then those revisions would have no real justification; rejecting those assumptions simply does not entail restricting political theorists to the materials that are latent in the public political culture. What remains is his attack on the third assumption on that list, namely the belief that we must go beyond the confines of the public political culture in order to justify the values it embodies, because such justification is a matter of establishing the degree to which they correspond to a reality that is somehow external to that culture. Why is this picture of justification as correspondence incoherent? And even if it is, does it follow that, in attempting to justify a given political system, we have no alternative but to restrict ourselves to the materials provided by that culture?

Although Rorty holds that this picture of justification is deeply embedded in the forms of political philosophy he opposes, he makes little attempt in his article on the communitarians to expound and clarify his reasons for regarding that assumption as flawed. To appreciate those reasons, we must turn to his book *Contingency, Irony and Solidarity*, from which it becomes clear that this assumption is a specific inflection of the general metaphysical tendency against which Rorty has set his face for more than a decade. In the first chapter of that book, he provides a critique of the idea that *anything* – mind or matter, self, society or any other entity in the world – has an intrinsic nature that a body of discourse might express or represent. If, as he argues, no sense can be made of the idea that any given vocabulary might stand in a relation of fitting or correspondence to the world or to any given part of it, then the incoherence of the idea that a given concept or theory of the person (or a

given political vocabulary) must be assessed in terms of its correspondence to the reality of human nature will be an inevitable
consequence. It is this general anti-foundational theme that is the
crucial backbone of Rorty's enterprise, in the domain of political
philosophy as well as elsewhere.

Rorty's view on this matter is clear:

> ... great scientists invent descriptions of the world which are useful
> for purposes of predicting and controlling what happens, just as poets
> and political thinkers invent other descriptions of it for other pur-
> poses. But there is no sense in which _any_ of these descriptions is an
> accurate representation of the way the world is in itself ... the very
> idea of such a representation [is] pointless ...[7]

According to Rorty, we have failed to see the pointlessness of this
idea because we have failed to bear in mind the distinction between
single sentences and vocabularies:

> For we often let the world decide the competition between alternative
> sentences (e.g., ... between 'The butler did it' and 'The doctor did it').
> In such cases, it is easy to run together the fact that the world contains
> the causes of our being justified in holding a belief with the claim that
> some non-linguistic state of the world is itself an example of truth, or
> that some such state 'makes a belief true' by 'corresponding' to it. But
> it is not so easy when we turn from individual sentences to vocabu-
> laries as wholes. When we consider examples of alternative language
> games – the vocabulary of ancient Athenian politics versus Jefferson's,
> the moral vocabulary of Saint Paul versus Freud's, the jargon of Newton
> versus that of Aristotle, the idiom of Blake versus that of Dryden – it
> is difficult to think of the world as making one of these better than the
> other, of the world as deciding between them. When the notion of
> 'description of the world' is moved from the level of criterion-governed
> sentences within language games to language games as wholes, games
> which we do not choose between by reference to criteria, the idea that
> the world decides which descriptions are true can no longer be given
> a clear sense.[8]

The sentence that contains the kernel of argument in the above
passage is the following: 'When the notion of "description of the
world" is moved from the level of criterion-governed sentences
within language games to language games as wholes, games which
we do not choose between by reference to criteria, the idea that the

world decides which descriptions are true can no longer be given a clear sense.' The concentration of Wittgensteinian terminology suggests that this sentence should be read as a reference to the considerations that led Wittgenstein to characterize grammar as autonomous, an insight that rests upon emphasizing an essential difference between grammatical remarks and empirical propositions. Empirical propositions are capable of being true and of being false; they claim that something is true of the world, and their claim is evaluated by reference to the facts, to the way the world is. If, for example, someone claims that the sea is blue, we need only observe the colour of the body of water referred to in order to assess the truth of the claim. Obviously, such propositions could only be framed if their constituent terms have meaning, that is if there is a set of rules governing their use, a set of what Wittgenstein sometimes calls criteria. These function as standards which distinguish correct from incorrect applications of a given term; they mark the boundary between sense and nonsense, between meaningful uses of the term and unintelligible ones. For example, if someone defines water as H_2O, then anyone who applies the term 'water' (as part of a factual claim) to something that does not have that chemical composition has misused the term, and so failed to say anything meaningful. Propositions that elucidate criteria or meaning-rules are what Wittgenstein calls grammatical remarks.

The crucial point to follow from these reminders is that, unlike empirical propositions, grammatical remarks are incapable of being true or false; this is because they are rule formulations, not descriptions or factual claims. It makes no sense to talk of a rule being true or false; that, one could say, is an aspect of the grammar of the term 'rule' – and an aspect of the grammar of the terms 'true' and 'false'. (How, for example, might it be *false* to define 'water' as 'H_2O'? Even if the world lacked any substance with that particular chemical composition, this would show only that there was no water in the world, not that our definition of the term had failed to represent it accurately.) Of course, in the absence of a grammatical or conceptual framework, no meaningful empirical proposition could be constructed, and in this sense the possibility of a true (as well as of a false) empirical proposition is a function of the existence of a set of grammatical rules; but the actual truth or falsity of the propositions thus constructed neither validates nor falsifies that set of rules. The world may be such as to make one grammar more useful or more appropriate than another, but it could not make it more accurate or closer to the facts. Since, then, sentences that formulate rules are not in the business of describing the world, they can neither correspond nor fail to correspond with that world. To imagine that they can is akin to treating a set of grammatical rules as a series of descriptions or factual claims, as if the expression of a rule governing the use of a word were part of a theory about the world – as if a definition were a truth-value candidate. In short, for Rorty it simply makes no sense to characterize the grammatical or conceptual framework of any language game as a description of the world, for it is not a description at all.

Communitarianism and correspondence

Such, on our reading, is Rorty's argument for his general anti-foundationalist attack upon the picture of justification as correspondence.[9] It seems powerful; but even if we grant its cogency, a question remains as to its consequences for political theory. What would follow from rejecting the general picture of justification as correspondence in that specific domain? If it *is* a piece of metaphysics, how might this new knowledge alter our understanding of political morality and its rational underpinnings? Rorty identifies two consequences of such a rejection: first, that it would allow us to dismiss the communitarian critique of liberalism, since that critique is couched in terms that imply the coherence of this picture; and second, that it would reveal the very idea of an external standard against which to assess the political vocabulary of liberalism to be chimerical, and so allow us to remain content with the standards of justification that are internal to that vocabulary and its supporting culture. In the following section of this chapter we shall examine this second, more general claim; but in this section we shall evaluate Rorty's first, more specific anti-communitarian conclusion. Does the communitarian attack on the liberal conception of the person as flawed, inaccurate or just plain wrong entail that communitarians are committed to the incoherent assumption that concepts of the person are in the business of accurately describing the metaphysical Reality of human nature?

The answer to this question varies from communitarian to communitarian. In the case of Taylor, Rorty's attack seems entirely misplaced: for the assumption that there is a timeless essence of the self against which conceptions of the self must be measured would contradict his conception of human beings as self-interpreting animals, as beings whose identity is fixed by the terms in which they understand it and so is transformable by a shift in those understandings and their concomitant social matrices. In the case of MacIntyre, Rorty seems to be equally inaccurate: MacIntyre does indeed think that he can demonstrate that an emotivist conception of the self is flawed, but it is flawed because it fails to provide the resources needed to comprehend the concepts of personal identity and morality; it is not that liberals misrepresent the true nature of those phenomena, but rather that their conceptual framework cannot make adequate sense of them. With respect to Sandel, however, Rorty seems to be on firmer ground. Certainly, Sandel articulates his criticisms of Rawls in terms that imply that Rawls has mis-described the nature of the human self – more specifically, that he has overlooked that self's capacity for constitutive attachments; and this is something that Sandel seems prone to think of as a meta-physical truth about distinctively human beings.

However, the most interesting question that Rorty raises is not that of measuring the degree to which the attacks made by the communitarians did or did not involve formulations and turns of phrase that might be read as entailing a commitment to the erroneous view Rorty has identified. The real issue is whether their criticisms can be articulated in ways that entirely dispense with such locutions, and yet maintain their original force. For, although this metaphysical confusion may be widespread in our culture, it seems entirely ex-trinsic to the content of any particular ethical system: it might be a part of the articulation of almost any ethic, and yet not be an in-dispensable part of any of them. When someone engaged in an ethical or political argument says 'This view of the self fails to capture the truth about human nature' or 'But my concept of human nature is the only right one!' or 'This is how all human beings ought to live, and anyone who doesn't is wrong!', no commitment to a metaphysical confusion need be inferred. It may simply be that these are manifestations of the sincerity with which someone cleaves to a vision of life, or an expression of his belief that the answer to such questions is not a matter of personal preference. As Rorty himself puts it in a slightly different context: 'Everybody is just insisting that the beliefs and desires they hold most dear should come first in the order of discussion. That is not arbitrariness but sincerity.'[10]

If we reread Sandel in such a light, then his attack on liberalism can easily be viewed as a passionate assault upon the values underlying the liberal social blueprint, which happens to be couched in terms of the conception of the person that he takes to be associated with that blueprint. And since, as we argued earlier, Rorty's view that the liberal need not articulate his values in those terms gives him no ground for believing that the liberal need not defend himself against criticisms that employ those terms, we find ourselves back where we started – with an obligation to understand, assess and respond to the specific content of the communitarian critique. In other words, Rorty's anti-foundationalist attack upon the picture of justification as correspondence does not provide us with any speedy way of dismissing the communitarians.

Metaphysics and politics

However, Rorty also makes a second claim about the consequences of rejecting the picture of justification as correspondence: the claim that this rejection entails that political argument and justification in general must be conducted within the confines of the prevailing public political culture. How does he reach this more sweeping conclusion?

> The realization that the world does not tell us what language games to play should not, however, lead us to say that a decision about which to play is arbitrary, nor to say that it is the expression of something deep within us. The moral is not that objective criteria for choice of vocabulary are to be replaced with subjective criteria, reason with will or feeling. It is rather that the notions of criteria and choice (including the idea of 'arbitrary' choice) are no longer in point when it comes to changes from one language game to another. Europe did not *decide* to accept the idiom of Romantic poetry, or of socialist politics, or of Galilean mechanics. That sort of shift was no more an act of will than it was a result of argument. Rather, Europe gradually lost the habit of using certain words and gradually acquired the habit of using others . . .[11]

The point upon which Rorty is fastening here is important: the concept of decision, as it is employed within the context of a given language game (for example, to decide between competing descriptions of a given state of affairs), has no obvious application at the level of language games as a whole. But he takes this to imply that cultural change is itself primarily a matter of shifts in vocabulary which are as little affected by human will and reason as is the weather. And what is true of culture *per se* must be true of political culture: in other words, for Rorty, liberalism is now simply a part of our cultural weather system. Just as Western Europe acquired Galilean vocabulary and dispensed with its Aristotelian predecessor, so our contemporary culture has got out of the habit of employing any political vocabulary other than that of liberalism. And since we cannot object to that vocabulary on the grounds that it misrepresents the Truth about the Reality of the self or of human nature (for the very idea of such an external measure or standard is incoherent), we should simply get on with the business of developing and refining the political vocabulary with which we find ourselves equipped, in accordance with the standards that are internal to that vocabulary and culture. In short, we should, as political theorists, restrict ourselves to the resources latent in our public political culture.

In this respect, the situation in politics is precisely analogous to the situation as Rorty describes it in contemporary philosophy:

> To say that we should drop the idea of truth as out there waiting to be discovered is not to say that we have discovered that, out there, there is no truth. It is to say that our purposes would be served best by ceasing to see truth as a deep matter, as a topic of philosophical interest, or 'true' as a term which repays analysis. 'The nature of truth' is an unprofitable topic, resembling in this respect 'the nature of man' and 'the nature of God', and differing from 'the nature of the positron', and 'the nature of Oedipal fixation'. But this claim about relative profitability, in turn, is just the recommendation that we in fact *say* little about these topics, and see how we get on.[12]

As his use of this analogy brings out, Rorty takes his discovery that vocabularies as a whole do not represent reality to show that the task of persuading someone to adopt a new vocabulary can amount to nothing more than simply ignoring their old vocabulary and elaborating the new one in a way that emphasizes its attractions. His advice is to 'try to ignore the apparently futile traditional questions by substituting the following new and possibly interesting questions'.[13] This is why he then goes on to expound the views of Davidson, Freud and Nietzsche (amongst others); and it is why he feels that he can safely ignore the doctrines of Loyola and Nietzsche (in his anti-liberal incarnation) – not to mention the communitarians. But does Rorty's argument actually support this sweeping reconception and restriction of political theory?

The difficulty with Rorty's strategy is not its positive side but its negative one. It seems eminently plausible that one way of persuading someone to adopt a new outlook on life would be to emphasize the scope, sophistication, flexibility etc. of the concepts that embody it; in fact, communitarians such as Taylor and MacIntyre would agree whole-heartedly that this is an essential aspect of practical reasoning. However, another equally important part of such reasoning must be that of engaging with the old vocabulary, for example by highlighting its unwieldiness, its failure to mark certain distinctions, its propensity to obscure or play down certain fundamental aspects of human behaviour and experience – and by responding to similar claims that its proponents make about the new vocabulary. Rorty assumes that this negative or combative part of the process can simply be dispensed with in the case of any fundamentally anti-liberal thinker; but his grounds for this assumption are inadequate. Critical engagements that employ terms of criticism of the sort mentioned above no more assume that concepts describe or represent reality than does the positive part of the process that Rorty endorses. So, his only reason for dispensing with them must be the implicit presumption that a cultural transformation in the West has already disposed of every serious opponent of liberalism.

To be sure, in the late twentieth century, it might be safe to assume that an Aristotelian or Samurai moral vocabulary is no longer a viable contender for the status of 'most favoured discourse'; in such cases, the idea of critically engaging with such a vocabulary seems to be one whose time has passed: they can, perhaps, be simply ignored or dismissed as irrelevant. But this does not allow us to ignore or dismiss *in advance* any attempts to reconstruct or reinterpret such moral codes in ways more adapted to the present time (an attempt that Alisdair MacIntyre, for example, has made on Aristotle's behalf). And it certainly does not permit us to ignore or dismiss in advance every non-liberal vocabulary in the sphere of ethics and politics; for in the case of a vast array of such frameworks it simply cannot seriously be claimed that the march of cultural history has left them entirely by the wayside.

One cannot respond *a priori* to every critique of liberalism with the suggestion that we simply ignore the questions it raises; for this is to assume in advance that our opponent has already lost, at the level of the culture as a whole, the 'argument' she wishes to have with us on a one-to-one basis. It is to assume the validity of a sociological conclusion without the provision of any sociological evidence, and then to utilize that conclusion in order to avoid engaging in personal, individual political argument. It may well be that the ethical and political vocabularies of Nietzsche and Loyola are losing their grip on Western culture as a whole; but any individual who regards this development as a good thing and wants to speed it up, must do so by revealing the poverty, ugliness and irrelevance of those vocabularies in argument, not by declaring that development to have been completed already. However devoutly to be wished this consummation may be, it will not be brought about by wishing alone – certainly not when the wishing takes the form of stipulation.

In conclusion, we can say that this examination of the three pillars of Rorty's philosophical anti-foundationalism has revealed them to be insufficient to justify either his specific attacks on the communitarians or his more general desire to restrict political theorizing to the resources latent in our public political culture. This form of political liberalism lacks foundations in a sense that even an anti-foundationalist cannot simply shrug off; so those liberals who wish to pursue the general methodological strategy of avoiding the use of comprehensive moral doctrines must look elsewhere for a tenable version of it.

Notes

1 Rorty, 'The Priority of Democracy to Philosophy', p. 190. All page references to this article refer to the collection Rorty, *Objectivity, Relativism and Truth*.
2 Ibid., p. 187.
3 Ibid., p. 189.
4 Ibid., p. 190.
5 Ibid., p. 190.

6 Ibid., p. 190.
7 Rorty, *Contingency, Irony and Solidarity*, p. 4.
8 Ibid., pp. 5–6.
9 For those interested in and familiar with the philosophical background to Rorty's work, it may be worth noting at this point that certain other aspects of Rorty's text suggest an alternative reading of his argument, one according to which he is indebted to Quine rather than Wittgenstein. On that reading, Rorty's reason for rejecting the picture of correspondence would not be that this picture mistakenly treats a grammatical system as if it were an empirical theory, but rather that any such vocabulary is a web of propositions whose complexity and capacity to accommodate a wide range of empirical phenomena is so great that it is almost impossible to refute it. Our reason for not pursuing this reading in the text, however, is that such an argument would not put paid to the correspondence picture; for if such a vocabulary *were* akin to an empirical theory, then it would to that degree be in the business of attempting to describe or characterize reality, and so could at least in principle be accused of failing to correspond to that reality.
10 Rorty, 'The Priority of Democracy to Philosophy', p. 193.
11 Rorty, *Contingency, Irony and Solidarity*, p. 6.
12 Ibid., p. 8.
13 Ibid., p. 9.

8

RAZ:
The politics of perfection

We saw in our chapter on the political liberalism of the new Rawls that there were various senses in which his conception of justice as fairness might be regarded as communitarian. In this our final chapter we consider the political philosophy presented by another theorist, Joseph Raz, which will also be seen to combine, though in quite different ways, strands of liberal and communitarian thought. In contrast to that strain of liberalism that holds that there are good reasons, of whatever kind, why we should exclude from politics reasons that quite properly apply to us as individuals, Raz argues that it is legitimate for the state to seek to promote the well-being of citizens in a way that involves it in the business of judging the value of particular ways of life. The kind of 'epistemic abstinence' modelled by Rawls's veil of ignorance, the idea that reasons emanating from comprehensive (and controversial) conceptions of the good are inappropriate in the sphere of politics, is rejected in favour of a perfectionism that holds that 'it is the goal of all political action to enable individuals to pursue valid conceptions of the good and to discourage evil or empty ones' (*MF*, p. 133). If not a political philosophy that seeks a neutral state, what makes Raz's perfectionism nonetheless *liberal* is his claim that, at least in modern societies, a good life must be an autonomous life: a person's well-being depends on her being the maker or author of her own life and on the availability to her of a multiplicity of valuable options. In attempting to sever the connection between liberalism and anti-perfectionism or neutrality whilst keeping autonomy and moral pluralism central,

Raz effects a synthesis that transcends, in a way rather different from Rawls's political liberalism, the opposition between liberalism and communitarianism.

In the course of our critical assessment of Rawls's position, we argued that his liberalism was not as political, and hence as neutral, as he claimed. In order to defend it against those, such as the religious fundamentalist, whose comprehensive doctrines do not have room for the kind of separation between the political and the non-political that Rawls favours, he has to invoke elements of his own comprehensive, or at least partially comprehensive, liberal understanding of what makes a person's life go well. If this is right, then he cannot, when it comes to the crunch, argue that his liberalism is merely political; it is not neutral where 'neutral' means that it presupposes the validity of no particular (partially) comprehensive doctrine. On the other hand, as we went on to point out, even if justice as fairness does, in the end, invoke a particular (partially) comprehensive doctrine, this does not mean that it is perfectionist. On the contrary, it is the particular comprehensive doctrine invoked that leads to the requirement that reasons based upon a person's non-political conception of the good be excluded from politics and hence to a form of political neutrality. It is the (partially) comprehensive liberal commitment to the idea that people should be free to frame, revise and pursue their own conceptions of the good that leads to the split between the political and the non-political, to the claim that reasons emanating from the latter should be excluded from the former, and to the idea that the state should be, in this sense, neutral between the conceptions of the good held by its citizens.

Read in the context of this analysis of the new Rawls, two aspects of Raz's liberalism stand out as distinctive. First, unlike Rawls, Raz is unashamedly happy to embrace the comprehensiveness of his liberalism. Where we had to argue, in the face of his protestations to the contrary, that Rawls's justice as fairness was not as merely political as he might wish, Raz is deeply suspicious of this kind of distinction between the political and the non-political and quite ready to defend his political philosophy by appeal to a thick and controversial conception of personal well-being. As he says, near the beginning of *The Morality of Freedom*:

> Influential voices among political theorists argue for the existence of
> a relatively independent body of moral principles, addressed primarily
> to the government and constituting a (semi-)autonomous political

morality. The critical evaluation of such views is one of the main tasks
of this book. Their rejection means that the positive conclusions argued
for in the book concerning the morality of political freedom are based
on the considerations of individual morality to a greater degree than
is common in many contemporary works of political philosophy. (*MF*,
p. 4)

Since it was our contention that Rawls's position did in fact presuppose a particular (partially) comprehensive doctrine, and since
we have no wish to deny that his writings can be regarded as
attempts substantively to present the attractions of that doctrine
and its implications for politics, this first difference between him
and Raz concerns not so much what they are actually doing as
what they take themselves to be doing. If we reject the claim that
Rawls's liberalism is political in the sense of not presupposing any
particular controversial or comprehensive doctrine, we can read
Rawls as arguing for an understanding of individual well-being
that gives priority to the individual's capacity to frame, revise and
pursue conceptions of the good and for an anti-perfectionist state
as necessary for the full exercise of that capacity. It is here that the
second difference between him and Raz, and that on which we
shall focus in the body of this chapter, comes into play: unlike that
of Rawls, Raz's understanding of personal well-being is of such a
kind that it permits the state to make, and to embody in its laws,
perfectionist judgements, judgements about the relative value of
different ways in which people might lead their lives. There is, for
Raz, no reason why the state should exclude from consideration
those reasons that lead people in their personal lives to judge some
way of life better, and worse, than others. In a phrase, Raz's liberalism is perfectionist and not exclusionary.

These two features of Raz's position make him an excellent way
to conclude our introduction to the debates between liberals and
communitarians. Since he does not pursue a strategy of avoidance
but seeks rather to argue for the merits of liberal politics based on
a comprehensive understanding of personal well-being, he can be
read as engaging in a defence of liberalism that is explicitly pitched
at the same level as were most of the strands of communitarian
critique. Given this, it is particularly interesting to observe the ways
in which his distinctively perfectionist liberalism is immune, or
sensitive, to particular aspects of that critique. Where Rawls claims
that his liberalism is communitarian precisely in being anti-
perfectionist, political decisions having to exclude, for the sake of

a community that is publicly justifiable, reasons arising from controversial understandings of how people should lead their nonpolitical lives, Raz's perfectionist liberalism connects with the communitarian criticisms in rather different, but equally interesting, ways. It is partly because Raz recognizes the dependence of the individual's personal well-being on the social forms available to her in her society that Raz advocates his perfectionism, so discussion of his position brings out, more clearly than we have been able to so far, aspects of what is at stake in the debate between liberals and communitarians.

A brief disclaimer: *The Morality of Freedom* is a long and difficult book, and one that addresses, in a highly sophisticated manner, a wide range of issues in political philosophy. We do not, in this chapter, pretend to do justice to the variety and complexity of argument to be found in it. Our presentation of Raz's ideas will necessarily be selective and, at least when compared with his own meticulous articulation of them, somewhat superficial. Our selection will inevitably be informed by the reading of the background themes and debates that we have presented heretofore. Thus, for example, in seeking to identify only those strands of argument of most immediate relevance, we all but ignore his important and influential discussion of political authority. And even within the bounds set by our particular area of concern, we aim to do no more than indicate the bare outline of his position; for example, we gloss over his distinction between neutral political concern and anti-perfectionism, regarding, for our purposes, the two as equivalent. There is an unavoidable trade-off between clarity or accessibility on the one hand and precision or complexity on the other, and we are happy to acknowledge that, for the purposes of this book, we value the former qualities above the latter. If, by presenting Raz's ideas in a relatively introductory way, we can encourage the reader to take up his own more advanced exposition of them, we shall have achieved our aim.

Raz's perfectionist autonomy

We have argued that Rawls can most cogently be read as a (partially) comprehensive liberal whose core value is autonomy. The same is true of Raz. Where the two differ, and differ crucially, is in the way they spell out what autonomy means and in what they take the implications of that value to be for politics. For Rawls, a person's highest-order interest in her capacity to frame, revise, and pursue conceptions of the good requires that the state be anti-perfectionist; this is modelled by the exclusion of knowledge of particular (and controversial) conceptions of the good from the original position. For Raz, on the other hand, 'the autonomy principle is a perfectionist principle. Autonomous life is valuable only if it is spent in the pursuit of acceptable and valuable projects and relationships. The autonomy principle permits and even requires governments to create morally valuable opportunities, and to eliminate repugnant ones' (*MF*, p. 417). The value of autonomy is not only consistent with but even requires the state to make and act on judgements as to the relative value of particular conceptions of the good.

Before getting into the details of Raz's arguments, it may be helpful to indicate in very general terms the issues at stake here. Let us take as an example a specific political issue which might exercise the liberal: the rights of homosexuals to live the sexual life of their choice, perhaps despite the moral views of the majority of their political community who regard such a life as depraved. Anti-perfectionist and perfectionist liberals will think about such issues in quite different ways, and their conclusions, even if they coincide, will be based on quite different reasons. The anti-perfectionist or exclusionary liberal will think that the question of the moral value of a homosexual life is irrelevant to the question of how the state should act; even if the majority view is correct, and such a life is indeed depraved, this view, because based on perfectionist considerations, should simply be excluded from political consideration and homosexuals should be free to live the sexual life of their choice. The perfectionist, on the other hand, will consider the question of the value of a homosexual life quite relevant to the political conclusion. If it is indeed the case that governments are permitted and even required to 'eliminate' repugnant opportunities, and if the majority is right to find homosexuality repugnant, then it follows that the government would be permitted and even required to eliminate homosexuality. When we come to spell out Raz's view in more detail, we shall see that things are by no means as straightforward as his unusually forthright formulation and this rather crude example suggest, but the general shape of the point will survive the qualifications that are to follow. Unlike the anti-perfectionist, the perfectionist liberal has to get involved in substantive debate as to the value of particular ways of life. She will have to argue, at least in certain circumstances, not only for the value of the individual's freedom to make her own choice but also for the value of the choice that she makes.

It is also important to be clear that contemporary liberal democratic states do not exclude reasons arising from perfectionist ideals. Consider here the question of whether a sexually promiscuous life, whether homo- or heterosexual, is as valuable as one devoted to the heterosexual monogamous ideal represented by the institution of marriage. While the anti-perfectionist liberal has to argue that all questions of this kind are irrelevant to politics, and that the state should be neutral between these different ways of life, it is clear that, in giving legal recognition and public status to a particular form of sexual union and not to others, contemporary states encourage their citizens to live one sort of life rather than another. This, of course, clearly violates the anti-perfectionist exclusion of political action based on consideration of the relative merits of the various sorts of life favoured by their citizens. If the reader has hitherto been sympathetic to the anti-perfectionist cause, the fact that it is challenged by something as apparently uncontroversial as state recognition of heterosexual marriage might begin to sway her in the other direction.

Having seen the general shape of the wood, the time has come to consider the trees. We shall begin, reproducing his own mode of exposition of his position, by identifying Raz's negative arguments against anti-perfectionism – his reasons for rejecting the view that we should exclude ideals from politics. Perfectionism, he maintains, does not have three worrying implications that it might appear to have. First, allowing controversial ideals into politics does not necessarily mean that the beliefs of some are being allowed to overrule the beliefs of others. Second, perfectionist politics do not necessarily involve the coercive imposition of styles of life by some groups upon others. Finally, permitting governments to act on reasons that arise from ideals does not necessarily imply a rigoristic moral outlook, in that it does not mean that all but one morally approved form of life will be suppressed. Presentation of these negative points will of course involve us in the articulation of Raz's more positive articulation of a perfectionist liberalism based on autonomy and pluralism.

Ideals qua valid not qua beliefs: perfectionism against scepticism

The anti-perfectionist liberal thinks that the validity of a moral ideal is not a reason for the state to act on it, that the state should exclude moral considerations arising out of perfectionist ideals, even where that ideal is valid. One way in which the motivation for such exclusion is sometimes put is that, since people disagree over the validity of such ideals, the state is failing to treat its citizens with respect if it takes them into account. Raz's response is quick:

> Is one treating another with respect if one treats him in accordance with sound moral principles, or does respect for persons require ignoring morality (or parts of it) in our relations with others? There can be little doubt that stated in this way the question admits of only one answer. One would be showing disrespect to another if one ignored moral considerations in treating him. (*MF*, p. 157)

Such a response might seem *too* quick. The anti-perfectionist intuition may be that people's beliefs about how they should live their lives are worthy of respect purely in virtue of being their beliefs, and it is this respect for the moral opinions of her fellow citizens that leads this kind of liberal to exclude even valid ideals from politics. Allowing controversial ideals into politics necessarily involves, it would appear, allowing the beliefs of some citizens about how people should lead their lives to overrule the beliefs of others. Since people have different beliefs about what makes a life valuable, it might seem that the only way to treat them with respect is to constrain the state to exclude such beliefs from its policies.

This way of formulating the anti-perfectionist case, that people's beliefs have moral status simply *qua* their beliefs, brings us directly to a crucially distinctive aspect of Raz's liberalism. For Raz, a person's well-being does not depend upon her living the life that she believes to be of value, it depends upon her living a life that is valuable for reasons independent of her belief in its value. While it is indeed the case that for a life to be valuable it must be consciously endorsed by the person living it, and, as we shall see must, at least in modern conditions, be autonomous in the sense we shall discuss below, it does not follow that any life that is consciously endorsed and autonomous is thereby endowed with value. On the contrary, for Raz 'a person's well-being depends on the value of his goals and pursuits' (*MF*, p. 298), and not, we may add, on her belief in their value.

It is perfectly possible for a person's belief about the worth of her conception of the good to be mistaken, and, if it is, we do not respect her, nor promote her well-being, by ignoring the fact.

The fundamental point here is the reason-dependent character of goals and desires.

> A person who spends all his time gambling has, other things being equal, less successful a life, even if he is a successful gambler, than a livestock farmer busily minding his farm . . . The reason is that they engage in what they do because they believe it to be a valuable, worthwhile activity (perhaps but not necessarily because of its value to others). They care about what they do on that basis. To the extent that their valuation is mistaken it affects the success of their life. (*MF*, pp. 298–9)

People pursue goals for reasons, because they believe that they are valuable. If they are mistaken, if they are acting in accordance with beliefs that lack (good) reasons, then they are not living successful lives. 'Satisfaction of goals based on false reasons does not contribute to one's well-being' (*MF*, p. 301). And once we admit that some ideals are valid and some are not, that there are (good) reasons for pursuing some ideals and none for pursuing others, and acknowledge that a person derives no well-being from a life spent in pursuit of the latter, then it will look as if we have little reason to respect a person's mistaken belief in the validity of an invalid ideal. We will be doing her no service, for, contrary to the anti-perfectionist intuition, one gets no well-being from living a life in accordance with an ideal in which one believes unless there are true reasons for the belief, that is unless the ideal is indeed valid.

Perfectionism does not, then, have to argue that it is justifiable for the beliefs of some to overrule the beliefs of others, for perfectionist ideals may enter politics not because people believe in them but because they are valid; they are supported by true reasons, they correctly identify a valuable form of life. As Raz puts it: '. . . the fact that the state *considers* anything to be valuable or valueless is no reason for anything. Only its being valuable or valueless is a reason. If it is likely that the government will not judge such matters correctly then it has no authority to judge them at all' (*MF*, p. 412). This way of presenting the point makes very clear the extent to which Raz's perfectionist liberalism rejects any form of moral subjectivism or scepticism. While we saw that Rawls seeks neither to assert nor to deny any controversial claim about the status of moral judgements, and it is important for his position that even people committed to the truth of their comprehensive conceptions have reason to exclude them from politics, Raz's argument can be read both as suggesting that this position is problematic and as revealing a latent affinity between anti-perfectionism and moral scepticism.

It is clear, as we argued in our Introduction, that the liberal cannot coherently regard all moral judgements as mere expressions of subjective opinion. She must at least regard the judgement that people should be free to make up their own minds about how they live their lives as objectively valid. What we are considering here is the thought that one reason for the objective judgement that people should be free to live the way of life that they choose is the claim that such choices themselves lack objective foundation. There is, then, for someone espousing this form liberalism, a distinction between two kinds of moral judgement: judgements about the good life, which are subjective and should be kept out of politics, and judgements about the rights and duties that people have and that should govern their relations with one another, which are objective and are properly protected and enforced by the coercive apparatus of the liberal state. Raz is deeply suspicious of the idea that these two types of judgement are different in this way: '... is there reason to think that one is more likely to be wrong about the character of the good life than about the sort of moral considerations which all agree should influence political action such as the right to life, to free expression, or free religious worship? I know of no such arguments' (*MF*, p. 160). In fact, as we shall see later, Raz is suspicious of the whole distinction between what he calls 'morality in the narrow sense', which is meant to include 'only all those principles which restrict the individual's pursuit of his personal goals and his advancement of his self-interest' and 'the art of life', on the other, which consists of 'the precepts instructing people how to live and what makes for a successful, meaningful, and worthwhile life' (*MF*, p. 214). Our specific concern here is his claim that we should be no more sceptical with regard to judgements that concern the art of life than with regard to those that concern, for example, the rights of others. If Raz is right to think that we can be as sure that the life of a livestock farmer is better than that of a gambler as we can that people should be free to worship the religion of their choice, then he removes a major motivation for anti-perfectionism. Taken in combination, his rejection of scepticism in matters concerning the art of life and his claim that a person's well-being depends on the value of the goals she pursues lead forcefully to the conclusion that the state should be allowed, and perhaps even required, to act on judgements as to what makes a life meaningful or valuable.

Sceptical doubts of a different kind may remain, however, and, because they form distinct motivations for anti-perfectionist politics that have played a significant role in the liberal tradition, they warrant attention here. Even if there is no reason in principle why judgements about the art of life are more likely to be wrong than judgements about people's rights and duties, might we not think that governments are not to be trusted to get them right? Perfectionist ideals should be kept out of politics, the role of government should be limited to that relating to morality in the narrow sense, not because we cannot not know which ideals are valid but because we cannot expect governments to act on those which are. Scepticism about how politics works might be more persuasive than philosophical scepticism.

Quite apart from the practical worry that governments may be corrupt, the theoretically important issue here is that those whose judgements as to the the validity of ideals determine what the government does may, however well-intentioned, make mistakes. As Raz says:

> ... it is possible that the appeal of anti-perfectionism is at least in part indirect. There is no way of acting, politically or otherwise, in pursuit of ideals except by relying on the judgement of some people as to which ideals are valid and imposing it on others who disagree. Those whose views are imposed on the community do not regard the fact that they hold those views as a reason for their imposition on others who reject them. They maintain that their conception of the good is valid and that is the reason which justifies its imposition. But such an action is constitutionally justified on the ground that the rulers, the majority, etc. chose to act in that way, regardless of the truth or soundness of their views. (*MF*, p. 158)

Once we recognize that, whatever the philosophical justifiability of perfectionist politics, what actually happens is that the beliefs of some overrule the beliefs of others, and that such beliefs may be wrong, we may feel that Raz's arguments have somehow missed the point.

Raz's theory of authority, the essence of which (that it is only if the government is likely to make correct judgements that it has the authority to judge at all) we have already glimpsed in passing, may seem rather to beg than to answer the question. But one way of rendering Raz's position plausible is simply to note that exactly the same worries apply to those moral judgements that the anti-perfectionist does think are proper within the realm of politics. Those who decide what rights people have, whether they be democratic majorities or constitution founding elites, may be wrong too, so the 'argument from the possibility of mistake' must apply there also. The tempting way to resist the implication that either states should act on all moral judgements or that they should act on none is to claim that some kinds of judgement are more likely to be right than others, but we have already seen that Raz rejects this view.

Raz recognizes the force of these worries. While holding that governments can play a more positive role in helping their citizens to achieve well-being than would be allowed by the anti-perfectionist liberal, he cannot disguise 'the dangers inherent in the concentration of power in few hands, the dangers of corruption, of bureaucratic distortions and insensitivities, of fallibility of judgement, and un-certainty of purpose, and the . . . insufficiency and the distortion of information reaching the central organs of government' (*MF*, p. 427). Taking considerations such as these into account, he acknowledges, may well mean that people should be freer from governmental action than is implied by the 'pure' theory he outlines. Our point, and the reason to emphasize this acknowledgement, is simply that such impure considerations have been influential in the motivation for anti-perfectionist liberalism.

The same is true of what Raz calls another 'regrettable source of political freedom', and it is with this that we shall conclude this part of our presentation of his argument. Although, as we saw, Rawls's anti-perfectionism does not value agreement on pragmatic grounds, as the only way to avoid social conflict between groups who disagree about conceptions of the good, this line of thought can indeed lead in the direction of anti-perfectionist conclusions. Raz sees this:

> The pursuit of full-blooded perfectionist policies, even of those which are entirely sound and justified, is likely, in many countries if not in all, to backfire by arousing popular resistance leading to civil strife.

> In such circumstances compromise is the order of the day . . . which
> will confine perfectionist measures to matters which command a large
> measure of social consensus . . . (*MF*, p. 429)

Given adverse circumstances, where the implementation of policies
based on perfectionist ideals, however valid, would lead to civil
strife, there are good reasons to exclude those ideals from politics.
Here again we see that Raz acknowledges the force of considerations
that have provided a great deal of the motivation for the view that
the state should keep out of the business of judging how its citizens
should lead their lives. Here the fear is neither that governments
will be wicked nor mistaken, it is that their well-intentioned
implementation of sound perfectionist policies may be counter-
productive.

Not coercive imposition

The second thought supportive of anti-perfectionism that Raz rejects
is that which sees it as necessary to prevent the coercive imposition
of styles of life by some groups upon others. This neatly breaks
down into two distinct components, the idea that perfectionist
politics must be directed by some groups against others and the
idea that it must be coercive. For Raz, both of these involve confusion.
    With respect to the first, it simply need not be the case that
perfectionist political action seeks to get one or more groups to
conform to the ways of life of another.

> Perfectionist political action may be taken in support of social institu-
> tions which enjoy unanimous support in the community, in order to
> give them formal recognition, bring legal and administrative arrange-
> ments into line with them, facilitate their use by members of the
> community who wish to do so, and encourage the transmission of
> belief in their value to future generations. In many countries this is the
> significance of the legal recognition of monogamous marriage and
> prohibition of polygamy. (*MF*, p. 161)

We have already come across the example of marriage, and noted
that recognition of its perfectionist character seems rather to defuse

the apparent threat of the perfectionist position. Here it may be helpful simply to note that it is crucial for this part of Raz's argument that the social institutions in question really do enjoy unanimous support. If any group of people in a political community practises polygamy rather than monogamy, for example, then legal recognition of the latter but not the former will indeed look like an attempt to get some to live the way of life favoured by others. While we have already seen that Raz has reasons why this may indeed be justified (if, that is, a monogamous life is indeed more valuable than a polygamous one – something which Raz himself does not assert), it is important to note that these are quite distinct from the point he is making here.

Raz's remarks about the possibility of unanimity take us back to the problem we identified in Rawls's position, which argues for anti-perfectionism via the desirability of a political community that is publicly justifiable. As we pointed out, and as Raz's example shows, these two aspects of his position can come apart. While it may be 'reasonable' for people to disagree about how they should live their sexual lives, there is no reason why such disagreement should be regarded as inevitable and permanent. In some societies, Raz claims, there is unanimity on the value of monogamy. If a particular non-political ideal, such as monogamous marriage, enjoys unanimous support in a society, then clearly it can be justified publicly, without appeal to any controversial doctrine and, in that case, Rawls would seem to have lost the reason to hang on to his anti-perfectionism. As we observed in our earlier discussion, either Rawls's anti-perfectionism is circumstantial, applicable only if and to the extent that people disagree, in which case he can have no objection to the kind of perfectionism proposed by Raz here, or his commitment to the freedom of the individual to live the life of her choice without any kind of interference from the state is not in fact grounded in the desire for public justifiability.

The second anti-perfectionist confusion is the view that state 'interference' which the perfectionist is prepared to countenance must involve coercion. Again we are touching on a point directly raised by the new Rawls, for the reader will recall that it was the distinctive nature of the political relationship, that it necessarily involves the coercive use of state power, that led, via the need for public justifiability, to his anti-perfectionist conclusions. For Raz, on the other hand:

not all perfectionist action is a coercive imposition of a style of life. Much of it could be encouraging and facilitating action of the desired kind, or discouraging undesired modes of behaviour. Conferring honours on creative and performing artists, giving grants or loans to people who start community centres, taxing one kind of leisure activity, e.g., hunting, more heavily than others are all cases in which political action in pursuit of conceptions of the good falls far short of the threatening popular image of imprisoning people who follow their religion, express their views in public, grow long hair, or consume harmless drugs. (*MF*, p. 161)

Indeed, our example of legal recognition of marriage could already have been used to show that there can be perfectionism without coercion. After all, the state does not force people to get married, and it can support marriage in many ways without criminalizing polygamy.

Later in this chapter we shall see that Raz thinks that some reasons can justify coercive action by the state, and a fuller discussion of this issue will have to wait until then. Here it may be helpful just to make a couple of introductory observations on the simple point that he makes here. The essence of his argument, which is surely right, is that there is a big difference between locking a person up if he performs (or fails to perform) certain actions, and using taxation or subsidy to discourage (or encourage) his performance of those actions. The former involves coercion in a way that the latter does not, and, since Raz's central value is autonomy, which seems straightforwardly to require the absence of coercion, it is not hard to see why this difference is important to him. Granted that a distinction between these two kinds of state action can be made, however, it is worth pointing out the issues raised by any attempt to do so, if only because they allow us to see why the anti-perfectionist might object even to the apparently innocuous non-coercive action that Raz endorses.

In the first place, it is undeniable that taxation and subsidy involve the deliberate alteration of the costs and benefits attaching to particular actions, and this already suggests a couple of problems. To begin with, it would seem that the the obvious way to think about the concept of coercion is in terms of the deliberate attaching of a sanction or penalty to a particular action: 'If you do not cut your hair, we will send you to prison' would seem to be a paradigm example of a coercive threat. What is the difference, the anti-perfectionist might ask, between this, which Raz acknowledges to be coercive, and the statement 'If you do not stop hunting, the state will tax you heavily,' which he argues is not. Clearly, the penalty for non-compliance is greater in the first case than in the second, but it is not obvious that this is a difference of quality rather than of quantity, that it warrants calling one coercion and the other not. Raz discusses at length the question of what makes a threat coercive, and we do not mean to suggest that he has no answer; it is our purpose only to alert the reader to the fact that there is an interesting issue here.

In addition to this, however, even if we allow that we can distinguish between coercive and non-coercive sanctions, this will not save taxation and subsidy from conflicting with the anti-perfectionist intuition that *any* deliberate alteration of the costs and benefits attaching to particular actions invades autonomy. The easiest way to see this as a distinct point is to consider cases of subsidy rather than taxation, since it is hard to argue that *reducing* the costs of an activity can amount to coercion. The thought here is that the state's decision to subsidize the arts, for example, while clearly not coercive, nonetheless involves an interference with people's choices, the introduction of deliberate bias into the options from which people choose to make their lives, which contravenes respect for their auto-nomy. If a life with art is more valuable than one without, should not people make this judgement for themselves, without artificial incentives to live one rather than another? The suggestion is that, even if not coercive, subsidy and taxation involve manipulation. If they do, then Raz concedes that they would be autonomy-invading: 'Manipulation, unlike coercion, does not interfere with a person's options. Instead it perverts the way that person reaches decisions, forms preferences or adopts goals. It too is an invasion of auto-nomy . . .' (*MF*, pp. 377–8). We have already seen why Raz thinks that respect for citizens cannot require that the state should ignore moral considerations in its dealings with them. But the idea that citizens are shown more respect, are better able to exercise their capacity for autonomy, if they are left to make up their own minds, without interference, about the value of different ways of life than if they make their choices in an environment biased by the state's judgements is not absurd.

In the second place, there is the crucial point that all state action involves taxation and taxation is compulsory. Even if we grant that perfectionist state action need not be *used* coercively, but merely to promote particular valuable ways of life, the fact is that the money used to do the promoting has been *raised* coercively. In the last resort, the penalty attaching to non-payment of taxation is imprisonment, so what happens when the state decides to tax some activities and subsidize others is that it is using its coercive power to enforce its judgements about the relative merits of different activities. We shall see later that Raz acknowledges this, and argues that taxation, since compulsory, is only justified where coercion is so. For now the point is simply to be clear that the state's encouragement of artistic pursuits does involve coercion, even though, of course, nobody is forced to go to the theatre.

Autonomy and value pluralism

The third and final notion that might lead one to endorse anti-perfectionism and that Raz rejects is the idea that perfectionism implies that the state will be permitted to give its approval to one, morally approved, style of life, and suppress all others. Perfection-ism, it might seem, goes together with a rigoristic moral outlook which holds one particular set of ideals to be valid and requires government to promote that set alone, suppressing the ideals held by those who are not in power. For Raz, on the contrary, perfection-ism is consistent with moral pluralism, which allows that 'there are many morally valuable forms of life which are incompatible with each other' (*MF*, p. 161). The anti-sceptical claim that some con-ceptions of the good are valid and some are not does not mean that only one set of ideals is so. We can know that the life of an artist is valuable and that of a foxhunter is not without knowing that the former is the only valuable form of life. If there are many valuable ways of life, then the state can be perfectionist and pluralist.

Here Raz's negative arguments against anti-perfectionism overlap with the more positive articulation of the concept of autonomy that lies at the heart of his liberalism. We have already seen his view that autonomy is only valuable if it is exercised in pursuit of the good, and this means that the ideal of autonomy requires only the availability of morally acceptable options. It is important now to see what this does not imply: 'This may sound a very rigoristic moral view, which it is not. A moral theory which recognises the value of autonomy inevitably upholds a pluralistic view. It admits the value of a large number of greatly differing pursuits among which individuals are free to choose.' (*MF*, p. 381). In contrast to the view that what matters is just that people choose for themselves how they live their lives and not what they choose, Raz's claim that autonomy is only valuable if exercised in pursuit of the good might seem to warrant state interference, even if not coercion, in support of a single set of options, a single conception of what makes life valuable. What rules out this implication is the relation between autonomy and pluralism.

Raz's discussion of value pluralism contains many different strands of argument, and our focus on its relation to autonomy picks out one of these in particular. It is important to acknowledge this because the strand on which we shall concentrate presents the case for pluralism in rather an unusual form. A more straightforward and direct line of argument would claim that there are many incompatible valuable forms of life, and that it follows from this that a state concerned to promote the valuable autonomy of its citizens has no reason to favour any particular one. While his chapter on the incommensurability of values does present an argument with this general shape, the particular train of thought we shall look at here seeks to establish a more distinctive position. The more usual argument allows him to reach his pluralistic conclusion but it regards the claim that a life is only valuable if it is in pursuit of a valid ideal that has been autonomously chosen, and the claim that there are many conflicting such ideals, as quite separate. The peculiar and particularly interesting feature of the argument we shall outline here is the way it seeks to establish an internal relation between these two claims. As he puts it: . . . 'if autonomy is an ideal then we are committed to such a view of morality: valuing autonomy leads to the endorsement of moral pluralism' (*MF*, p. 399). His conception of autonomy seems to presuppose the truth of moral pluralism, not merely to be compatible with it.

The crucial step in Raz's argument is the claim that a person's life can only be autonomous and valuable if the person living it has a variety of morally acceptable options to choose from. If this is right, then it follows that if valuable autonomy is to be possible then moral pluralism must be true. It is relatively unproblematic to see why a person cannot be autonomous unless she has choices to make.

'The ruling idea behind the ideal of personal autonomy is that people should make their own lives' (*MF*, p. 369) and it is hard to see how someone who has only one option available to her can be thought of as fitting this description. But it should be clear that the mere availability of options is not sufficient to establish Raz's claim, for this would be satisfied by a situation in which a person has a variety of options from which to choose but only one of them is good, which is exactly what the monist, the person who thinks that there is only one valuable way of life, asserts, and exactly what Raz is arguing against.

To understand why Raz thinks that autonomy requires a choice between *good* options we need only to see that he regards the choice between good and evil as no choice at all. Someone with the choice between becoming an electrician and having to murder someone is not choosing autonomously if he chooses to become an electrician, for his choice is forced. If he is to be moral, then he has no choice. Just as autonomy cannot be achieved by a person whose every thought and action is concerned with avoiding death, with the fight for physical survival, so it cannot be obtained by a person who is constantly fighting for what Raz calls 'moral survival' (*MF*, p. 380).

This argument is so simple that it resists any elucidation. What is happening here is that Raz is further enriching his ideal of autonomy, and further distinguishing it from any thin notion, associated with anti-perfectionism, such as the individual's mere capacity to choose for herself how she lives her life. Not only is autonomy only valuable in pursuit of the good, it is only autonomy if a plurality of valuable options are available, so that the agent is choosing between goods. The thickness of Raz's ideal autonomy ties in with our observation about the unusual structure of his case for pluralism, for the more controversial that ideal, the more surprising it is to find an argument for pluralism that takes its validity as a premise. Raz's argument says that if autonomy, thickly understood, is to be possible, then value must be plural. Just as the anti-perfectionist may reject the claim that autonomy is only valuable in pursuit of the good, so the monist may simply deny that autonomy in Raz's strong sense is possible. We do not at all mean to suggest that either would be right to do so, our point is just that a lot of work is being done by the notion of autonomy. Here, as we have seen, it is spelled out in a way that not only renders it compatible with value pluralism but presupposes that doctrine. That is why, first appearances to the contrary, Raz's perfectionism by no means warrants the state seeking to promote a particular way of life above all others.

Autonomy, social forms and state perfectionism

The arguments so far are negative in the sense that they are intended to show why perfectionism does not have some of the counter-intuitive implications that would tell against it. The general thrust of the previous section has been to argue that the state *can*, contrary intuitions notwithstanding, be justified in acting in pursuit of perfectionist ideals. This raises the question of why the state *should* act in such ways, and it is to this aspect of Raz's position that we must now turn our attention. It is here that the communitarian strands in that position come to the fore: in arguing that personal well-being depends to a large extent on social forms, Raz accommodates the communitarian insistence on the priority of the social matrix to the individual. It is by adding to this the claim that political action is needed to ensure that such forms are and remain available, that he turns it into an argument for state perfectionism. We shall also see, at the end of this section, that Raz's recognition of the importance of social forms leads him rather further in a communitarian direction than might have been expected: autonomy, he argues, is only of value to people living in certain kinds of society, those whose social forms are such that they are based on individual choice. In order to keep things as clear as possible, we shall not in this section attempt to point out in any detail the various ways in which Raz's liberalism relates to the communitarian critique. Rather, we shall defer a full discussion of Raz's communitarian leanings until our final section, and concentrate here upon that aspect of his argument that links his recognition of the importance of the social matrix to the case for state perfectionism.

Well-being depends on social forms

The reasons for Raz's claim that 'A person's well-being depends to a large extent on success in socially defined and determined pursuits and activities' (*MF*, p. 309) can best be approached by dividing it into its two component sub-claims. First, that well-being depends important-antly upon success in one's comprehensive goals, and second, that comprehensive goals must be based on social forms of behaviour.

Comprehensive goals are, for Raz, the goals that people have, the ramifications of which pervade important dimensions of their lives, those that provide the structure within which their lesser goals are nested, that provide their lives with overall shape and orientation. If he is right to think, roughly speaking, that a person's well-being consists in the successful pursuit of her (valuable) goals then it is easy to see why success in her comprehensive goals (assuming they are valuable) will be the major source of her well-being. It is hard to characterize this conception of well-being, itself a notoriously slippery concept, except by regarding it as occupying a kind of middle ground between two diametrically opposed views, one of which holds that a person's life can go well even if she is not content in her situation, even if she does not willingly accept the goals set for her, the other of which holds that something is only valuable for a person if it seems so to her. If we accept that when we consider a person's well-being we are considering how good or successful her life is from her point of view, then it would seem clear that this is a question of how she is doing in relation to the (valuable) goals that she has set herself. If I decide to devote my life to becoming a concert pianist, in such a way that it becomes a comprehensive goal for me, then it seems plausible to hold that my well-being depends, at least in large part, on my success in the venture.

It is the claim that 'a person can have a comprehensive goal only if it is based on existing social forms ie on forms of behaviour which are in fact widely practised in his society' (*MF*, p. 308) that most clearly brings Raz's position into contact with some of the communitarian strands of argument that we have looked at. He presents two kinds of reason in support of it. First, there is the point that the significance of individual behaviour depends on the existence of social forms. While this is most obvious in the case of activities that directly involve social institutions – 'one cannot pur-sue a legal career except in a society governed by law, one cannot practise medicine except in a society in which such a practice is recognized . . .' (*MF*, p. 310) – the idea that what my actions *mean* depends necessarily upon the social or cultural practices and con-ventions that surround them embraces less thoroughly institutionalized areas also. Although any sighted person in the vicinity of birds can watch them, this does not make him into a bird watcher. To be that he must live in a society that recognizes bird watching, or something like it, as a leisure activity, that has certain attitudes to nature, and so on. What it means to be a bird watcher depends upon the inevitably social environment of significance that surrounds the activity of watching birds. Comprehensive goals, those that pervade important dimensions of a person's life, are inevitably going to be bound up with, perhaps straightforwardly to instantiate, social forms in this way.

Not only do the activities of individuals derive their meaning from society, but also, and this is Raz's second point, individuals can only acquire and maintain goals through continuous familiarity with social forms. We learn how to be friends, for example not through any process of explicit instruction – indeed, the conventions governing appropriate behaviour in specific friendship contexts, for example, are too dense to be codified – but through an ongoing process of participation in and observation of the social form of friendship. Micro-sociologists who study the minutiae of personal interaction tell us, what we already know but leave unspoken, that the development of a relationship between two people depends upon the significance of thousands of tiny bits of body language. As Raz says:

> All these are derived from the common culture, from the shared social forms, and though they receive the individual stamp of each person, their foundation in shared social forms is continuing and lasting. Just as the eye continues to guide the hand all the way to its target, and is not limited to determining its original trajectory, so our continued awareness of the common culture continuously nourishes and directs our behaviour in pursuit of our goals. (*MF*, p. 312)

Raz can hardly be accused of grounding his liberalism in an asocial individualism of the kind to which communitarians object.

It is important to see that there are two things that Raz is not claiming. First, he is very clear that his argument for the dependence of personal well-being on social forms is 'not a conventionalist thesis. It does not claim that whatever is practised with social approval is for that reason valuable' (*MF*, p. 310). We should have expected him to take this position: just as a person can be wrong about what is good for her, and her belief in the value of a goal does not make it valuable, so the same is true of societies. Second, the fact that a person's comprehensive goals will necessarily be derived from social forms does not mean that there is no place for deviation from, or even transcendence of, existing conventions. His thesis that comprehensive goals are inevitably based on socially existing forms is meant to be consistent with experimentation and with variations on a common theme, and sometimes these may be so extensive as to constitute real innovation.

> It is not that a person cannot, through the development of his own variations and combinations, transcend the social form. People can, and sometimes do, do this, but inevitably in such cases the distance they have travelled away from the shared forms is, in these cases, the most significant aspect of their situation. It more than anything else then determines the significance of their situation and its possibilities for those people. (*MF*, pp. 312–13)

Deviations from social forms always derive their meaning from the matrix of meanings in which they are embedded, a matrix that is itself necessarily social. Although the individual is not bound by existing practices, nor can she only live a valuable life if she goes along with them, she cannot escape the social web of significance.

Since, as we saw above, autonomy requires the availability of a variety of valuable options, and since, as we have just seen, valuable options depend in large part on social forms, it follows that autonomy requires the existence of a variety of social forms. If Raz is right, then the liberal ideal of individual autonomy is nothing like as individualistic as it seems:

> ... autonomy is only possible if various collective goods are available. The opportunity to form a family of one kind or another, to forge friendships, to pursue many of the skills, professions and occupations, to enjoy fiction, poetry, and the arts, to engage in many of the common leisure activities: these and others require an appropriate common culture to make them possible and valuable. (*MF*, p. 247)

Without getting into the details of Raz's understanding of what makes a good 'collective' and his more general rejection of what he calls 'moral individualism', we can see the general thrust of his position. Since 'the provision of many collective goods is constitutive of the very possibility of autonomy' (*MF*, p. 207), we are a long way indeed from any form of liberalism that builds upon the abstract individual and neglects the role of the community in providing the conditions necessary if individuals are to live valuable lives.

Even things as apparently individualistic as rights are given a communitarian defence. First Raz rejects the idea that people have a right to autonomy:

> A right to autonomy can be had only if the interest of the right-holder justifies holding members of the society at large to be duty-bound to him to provide him with the social environment necessary to give him a chance to have an autonomous life. Assuming that the interests of one person cannot justify holding so many to be subject to potentially burdensome duties . . . it follows that there is no right to personal autonomy. (*MF*, p. 247)

For Raz, as we have just seen, collective goods are constitutive of the very possibility of autonomy, yet no individual can have a right to collective goods, for that would imply implausibly onerous duties. It follows that no individual can have the right to autonomy.

Rather than being tied to an individualistic picture of the relation between the individual and society, however, rights should be conceived and defended in terms that relate to their contribution to the public culture. Raz argues

> that the liberal tradition is not unequivocally individualistic, and that some of the typically liberal rights depend for their value on the existence of a certain public culture, which their protection serves to defend and promote . . . their role is not in articulating fundamental moral or political principles, nor in the protection of individualistic personal interests of absolute weight. It is to maintain and protect the fundamental moral and political culture of a community through specific institutional arrangements or political conventions. (*MF*, p. 245)

In contrast to the asocially individualistic liberal scheme, which would see rights such as freedom of expression, association and assembly, of the press and of religion, as grounded ultimately in the freedom of the pre-social individual, Raz holds that these rights are really justified as helping to promote goods that are inherently social, such as the good of an open society. For him 'the importance of liberal rights is in their service to the public good' (*MF*, p. 256).

Social forms require perfectionist political action

Granted that personal autonomy requires the availability of an adequate range of acceptable options and that such options depend necessarily upon social forms, how does this justify state perfectionism? Raz's answer is that the state must do what it can to ensure that its citizens live autonomous lives and that perfectionist political action is needed to sustain those social forms necessary for autonomy. It is the duty of the state to promote the well-being of its citizens, and without state action there will not be the social preconditions of such well-being. Here, then, we have in effect two quite distinct claims, one a normative argument concerning the proper role of the state, what the state is permitted to do for its citizens, and one an empirical claim concerning the necessity of its doing it.

On the first, the point about political action, and what lies at the bottom of Rawls's anti-perfectionism, is that it involves coercion, and Raz is quite prepared to acknowledge this. Although, as we saw, Raz is keen to point out that perfectionist goals need not be pursued by the use of coercion, that the government can encourage activities by non-coercive means such as subsidy and advertisement, he at the same time recognizes the point that we made earlier:

> It is no objection to point out that the funds necessary for all these policies are raised by compulsory taxation. I assume that tax is raised to provide adequate opportunities, and is justified by the principle of autonomy in a way consistent with the harm principle . . . The government has an obligation to create an environment providing individuals with an adequate range of options and the opportunities to use them. The duty arises out of people's interest in having a valuable autonomous life . . . A tax which cannot be justified by the argument outlined here should not be raised. (*MF*, pp. 417–18)

For Raz, coercion is justified as long as it is used to enforce the duty to provide people with the conditions of autonomy, for then it will be consistent with the harm principle. We shall now see what he means by this.

According to Raz, we all have autonomy-based duties, duties to provide one another with the conditions of autonomy, and the state is justified in using coercion to enforce these duties, for, and here we again glimpse his theory of authority, it is then only discharging on our behalf obligations that we have in any case. There are three kinds of condition of autonomy and correspondingly three kinds of duty. It is relatively straightforward to see that in order to be autonomous people need to be independent, to be free from coercion and manipulation, and this leads to the standard liberal duty to refrain from coercing and manipulating others and the standard justification of state action to ensure that we do so. To this Raz adds two further conditions and duties. First, there are those conditions that he describes as 'mental abilities'. We all have duties to

> help in creating the inner capacities required for the conduct of an autonomous life. Some of these concern cognitive capacities, such as the power to absorb, remember and use information, reasoning abilities, and the like. Others concern one's emotional and imaginative make-up. Still others concern health, and physical abilities and skills. Finally, there are character traits essential or helpful for a life of autonomy. They include stability, loyalty and the ability to form personal attachments and to maintain intimate relationships. (*MF*, p. 408)

The second additional condition of autonomy we have already touched on in our discussion of the relation between autonomy and pluralism: for Raz a person cannot be autonomous unless she has available to her an adequate range of valuable options. This gives rise to an autonomy-based duty to create for all people an adequate range of valuable options from which to choose.

There are, then, three kinds of condition of autonomy, three kinds of autonomy-based duty, and three kinds of reason why the state might be justified in using coercion. For Raz, and contrary to appearances, these do not contravene the traditional liberal view, famously formulated by Mill and usually referred to as the 'harm principle', which asserts that the only justification for coercively interfering with a person is to prevent harm to others. Once we see that one can harm another by denying her what is due to her, that someone who fails to fulfil his autonomy-based obligations towards another is harming her, even if the obligations are designed to promote her autonomy rather than to prevent its deterioration, then

> It follows that a government whose responsibility is to promote the autonomy of its citizens is entitled to redistribute resources, to provide public goods and to engage in the provision of other services on a

compulsory basis, provided its laws merely reflect and make concrete autonomy-based duties of its citizens. If the law reflects autonomy-based duties then failure to comply harms others and the harm principle is satisfied. (*MF*, p. 417)

The state can coercively enforce people's autonomy-based duties to provide one another with the conditions of autonomy and this is consistent with the harm principle properly understood.

It may be helpful to point out a possible difference between the first two kinds of condition (or duty) and the third: the former can be argued to be consistent with anti-perfectionism, as not involving the state in judgements about the relative merits of different ways of life, in a way that the latter cannot. This is obvious in the case of the duty to refrain from coercion or manipulation, but applies also to the provision of the mental capacities necessary for autonomy. The advocate of autonomy who rejects Raz's view that it is appropriate for the state to act on judgements as to the relative merits of different forms of life, might nonetheless think it proper for the state to provide people with whatever they need to make their own choices. One does not have to be a perfectionist to support taxation for health care and education, one need only hold that physical and mental health, and the capacity to acquire, process and rationally reflect upon information, are conditions of an agent's being able to make genuinely autonomous choices. Similarly, it is quite usual for the anti-perfectionist to advocate redistributive taxation on the grounds that autonomy requires a certain level of control over material resources. In principle, there is no reason why she should not recognize that autonomy requires other abilities also: perhaps, for example, one can only make an autonomous choice between two courses of action if one has the capacity to imagine what it would be like to choose each course. What is crucial about all these cases, however, is that here the state is using coercion to provide people with the conditions of autonomy without making any judgements as to the value of particular options that people might choose.

Of course, Raz's particular list of the inner capacities necessary for autonomy might well be disputed by the anti-perfectionist. It might be argued that, by including, for example, particular character traits such as loyalty, he so enriches or thickens the concept of autonomy as to obscure the distinction between the conditions of choosing and proper objects of choice. For Raz of course, since there is no reason to make that distinction, this is not a problem, and we may well feel that the very recognition that not just any choice can count as an autonomous one already sets the anti-perfectionist on a slippery slope which leads unavoidably to a rejection of the distinction with which she started. While the anti-perfectionist might seek to argue that the state can support the arts purely on the grounds that they promote the capacities necessary for people to make autonomous choices, and without making the perfectionist judgement that people choosing to go to art galleries or theatres are making better choices than those frequenting casinos, that the arts come in, along with education, solely as providing people with what they need to make their own autonomous choices in a neutral framework, we might have doubts about whether such a position can be sustained. Since there is clearly here the judgement that a life with the arts is better than one without, what reason do we have to deny that theatre-going is more valuable than gambling?

Whatever one's conclusions on such matters, it is the third condition and coercively enforceable duty that is most clearly distinctive of Raz's approach, and it is here that we can begin to think about our second question, that which concerns whether it is necessary for the state to act if people are to have the conditions of autonomy. While the anti-perfectionist need perhaps have no problem with the idea of taxation for health, education and even straightforward redistribution of resources, and can acknowledge that the state must tax for these reasons if its citizens are to be autonomous, she must clearly resist the idea that the state can use its coercive power to provide people with an adequate range of valuable options, for that necessarily involves the state in the business of acting on judgements as to which options are valuable. Raz's empirical claim is thus crucial:

> Supporting valuable forms of life is a social rather than an individual matter. Monogamy, assuming that it is the only morally valuable form of marriage, cannot be practised by an individual. It requires a culture which recognises it, and which supports it through the public's attitude and through its formal institutions . . . perfectionist ideals require public action for their viability. Anti-perfectionism in practice would lead not merely to a political stand-off from support for valuable conceptions of the good. It would undermine the chances of survival of many cherished aspects of our culture. (*MF*, p. 162)

We said in our Introduction that the kind of neutrality sought by the anti-perfectionist liberal was not neutrality of effect or consequences but that of justification or intention, and this suggests that she might seek simply to dismiss the relevance of this kind of consideration. If it is simply inappropriate to take consequences into account when evaluating a political theory, then Raz would seem to be missing the point. On the other hand, of course, to those, like him, who hold that consequences *are* relevant, recognition of the fact that the justificatorily neutral state will not be neutral in its effects seems to open the door to a different approach. Since we are not confronted with a choice between a state with effects and one without, the question can only be whether we should take those effects into account when thinking about state action. And if we should, it may be hard to see why we should not seek to achieve good ones rather than bad. Granted that considerations of this kind are relevant, and if Raz is right to think that valuable options require perfectionist political action, then it would seem that the anti-perfectionist faces a real problem. If the cost of anti-perfectionism is indeed the withering away of cherished aspects of our culture, then the anti-perfectionist may feel the need to rethink her position.

But is he right? We can grant the point that valuable ways of life require social and cultural recognition, support, and even institutionalization, without conceding that political action is necessary for their survival. Consider all those associations and organizations that exist below or above the level of the state and of which the anti-perfectionist Rawls was so keen to remind us, such as churches or scientific associations. Surely these promote and sustain valuable forms of life within a neutral framework and without requiring state support. Raz's own example of bird watching is clearly an example of a valuable social form which can survive without state action. Is Raz too quick in jumping from his recognition of the dependence of valuable ways of life, and hence of autonomy, on *social* forms to the claim that this warrants perfectionist political action by the *state*? It is true that some valuable social forms may derive part of their significance from the very fact that they are endorsed or recognized by the state. It is arguable that part of what makes marriage the institution that it is in our culture is precisely the fact that it is the form of sexual union that enjoys official state support and encouragement. Social forms of this kind, what we might call inherently political forms, would indeed lose or change their meaning in an anti-perfectionist state, but it is hard to see that this point is very wide in its application.

The thought that perfectionist action may not be necessary after all gains strength when we remember that even if some valuable forms of life would indeed fail to survive without state support, this is not enough for Raz's argument to justify coercive action on their behalf. For people to be autonomous they need only to have available an adequate range of options, and this means that there is no justification for the state's using coercive action to support valuable options if there would be an adequate range even without such action. The anti-perfectionist may acknowledge that it would be a problem for her position if the society she advocates was likely to fail to provide people with a range of valuable ways of life to live, but she may respond simply that it is unlikely; that even if *some* ways of life would disappear, Raz's own argument would not justify state action on their behalf. Such action would only be justified if society, in the absence of state action, failed to sustain an adequate range of valuable options.

Clearly it might matter a great deal what counts as 'adequate', and it is true that Raz has rather a wide notion of adequacy: 'To be autonomous and to have an autonomous life, a person must have options which enable him to sustain throughout his life activities which, taken together, exercise all the capacities human beings have an innate drive to exercise, as well as to decline to develop any of them' (*MF*, p. 375). But even on this definition, and even granting that these 'innate drives' include the drive to engage our imagination and to occupy our mind, it is not clear that Raz has any reason to worry about the loss of that perhaps rather limited set of valuable options whose continued survival depends upon state action on their behalf. Even if it were the case that opera, for example, would not survive without state subsidy, and even if opera is one of the most valuable and cherished forms currently available to people, it would be hard to argue that a society without opera fails to provide its members with an adequate range of valuable options from which to choose.

Two aspects of this point are worth emphasizing. First, we assume that when Raz talks about the duty to provide one another with the conditions of autonomy, he has in mind some sort of threshold notion; that there is a range of options, hard to define but in principle definable, that is sufficient for someone to be autonomous even if there is another set of of options that would enable him to live a more valuable life. The point here is that one does not have to deny that a life with opera is more valuable than one without in order to deny that, on Raz's own account, the state is justified in coercing people to provide one another with opera. The alternative would be the view that we have a coercively enforceable duty to provide one another with as valuable a life as is possible, which is surely too strong. Second, it may well be that our focus on the issue of the survival of valuable forms, although encouraged by Raz himself, misses the real impact of his position. Even if an adequate range of valuable forms would survive without state support, it might be argued, they would do so in such a way that they are available only to a wealthy elite. If some forms of art must be available to people for them to be autonomous, they must really be available, not just present somewhere in the society at prohibitive cost. Political action, according to this line of argument, is needed not so much to secure the survival of a valuable range of options as to give people the opportunities to enjoy them. But this raises again the question of why such action must be perfectionist in the sense identified as specific to the third condition of autonomy, why this must involve judgements as to the relative value of different options. If we grant that valuable forms will survive without state support, and argue that such support is needed only to give people effective opportunities to choose them, then it looks as if this could done simply by the kind of egalitarian redistribution of resources that is consistent with anti-perfectionism. This is the beginning rather than the end of the argument, and we do not mean to suggest that Raz has no response. Perhaps the kind of egalitarian redistribution envisaged would itself lead to the withering away of valuable forms, so that their survival depends on the same unequal distribution of resources that puts them beyond the reach of most people. In that case the anti-perfectionist's move to avoid the unpalatable consequences of her position may be unavailable to her: if all people are to have genuine access to valuable art forms, then state action to subsidize those forms specifically, involving judgements as to their value, may be necessary after all. These are complex and difficult issues which we cannot address here. Our aim is only to point out their existence.

We have seen, then, that Raz thinks that the state is justified in using its coercive power of taxation to support valuable social forms because the availability of an adequate range of such forms is a condition of autonomy and because the very fact that they are social means that they will not survive without such support. Having raised some questions about this aspect of his argument, we can now turn to what we can think of as the other side of the coin. If the state can use coercion to encourage some ways of life, can it do so to discourage others? We saw early on in the chapter his claim that the autonomy principle permits and even requires governments to eliminate repugnant opportunities, and it is now time to see what he means by this. Should the state tolerate repugnant options?

We have already seen that Raz thinks that autonomy is only valuable in pursuit of the good. In fact, he argues the stronger claim that autonomously doing wrong is worse than doing it non-autonomously:

> Has autonomy any value qua autonomy when it is abused? Is the autonomous wrongdoer a morally better person than the non-autonomous wrongdoer? Our intuitions rebel against such a view. It is surely the other way round. The wrongdoing casts a deeper shadow on its perpetrator if it is autonomously done by him. A murderer who was led to his deed by the foreseen inner logic of his autonomously chosen career is morally worse than one who murders because he momentarily succumbs to the prospect of an easy gain. (*MF*, p. 380)

It would seem to follow that the state would be promoting the well-being of its citizens if it banned bad options. If, as Raz thinks, there are some options that one is better off not having, if autonomously choosing the bad makes one's life worse than a comparable non-autonomous life, then there would seem to be no reason to desist from using coercion to prevent people making such choices.

In fact, Raz resists such a conclusion. Even though one cannot defend pursuit of the morally repugnant from coercive interference on the ground that being an autonomous choice endows it with value, nonetheless such interference violates the autonomy of its victim, and in two ways.

> First, it violates the condition of independence and expresses a relation of domination and an attitude of disrespect for the coerced individual. Second, coercion by criminal penalties is a global and indiscriminate invasion of autonomy . . . there is no practical way of ensuring that the coercion will restrict the victims' choice of repugnant options but will not interfere with their other choices. (*MF*, pp. 418–19)

This is surprising. The second consideration, the idea that it is impossible to stop choosing bad options without interfering with her choice of others, seems to depend on contingencies, but it at least makes sense in the context of Raz's overall argument. The first, on the other hand, seems to go against the whole thrust of his position. If people derive no well-being from bad choices, what is it about autonomy that means we should respect the individual's autonomous but bad choice? What happened to the idea that respect for people cannot require us to ignore moral considerations in our dealings with them?

Although it looks as if Raz is here endorsing, willy-nilly, that understanding of autonomy that means that there is value in the very fact of the individual choosing for herself, all is not what it seems. As the following passage makes clear, it is only because the state is likely to make mistakes in its judgements as to which options are immoral that coercive action based on such judgements violates the independence of agents who might choose them. *Both* the first and the second points depend on contingent facts; namely

> the non-existence at the present time of means of coercion which do not infringe autonomy, and the fact that conditions justify suspecting governments of lacking respect for individuals. What if it became possible to coerce people to avoid immoral but harmless conduct without restricting them in any other way; suppose we had institutions which could be relied on to do so only to stop immoralities, and would not mistake what is worthwhile for what is evil nor would they abuse their power? They would be free from suspicion that they do not respect their subjects. In such a case both the conditions of adequacy of options and of independence will be satisfied. (*MF*, p. 419)

This scepticism about the government's ability to make the right judgements about which ways of life are immoral, which is one of his two reasons for rejecting coercive action to prevent people choosing repugnant options, sits oddly alongside his rejection of such scepticism about its ability correctly to identify valuable forms of life. While he rather backs away from his early claim that the state may be permitted and even required to eliminate repugnant opportunities, at least if we assume that 'elimination' involves coercion, Raz's reasons for doing so are in both cases oddly, though avowedly, contingent and in one case apparently contrary to the anti-scepticism on which his perfectionism depends.

Autonomy only conditionally valuable

One further, and at first sight surprising, aspect of Raz's position, relevant to our general theme here, can be presented very quickly. Given the whole-hearted endorsement of the ideal of personal autonomy that pervades Raz's argument, it comes as rather a shock to be told, initially in a footnote, that 'not everyone has an interest in autonomy. It is a cultural value ie of value to people living in certain societies only' (*MF*, p. 189 n. 1). The reason, however, lies in the very claim presented above, and the implications of which we have just been discussing; namely, that personal well-being is dependent on social forms. It is because our social forms are autonomy-presupposing that autonomy is necessary for our well-being.

This aspect of Raz's position can give his formulations an air of resignation rather than exaltation, as if autonomy were something we have to put up with, something demanded of us by the society in which we live, rather than, as it might seem to liberals of a more universalistic kind, the realization of our essential nature. As he puts it:

> For those who live in an autonomy-supporting environment there is no choice but to be autonomous, there is no other way to prosper in such a society ... The value of personal autonomy is a fact of life. Since we live in a society whose social forms are to a considerable extent based on individual choice, and since our options are limited by what is available in our society, we can prosper in it only if we can be successfully autonomous. (*MF*, pp. 391, 394)

Our institution of marriage, to take our by now familiar example, has built into its very nature the idea that people have chosen their partners for themselves; one cannot prosper in that institution if one's marriage has been arranged.

In other kinds of society, however, where social forms do not presuppose or depend upon the value of autonomy, one can live a successful and valuable non-autonomous life: 'Autonomy is, to be sure, inconsistent with various alternative forms of valuable lives. It cannot be obtained within societies which support social forms which do not leave enough room for individual choice' (*MF*, p. 395). While, as we have already seen, Raz denies the conventionalist thesis that 'whatever is practised with social approval is for that reason valuable', and while he thinks that a non-autonomous but morally worthy subculture can nonetheless be judged inferior to the dominant liberal culture in the midst of which its members may live, he is clearly sensitive to the relation between personal well-being and social or cultural context.

Raz and communitarianism

We have, in passing, made various observations about the extent to which Raz's liberalism recognizes and endorses aspects of the communitarian critique. In this last section we seek rather more systematically, and summarily, to identify the points of connection; once again, and for the last time, we shall organize our discussion around the five themes that have guided us from the beginning. In very broad terms, Raz is a liberal who clearly recognizes the senses in which the community is prior to the individual. Where Rawls's political liberalism can be read as communitarian specifically in that it regards a certain kind of community, one publicly justifiable to its citizens, as of overriding value, and as giving people a reason to refrain from using political action to support their particular conceptions of the good, Raz's perfectionist liberalism points rather to the extent to which those conceptions themselves depend upon social forms that require political support. While both regard the value of autonomy as central – this is what makes them both liberal – they understand that value in very different ways: for Rawls it requires an anti-perfectionist state, one that leaves citizens free to make their own judgements about how they should live their lives and does not seek to influence those judgements; for Raz it demands a range of valuable options, something that the state can use its coercive power to provide and that necessarily involves it in the business of discriminating between the valuable and the worthless.

Conception of the person

Although he does not use the term, much of Raz's argument can readily be seen to be relevant to this first theme, and it is clear that his understanding of autonomy does not commit him to anything like the views identified as endemic to liberalism by its communitarian critics. That his self is not emotivist in MacIntyre's sense will be seen under the heading of objectivism and subjectivism; that he recognizes Sandel's insistence on the extent to which it is our community that provides the social matrix that contributes to the constitution of our self-understandings will be dealt with in our observations on asocial individualism. Here we point out simply that Raz's autonomy not only does not rule out the possibility of attachments and commitments, but in fact requires them.

We already touched on this point when we presented his account of the inner abilities that are the among the conditions of autonomy, for the reader will recall that these included character traits such as stability, loyalty and the ability to form personal attachments and to maintain intimate relationships. Another passage indicates clearly how far Raz's autonomy is from the idea that the person is necessarily and always detached from her goals and projects:

> (Significantly) autonomous persons are those who can shape their life and determine its course. They are not merely rational agents who can choose between options after evaluating relevant information, but agents who can in addition adopt personal projects, develop relationships, and accept commitments to causes, through which their personal integrity and sense of dignity and self-respect are made concrete. Persons who are part creators of their own moral world have a commitment to projects, relationships, and causes which affect the kind of life that is for them worth living. (*MF*, p. 155)

Indeed, Raz goes so far as to say that, in extreme cases, an autonomous person may be so committed to a particular cause or project that certain actions, betraying or compromising that commitment, would render their life 'worthless or even impossible (in a moral sense)' (*MF*, p. 155). Clearly there is room here for Sandel's point that there are certain commitments that we cannot imagine ourselves not having, that we regard as constitutive of our identity.

He is similarly alert to MacIntyre's related emphasis on the importance of narrative unity to a person's life. Far from autonomy involving the notion of discrete moments of existential, arbitrary and radical choice, the fact that our life comprises the pursuit of goals means that it is sensitive to our past; the very fact that one has embraced certain commitments gives one new ways of succeeding and failing. Although one can be autonomous without imposing any particular unity on one's life, in that an autonomous life may consist of diverse and heterogeneous pursuits, one cannot be so without the capacity to form commitments and attachments that change one's subsequent reasons for action. It is partly because one has these reasons that Raz's account is immune from Sandel's charge that the liberal must regard the choice of how to live one's life as the mere expression of preference or non-rational desire.

> Saying 'I want to . . .' can be a way of indicating that one is committed to a project, that one has embraced a certain pursuit, cares about a relationship. It is . . . part of a valid reason for action, once the initial commitment has been made. In this usage it does not signify the existence of a particular mental state, a desire. It signifies a commitment, deep or shallow, to a pursuit, which may be limited or lasting or comprehensive. (*MF*, p. 389)

The understanding of the way a person relates to her ends implied by Raz's notion of autonomy is a long way from that criticized as implicit in the liberal commitment to individual freedom of choice.

Asocial individualism

It will already be clear that Raz's liberalism is not susceptible to the first communitarian charge that we identified under this heading. His claim that comprehensive goals, and hence personal well-being, depend on social forms clearly involves recognition of the idea that society is prior to the individual in the sense that it provides her with the matrix of significance within which she can come to acquire the goals and the identities that make her moral life possible. We can perhaps identify two distinct points here, for not only is it the case that we need society in order to pursue particular comprehensive goals but, as we saw at the end of our discussion, the very value of autonomy itself, that which requires as its condition an adequate range of valuable options is, so to speak, secreted by the social forms within which we live our lives. There is no incompatibility here with either Taylor's or MacIntyre's arguments for the importance of the social matrix.

The second, substantive, issue, it will be recalled, concerns liberalism's purported failure to attend to the importance of social ties that are more than those of association between individuals, and its blindness to, or at least downgrading of, the value of goods that are strongly communal in content, whether these goods be political or non-political. Here, although he says little explicitly on this point, it is clear that Raz does not think that the only good way to live one's life is as a family man, or as a member of a community of religious believers, or as a citizen participating in the common life of one's political community. So much is implied by his understanding of personal autonomy and its relation to value pluralism; if the communitarian claim is that there is one, strongly communal, valuable way of life, then Raz rejects it. If, on the other hand, the claim is just that there are valuable ways of life that are of this kind, then it would seem that Raz's perfectionism enables him not only to leave room for them as consistent with the liberal political framework, which is roughly Rawls's position, but also, unlike Rawls, to envisage political action on their behalf. If family life, for example, is indeed valuable, then it may be perfectly legitimate for the state to use social policies to support and promote it. A way of life whose content is essentially communal and which is indeed valuable (and of course its value would need to be established in the particular case) would be more likely to survive in Raz's perfectionist state than in Rawls's anti-perfectionist one, though Raz would have no place for any which conflicted with his central commitments to autonomy and pluralism.

More generally, Raz is suspicious of the whole idea that there is an essential tension between society and the interests of the individual. For him:

> ... individuals inevitably derive the goals by which they constitute their lives from the stock of social forms available to them, and the feasible variations on it. If those social forms are morally valid, if they enshrine sound moral conceptions, then it is easy for people generally to find themselves with, and to choose for themselves, goals which lead to a rough coincidence in their own lives of moral and personal concerns. In their careers, personal relations and other interests they will be engaged on activities which serve themselves and others at the same time. By being teachers, production workers, drivers, public servants, loyal friends and family people, loyal to their communities, nature loving, and so on, they will be pursuing their own goals, enhancing their own well-being, and also serving their communities, and generally living in a morally worthy way. (*MF*, p. 319)

While the first sentence claims that it is the social matrix that is the source of the individual's aims and purposes (which is our first strand), his insistence on the point that individual interests will tend to coincide, rather than conflict, with those of others in their community can be read as a variation on the idea (which constitutes our second strand) that valuable ways of life will be communal in content. By pointing out the extent to which the goals we have as individuals, the attainment of which constitutes our individual well-being, are connected to the service of others and of our community, so that even individual goods are in this sense communal in content, Raz calls into question the whole opposition between individual and community in a way that seems to transcend the terms of debate between liberal and communitarian.

Universality

The issue of whether Raz's liberalism is universal in its application, is applicable cross-culturally, is complicated. On the one hand, as we have seen, his recognition of the dependence of well-being on social forms leads him to hold that autonomy is only conditionally valuable, valuable only in societies whose forms are based on the value of individual choice, and that a person in a different kind of society can live a valuable life that is non-autonomous. On the other hand, he thinks that even a non-autonomy-supporting culture that is morally worthy, one that provides its members with social conditions that enable them to live valuable and successful lives, can nonetheless be judged inferior to our autonomy-supporting liberal culture. While it does not follow from that judgement that we would be justified in coercively wrenching people out of their non-autonomy-supporting communities, for those brought up in such communities will not have acquired the capacities necessary to live a successful autonomous life, Raz does think that a liberal culture can act gradually to assimilate such people, even at the cost of letting their illiberal culture die. The judgement that an autonomous life is better than a non-autonomous one does seem to be universal in its application. It just does not follow from this that the lives of those brought up in non-autonomy-supporting cultures will be improved by having autonomy thrust upon them.

Objectivism/subjectivism

That Raz's liberalism is not based in any subjectivist or sceptical meta-ethical position should be clear enough and requires only cursory restatement here. Where Rawls seeks neither to assert nor to deny any position on the status of moral judgements and pursues a strategy of avoidance, Raz's perfectionism follows in part from his view that some ways of life are objectively better than others and we can know which are which. Not only is the value of autonomy substantively endorsed, but his rejection of the view that judgements concerning the 'art of life', those pertaining to the goals and ends that constitute people's conceptions of the good, are any more doubtful than those concerning the requirements of justice or 'morality in its narrow sense', leads him to his perfectionist conclusions. Since we can know some ways of life to be valuable and others not, and since people derive well-being only from those which are valuable, we have no reason to ignore such knowledge even in our political dealings with others.

As we observed in our Introduction, there is a quite distinct issue which tends to arise alongside this meta-ethical question about the status of value judgements. This concerns the relation between the value of a person's life and its having been freely or autonomously chosen or endorsed by that person. Rather than grounding one's liberalism in the the meta-ethical claim that value judgements, or more specifically judgements concerning the relative merits of particular ways of life, are nothing more than expressions of preference, it might be argued substantively that what makes a person's life valuable is so closely related to her having autonomously chosen it as to make the fact of its being chosen or endorsed sufficient to endow it with value. We find it hard to make sense of such a view, and it is clear in any case that Raz has no time for it: a life that is freely endorsed can nonetheless be worthless. What matters to a person is not that she lives a life in the value of which she believes, but that she lives a life that she has reason to value, and her beliefs can be mistaken. The fact that mistakes are only possible if there is something to be right or wrong about makes clear how Raz's position on this second issue presupposes the rejection of any meta-ethical subjectivism or scepticism. While MacIntyre's characterization of contemporary liberal culture as essentially emotivist may be justified, Raz's brand of liberalism is firmly grounded in the repudiation such a view.

Anti-perfectionism/neutrality

The perfectionist character of Raz's liberalism has been so central to this chapter that it hardly needs further discussion here. The claims that the state has a duty to promote the well-being of its citizens, that well-being consists in the autonomous pursuit of valuable ways of life, and that valuable of ways of life are necessarily social in form, combine to yield the conclusion that governments can be justified in acting on judgements about the relative merits of the conceptions of the good espoused by their citizens. Rather than regarding the proper role of the state as that of guaranteeing a neutral framework within which citizens should be left to make their own choices without interference and bias, Raz holds that the state can be justified in acting to encourage particular ways of life and discourage others. While direct coercion in the name of particular ideals would be self-defeating given the centrality of autonomy to well-being, it is permitted and even required that the state should use compulsory taxation to provide its citizens with the conditions of autonomy. Since such conditions include not only freedom from coercion and manipulation, and certain mental capacities necessary for a choice to be regarded as genuinely autonomous, but also the availability of an adequate range of valuable options, it is clear that, at least in certain situations, perfectionist political action will be justified. Where Rawls thinks that a community that is publicly justifiable to its citizens is of such value that it can give those citizens reason to ignore, when it comes to politics, reasons arising from their comprehensive conceptions of the good, Raz holds that what matters is that people live valuable lives, and that it is appropriate that we should use politics to help them do so.

CONCLUSION

Having completed our exploration of liberal positions other than that of Rawls, we will bring this book to a close by attempting to specify what that widening of focus has added to our understanding of the debate between Rawlsian political liberalism and its communitarian critics.

In essence, it has shown that justice as fairness is under siege from (at least) two apparently different directions. In the first place, our evaluation of Rorty's anti-foundationalism suggests that it offers no hope of providing a version of liberalism that might avoid the difficulties encountered by Rawls in his own attempts to respect the limits of the purely political. Nothing that we met with in chapter 7 gives us any reason to alter our provisional conclusion at the end of chapter 6 that, if Rawls wishes to maintain a full-blooded commitment to anti-perfectionism in politics, he must draw upon and defend a comprehensive liberal moral doctrine of human well-being. There is no reason to think that a comprehensive anti-perfectionist doctrine of the requisite sophistication is not available to him; but by committing himself to it, Rawls deprives himself of the means with which to argue (as he has argued in the past) that the main elements of the communitarian critique of his theory of justice are ones that have no relevance to it. It may turn out that these criticisms can be dismissed as irrelevant or insufficiently powerful on other grounds, but they cannot be ignored for the reasons Rawls has hitherto offered. So, if we cannot be certain of the outcome of the next stage of this debate, we can at least venture the prediction that it will involve a more direct engagement between Rawls and those of his critics who are opposed to justice as fairness for the sorts of reason that we spelt out in part 1 of this book.

This renewed communitarian opposition would, of course, be mounted from a position that is in large part external to the liberal tradition; it would be an attack from a perspective opposed to some of liberalism's most central values. But in chapter 8, we saw that Rawls is also facing a fundamental attack from a fellow liberal. Raz shares Rawls's commitment to the view that individual autonomy is central to human well-being; but he argues that this value must be defended by drawing upon comprehensive moral doctrines *and* that it should be understood as requiring a perfectionist state – one that does not observe a split between the sphere of politics and that of private morality. Once again, predicting the outcome of this second, internecine debate is beyond the scope of our book; but we can at least claim to have clarified the main lines of argument in chapter 8.

We intend to end our discussions by offering a more substantial (even if extremely tentative) set of suggestions as to how the dispute between liberalism and communitarianism might be reformulated in the light of our investigations. This will not only permit us to make a small contribution to defining the direction, and maintaining the momentum, of the debate; it will also underline the degree to which liberalism is a broad church. In particular, it will demonstrate that forms of liberalism that are not anti-perfectionist might offer a very different – and perhaps a more elusive – target for communitarian fire from that of Rawlsian justice as fairness. For, as we stressed in chapter 8, Raz's perfectionist liberalism is not only a comprehensive doctrine: it is also strongly communitarian. In this way, we might come to see that the two directions from which Rawls is open to attack are not as unconnected as they appear.

We want to suggest that the array of communitarian criticisms of Rawlsian liberalism can be reinterpreted as being focused upon the substantive value of autonomy in human life to which Rawls now seems committed. The main reason for being sceptical of such a rereading of communitarianism is the following: it has standardly been taken to be distinctive of the communitarian critique that it appears to engage with the methodological presuppositions of liberalism rather than with the values that are at the heart of its substantive message; the focus is not upon the worth of autonomy, but upon the nature and extent of liberalism's reliance upon a comprehensive conception of the person, of human nature and the human good when articulating that worth. So, for example, communitarians have argued that Rawls is committed to an ontological account of the person rather than to a purely political conception that is the focus of an overlapping consensus; that despite claiming to assign priority to the right over the good, Rawls does not derive his principles of justice in a manner that makes them prior to or independent of a thick (rather than thin) conception of the good; and that Rawlsian liberalism tends to secrete an Archimedean conception of political theorizing, not only regarding its pronouncements as having universal application, but also regarding them as originating from a position or perspective that transcends the constraints and limitations of its cultural context. Accordingly, a communitarian picture of the liberal theorist's understanding of his or her own status as a theorist might be summarized as follows: the liberal theorist tends to think of himself or herself as essentially tradition-free.

According to a communitarian such as MacIntyre, such a self-image represses, ignores or minimizes the following points. The work of a contemporary liberal theorist stands at the end of a long tradition of political and moral thought; it is the latest episode in a narrative quest whose origins lie in specific social circumstances and the particular theoretical disputes and requirements that they threw up. It draws upon conceptions of human worth and well-being embedded in the texts of previous thinkers (themselves addressing specific problems) and in the structures of social institutions both past and present. And it relies upon, as well as helping to refine and contribute to, fellow liberals' understandings of the nature of their shared project and of the standards by which its success might be judged. In short, the liberal theorist's activities take place within, and presuppose resources that can only be provided by, the communal matrix of a tradition.

And of course, the very obviousness of the last claim makes it seem to many people that the communitarian is setting up a straw man. Even if past liberal theorists have explicitly thought of themselves in Archimedean ways, and even if contemporary theorists needed a little prodding in order explicitly to disown such self-images, there can be no reason for thinking that there is any fundamental contradiction between the content of a liberal theory of justice and an explicit acknowledgement of the elementary truth that this theory (like any other product of human intellectual endeavour) emerged from a tradition of enquiry. To think otherwise is simply to commit a version of the genetic fallacy, to conflate the question of a theory's origins with that of its content.

However, what if the communitarian claim is not that the liberal theorist cannot *consistently* acknowledge this truth about herself, but rather that she is not giving *sufficient* weight to its implications? What if the claim is that the elementary nature of this truth about the theorist's own position highlights in as striking a way as possible the fact that she places a degree of emphasis upon individual autonomy that is belied by a range of mundane facts about her own life *qua* theorist? The structure of the communitarian claim would then be: 'If one of the most fundamental facts about the people who are engaged in propounding a political theory that assigns absolute priority to individual autonomy is that they are not and cannot be autonomous of a communal matrix of enquiry, then perhaps they should question their substantive claim that the most fundamental fact about people is their autonomy.'

In other words, according to this rereading, the seemingly abstract methodological focus of communitarianism is in reality a way of questioning the worth of autonomy by emphasizing the non-autonomous status of the defenders of autonomy. Of course, this point could be made in other ways to other liberal interlocutors: since the communitarians are primarily dealing with political theorists, they have focused upon the essentially communal nature of political theorizing, but the same point can be made to people whose life and work places them in different circumstances. When asked to reflect upon the degree to which their own lives match up to the liberal vision of persons as autonomous beings, as self-contained and self-originating sources of moral value, most people will see that they do so to a very limited extent. They will see that they are physical beings, just one part of a complex natural world upon which they depend for sustenance and shelter – indeed, for life itself. They will see that the fabric of their lives – their homes, clothing and consumer goods – is woven from and by the efforts of other members of their society. They will also see that their life derives its meaning not from themselves alone but from their children, lovers, family and friends; and that they make sense of their lives by means of a language and culture with a history and a future that transcends their own. They may even see themselves as dependent on something other than nature, culture and the society of other human beings, on something that is extra-human and supernatural: they may see God as the medium in which they live and move and have their being. In this respect, however, religious belief constitutes one mode of an awareness that is elemental to human life – an awareness that, in many ways, the things that make life possible and that give it whatever distinctively human meaning it has are to be found outside the individual.

It should be obvious that such a set of reminders does not amount to a knock-down, logically valid ethical conclusion derived from uncontroversial premises. The aim is rather to construct a species of *ad hominem* argument, one that explicitly fits itself to the particular circumstances of its recipient and attempts to generate in her a sense of existential paradox – a sudden perception that her essentially individualistic beliefs do not correspond to the real circumstances of her life. The examples mentioned in the previous paragraph are heterogeneous enough: coming to a belief in God's existence will not revolutionize someone's values in the same way as a growing conviction in the importance of ecological issues; and someone who regards the well-being of her family as her central goal will not live in accordance with the same principles as someone who devotes herself to the preservation of her culture's language. However, it does not seem misleading to regard such people as having this much in common: they have conceptions of the good in which the value of individual autonomy, the notion that what matters most in life is their own and other's individual capacity to choose how to live, no longer has pride of place. They have, each in their different ways, de-centred the human individual in their system of values; the Enlightenment sun has become just one more star.

But, of course, in criticizing the liberal in this way, the communitarian aim need not be to suggest that individual autonomy has no worth whatever as a value; the claim could rather be that its worth must be understood against this backdrop of individual dependence upon and respect for structures and resources external to the individual. Seen from such a perspective, it may be easier to accept that limits should be placed on the value of individual autonomy; rather than viewing it as a human good with unquestionable and absolute priority, we should see it as one good amongst others, and so as one that in some circumstances it might be permissible and even advisable to sacrifice or trade off against those other goods. If we do not, if we regard autonomy as a hypergood, then we open ourselves and our society to a form of self-understanding that is delusive, arrogant and ultimately hubristic. In short, against the liberal's emphasis upon autonomy, the communitarian sets an emphasis upon dependence; against the liberal claim that my life is my own to make of what I will, the communitarian sets the claim that the loci of value in my life are often to be found outside myself. We might therefore entitle the reformulated communitarian critique of liberalism: 'Liberalism and the limits of autonomy'.

Such a reformulation cannot, however, be allowed to stand as our conclusion, as if the battle lines were thereby clearly defined – (liberal) autonomy versus (communitarian) dependence. For that would be to ignore the brand of perfectionist liberalism developed by Raz which, whilst giving a central role to the value of autonomy, can be seen to accommodate that recognition of the dependence of the individual on factors external to her of precisely the kind that, on our reading, communitarians insist upon. While Raz, by invoking it as a comprehensive and not merely as a (purportedly) political ideal, accords autonomy greater explicit importance than does Rawls, and thus might seem to be more susceptible to doubts about its worth or attractiveness, his understanding of what it means, of its value and preconditions, indicates that he takes very clearly on board the communitarian point that value can exist in structures – in social forms, in particular kinds of social relationship – external to the individual. Just as the communitarian need not deny altogether the value of the individual's freedom to choose how she lives her life but merely observe that it is just one good among many, so the liberal need not regard the protection of that freedom, or of individual rights more broadly understood, as the sole legitimate purpose of politics. In granting, with Raz, that autonomy is only valuable in pursuit of the good and that goods are in various senses external to the individual, one opens up the possibility of a reconciliation of the liberal value of autonomy with the communitarian recognition of dependence. Instead of regarding Rawls as under attack on two flanks, then, we would suggest that he might regard Raz as offering, from within the liberal camp, a reading of autonomy that at once comes from the same direction as the communitarian critique and indicates that liberalism has the resources to accommodate it.

Bibliography

Ackerman, B., *Social Justice and the Liberal State* (Yale University Press: New Haven, 1980)

Arblaster, A., *The Rise and Decline of Western Liberalism* (Blackwell: Oxford, 1984)

Berlin, I., 'Two Concepts of Liberty', in *Four Essays on Liberty*, I. Berlin (Oxford University Press: Oxford, 1969), pp. 118–72

Buchanan, A., *Marx and Justice* (Methuen: London, 1982)

Dworkin, R., 'What is Equality? Part II: Equality of Resources', *Philosophy and Public Affairs*, 10, 4 (1981), pp. 283–345

——, 'Rights as Trumps' in *Theories of Rights*, ed. J. Waldron (Oxford University Press: Oxford, 1984), pp. 153–67

——, *A Matter Of Principle* (Oxford University Press: Oxford, 1985)

——, 'Bakke's Case: Are Quotas Unfair?' in *A Matter of Principle*, R. Dworkin (Oxford University Press: Oxford, 1985), pp. 293–303

——, 'What Justice Isn't', in *A Matter of Principle*, R. Dworkin (Oxford University Press: Oxford, 1985), pp. 214–20

Gramsci, A., *Selections from the Prison Notebooks*, ed. and trans. Q. Hoare and G. Nowell Smith (International Publishers: New York, 1971)

Gray, J., *Liberalism* (Open University Press: Milton Keynes, 1986)

Habermas, J., *Legitimation Crisis*, trans. Thomas McCarthy (Beacon Press: Boston, 1975)

Holmes, S., 'The Permanent Structure of Antiliberal Thought' ed. N. Rosenblum (Harvard University Press: Harvard, 1989) pp. 227–53

Jaggar, A., *Feminist Politics and Human Nature* (Harvester: Brighton, 1983)

Kukathas, C. and Pettit , P., *Rawls: A Theory of Justice and its Critics* (Polity: Cambridge, 1990)

Kymlicka, W., *Liberalism, Community and Culture* (Oxford University Press: Oxford, 1989)

MacIntyre, A., *After Virtue* (Duckworth: London, 1981)

——, *Whose Justice? Which Rationality?* (Duckworth: London, 1988)

——, *Three Rival Versions of Moral Enquiry* (Duckworth: London, 1990)

Malachowski, A. (ed.), *Reading Rorty* (Blackwell: Oxford, 1990)

Marx, K., *The German Ideology*, ed. C. J. Arthur (Lawrence and Wishart: London, 1970)

Nozick, R., *Anarchy, State and Utopia* (Blackwell: Oxford, 1974)

Peterson, M. D. and Vaughan, R. C. (eds), *The Virginia Statute on Religious Freedom* (Cambridge University Press: Cambridge, 1988)

Rawls, J., *A Theory of Justice* (Harvard University Press: Cambridge, MA, 1971)

——, 'Fairness to Goodness', *Philosophical Review*, 84 (1975), pp. 536–54

——, 'Kantian Constructivism in Moral Theory', *Journal of Philosophy*, 77, 9 (1980), pp. 515–72

——, 'Social Unity and Primary Goods', in *Utilitarianism and Beyond*, ed. A. K. Sen and B. Williams (Cambridge University Press: Cambridge, 1982), pp. 159–85

——, 'Justice as Fairness: Political not Metaphysical', *Philosophy and Public Affairs*, 14, 3 (1985), pp. 223–51

——, 'The Idea of an Overlapping Consensus', *Oxford Journal of Legal Studies*, 7, 1 (1987), pp. 1–25

——, 'The Priority of Right and Ideas of the Good', *Philosophy and Public Affairs*, 17, 4 (1988), pp. 251–76

——, 'The Domain of the Political and Overlapping Consensus', *New York University Law Review*, 64, 2 (1989), pp. 233–55

Raz, J., *The Morality of Freedom* (Oxford University Press: Oxford, 1986)

Rorty, R., 'The Priority of Democracy to Philosophy', in *The Virginia Statute on Religious Freedom*, ed. M. D. Peterson and R. C. Vaughan (Cambridge University Press: Cambridge, 1988), *Reading Rorty*, ed. A. Malachowski (Blackwell: Oxford, 1990), and *Objectivity, Relativism and Truth*, R. Rorty (Cambridge University Press: Cambridge, 1991)

——, *Contingency, Irony and Solidarity* (Cambridge University Press: Cambridge, 1989)

——, *Philosophical Papers*, Vol. 1: *Objectivity, Relativism and Truth* (Cambridge University Press: Cambridge, 1991)

Rosenblum, N., (ed.), *Liberalism and The Moral Life* (Harvard University Press: Cambridge, MA, 1989)

Sandel, M., *Liberalism and the Limits of Justice* (Cambridge University Press: Cambridge, 1982)

Scruton, R., *The Meaning of Conservatism*, 2nd edn (Macmillan: London, 1984)

Sen, A. K. and Williams, B. (eds), *Utilitarianism and Beyond* (Cambridge University Press: Cambridge, 1982)

Taylor, C., 'Interpretation and the Sciences of Man', *The Review of Metaphysics*, 25, 1 (1971), pp. 3–51 and in *Philosophical Papers*, Vol. 2, C. Taylor (Cambridge University Press: Cambridge, 1985), pp. 15–57

——, *Philosophical Papers* (Vol. I: Human Agency and Language, Vol. II: Philosophy and the Human Sciences) Cambridge University Press: Cambridge, 1985

——, 'Cross-Purposes: The Liberal–Communitarian Debate', in *Liberalism and the Moral Life*, ed. N. Rosenblum (Harvard University Press: Cambridge, MA, 1989), pp. 159–82

——, *Sources of the Self* (Cambridge University Press: Cambridge, 1990)

Waldron, J. (ed.) *Theories of Rights* (Oxford University Press: Oxford, 1984)

Walzer, M., 'Philosophy and Democracy', *Political Theory* 9, 3 (1981), pp. 379–99

——, *Spheres of Justice* (Basic Books: New York, 1983)

——, 'Liberalism and the Art of Separation', *Political Theory*, 12, 3 (1984), pp. 315–30

——, *Interpretation and Social Criticism* (Harvard University Press: Cambridge, MA, 1987)

——, *The Company of Critics* (Peter Halban: London, 1989)

Wittgenstein, L., *Zettel*, 2nd edn (Blackwell, Oxford: 1981)

Index

Ackerman, B., 130
antecedently individuated self,
    40–1, 45–7, 48–69, 77, 94, 102,
    114, 121–2, 158, 160, 163, 177,
    199–201, 205
    see also metaphysical conception
    of the person
anti-foundationalism, 230, 232–47,
    289
anti-perfectionism, 25–33, 41,
    153–4, 159, 189, 209, 115–26,
    229–31, 252–67, 285, 288,
    289–94
    see also neutrality
Aquinas, T., 92
Aristotle, 78–82, 92, 220, 240, 245
art of life, 257, 287
arts, 263–4, 270, 275, 278
    see also opera
asocial individualism, 13–18, 41,
    56, 114, 159
    vs. social matrix, 14–15, 94, 102,
    110–12, 121, 127–46, 158,
    195–7, 210–12, 267–82, 284, 286
    vs. strongly communal
    conception of the good, 15–16,
    52–3, 59–69, 71, 94, 158,
    198–9, 210–12, 219, 285–6

authority, 252, 259, 273
autonomy, 43–5, 53–5, 67–9,
    117–18, 119, 124, 131, 159,
    163–4, 175–8, 197, 209, 212,
    224–6, 230–1, 235, 249, 252–8,
    264–88, 290–4
    conditions of autonomy, 272–8
    see also freedom

basic structure, 171–2, 179–80,
    182–3, 196
burdens of reason, 185, 222–4

citizens/citizenship, 54–5, 135–6,
    149, 174–205, 206–26
    see also persons as free and equal
civic humanism, 219
civil liberties, xi
classical republicanism, 219
coercion, 262–4, 275–9
communitarianism, viii–xii, 10–33,
    35–164, 167–80, 184, 193–205,
    206–20, 225–6, 233–4, 235–9,
    242–4, 251–2, 267–88, 289–94
complex equality, 146–64
comprehensive conceptions of the
    good, 168–9, 171–205, 206–26,
    249–50, 291

partially vs. fully comprehensive,
222, 250
comprehensive goals, 268–72, 284
conception of the person, 10–13,
45–69, 71, 121–2, 128–9,
138–9, 158, 162–4, 174–8, 194,
196–7, 206–9, 233–4, 235–6,
239–40, 242–4, 282–4, 291
conceptions of the good, 5–7,
10–18, 25–33, 42–55, 71, 88–9,
90–1, 97–100, 102, 104, 112,
116–18, 130–1, 155, 159, 182,
184, 196–7, 214, 253, 255–6,
263–7, 291
see also comprehensive
conceptions of the good
conservatism, ix, xiii, 84, 111,
140, 143
constitutive attachments, 15–16,
41, 49–55, 66, 93, 113, 158,
161, 162, 199–201, 210, 243
contract theory, 14–18, 64–6, 94–7,
174, 188, 210
cultural particularity, 19–21,
127–34, 137, 146, 154–5, 158,
178–80, 201–2, 212–14

democracy, 135–8, 154–5, 171,
172–3, 202, 232
deontological liberalism, 42–5, 119
desert, 60–3, 95
difference principle, 7–8, 59–63,
66, 68
dominance, 147–50
Dworkin, R., 61, 69, 156

emotivism, 73–7, 85, 93, 287
emotivist self, 75–7, 90, 93–4, 243,
283
Enlightenment, 20, 77–9, 82, 234,
293
epistemological crisis, 91–2, 115
equality, 4–5, 67, 125, 138, 143,
145, 151–4

equality of opportunity, x, 7–8
exclusionary liberalism, 251

fact of pluralism, 181, 184–5,
188–9, 190, 198, 202, 223–5
see also pluralism
feminism, ix
fraternity, 67–8
freedom, x–xii, 5–7, 117, 125,
128–9, 131, 151–4, 196–7, 238,
251, 254, 261, 284
see also autonomy

grammar, autonomy of, 241–2
Gramsci, A., xii, 142

Habermas, J., 130, 135
harm principle, 272–4
Hegel, G. W. F., xii
Hobbes, T., 188–9, 204
homosexuality, 27, 253–4
hypergoods, 114–18, 124, 294

individualism, 14, 63, 96, 125,
211–12, 270–1, 292–3
internal and external goods, 82–4,
85, 88, 91
intersubjective conception of the
self, 41, 51–2, 59–66

judicial review, 136
justice, 95–6, 132, 139, 140, 148,
178, 179, 195
justice as fairness, x, 3–9,
167–205, 206–26, 289–90

Kant, I., xii, 43–4, 45, 62, 77, 98,
197
Kymlicka, W., 33

Lenin, V., 142
liberalism, viii–xii, 1–33, 175, 190–1,
220–6, 229–31, 244–7, 291–4
classical liberalism, xii

Rawlsian liberalism, *see* justice
  as fairness; political liberalism
libertarianism, ix
  see also Nozick, R.
Locke, J., xi, xii
Loyola, I., 234, 238, 246, 247

MacIntyre, A., 10, 22, 37, 40,
  70–100, 101, 112, 113, 115, 117,
  120–1, 122, 124, 127, 132, 155,
  158–64, 206–19, 243, 246, 283,
  287, 291
manipulation, 263
market, 152–4, 182
marriage, 27, 32, 77, 86, 224, 254,
  260–2, 275, 276–7, 281
Marx, 142
Marxism, ix–x
metaphysical conception of the
  person, 41, 45–7, 48–55, 69,
  163, 176–7, 234, 235, 243
  see also antecedently
  individuated self
methodology, 127–9, 130–46,
  154–5, 159–60, 180, 191,
  194–5, 201, 233–47, 290–2
Mill, J. S., xii
modus vivendi, 187–9
monopoly, 147–50

narrative unity of a human life,
  76, 82, 86–9, 92, 113–14, 116,
  120, 283–4
natural talents/endowments, 4,
  60–3, 213
Nietzsche, F. W., 234, 238, 246, 247
neutrality, 29–33, 41, 53–5, 71,
  97–100, 121, 123–5, 130–1, 153,
  155, 159, 212, 214, 215–26,
  249–88
  of effects vs. of justification, 30,
  99, 217, 276–80
  see also anti-perfectionism
Nozick, R., x, 14, 153

objectivism, 21–5, 28–9, 41, 55–9,
  85, 159, 214–15, 287–8
opera, 26, 30–1, 277–8
original position, 3–33, 47–50,
  63–6, 94–7, 135, 150, 168,
  172–4, 177, 180, 183, 214, 253
overlapping consensus, 181, 185–8,
  192, 221–2, 291

perfectionism, 26, 209, 212, 215,
  224, 226, 230–1
perfectionist liberalism, 212,
  249–88, 290, 294
persons as free and equal, 4–9, 96,
  173–205, 206–26, 232
  see also justice as fairness
philosophical anthropology, 45
pluralism, 181–2, 215, 219, 249,
  254, 264–7, 285
  see also fact of pluralism
political liberalism, 167–205,
  206–26, 289–94
  as response to MacIntyre,
  206–19
  as response to Sandel, 174–8,
  193–5, 199–201, 205, 206–19
  as response to Taylor, 195–7,
  206–19
  as response to Walzer, 174,
  178–80, 193–5, 201–3, 206–19
  see also the new Rawls
positive discrimination/affirmative
  action, 61
practical reasoning, 91, 100,
  115–18, 119, 123, 161–2
  procedural vs. substantive,
  116–18, 123
practice, 82–6, 90, 91, 92, 144, 161,
  162
pragmatism, 181, 183, 185–9, 207,
  259–60
primary goods, 8, 130, 133–4, 150,
  154–5, 178–80, 194–5, 202,
  216–17

public justifiability, 181–205,
206–26, 232, 261
public political culture, 172,
172–205, 206–26, 232, 234,
244–7
public/political vs. private, 27–33,
99–100, 155, 175–6, 178,
203–5, 209, 220–6, 229–31,
250, 290
publicity, 196–7

qualitative discriminations, 104–5,
113, 114–15, 119, 121, 122
Quine, W. V. O., 248

Rational and Reasonable, 211
rational choice, 8–9, 57, 211
Rawls, J., x–xii, 1–33, 40–69, 70,
93–100, 101, 119–26, 127–9,
130–1, 133–4, 135, 137–9, 146,
150, 154–5, 157–64, 167–205,
206–26, 229–31, 232–4, 249–53,
256–7, 261, 272, 276, 282, 285,
287–8, 289–91, 294
the new Rawls, vii, 39, 167–205,
206–26, 229–31, 232–3, 235–6,
249–53
Raz, J., 212, 229, 231, 249–88, 290,
294
redistribution, 62
relativism, 20, 91, 139–46, 195, 202
right prior to the good, 31–3, 42,
118–20, 123–5, 211, 216–19, 291
rights, 31, 71–2, 125, 136–8, 155,
197, 214, 216, 219, 253, 257,
271
roles, 79–81, 89, 179–80
Rorty, R., 229–31, 232–48, 289

Sandel, M., 10, 37, 40–69, 70, 71,
77, 93, 94, 101, 113, 117,
120–1, 122, 123, 126, 127, 128,
158–64, 174–8, 191, 193–5,

199–201, 205, 206–19, 243–4,
283–4
scepticism, 21–3, 59, 102, 181,
183–5, 189, 214–15, 222–3,
255–9, 280, 287
self-interpretation, 101, 107–10,
112, 121, 124, 125, 139, 155,
161, 195, 243
simple equality, 147–50
social criticism, 140–6
social forms, 252, 267–82, 284, 286,
294
social goods, 127–8, 132–4, 141,
161, 218
social matrix, 13–18, 93, 96, 102,
125, 195–7, 210, 243
social meanings, 132–4, 139–46,
147, 149–50, 153, 161, 179–80,
194, 201, 207
society as private association or
scheme of cooperation, 15, 48–9,
56, 60, 94–7, 173–4, 180, 183,
188, 203, 204–5, 210–12,
218–19
stability, 181, 185–9, 192–3
state, 16, 27–33, 148, 188, 190–1,
193, 249, 251, 256–9, 261–4,
267, 272–82, 288
state of nature, 13–19, 188
strong evaluation, 102–4, 106
strongly communal conceptions of
the good *see* asocial
individualism
subjectivism, 21–5, 28–9, 41, 55–9,
71, 94, 102, 105, 114, 122, 159,
214–15, 287–8
global vs. restricted, 22–3

taxation, x, 63, 262–4, 274,
275–9, 288
Taylor, C., 37, 100–26, 127, 132,
139, 155, 158–64, 195–7,
206–19, 236, 243, 246
telos, 78–82, 87–9

thin conceptions of the good, 102, 114, 119–20, 123, 130, 216–17, 291

tradition, xii, 82, 89–93, 97–100, 161, 162, 291

universalism, 19–21, 128, 139, 154, 158, 178–80, 212–14, 286

veil of ignorance, 3–9, 19, 27, 47, 64, 183, 214, 217, 249
virtues, 60, 83, 85, 86, 89, 95, 217–19
    political virtues, 217–19

vocabulary, 107–10, 237–9, 239–47
voluntary exchanges, 148, 153

Walzer, M., 19–37, 127–56, 158–64, 174, 178–80, 193–5, 201–3, 206–19, 238
welfare state, viii, x
well-being, 250–2, 255–8, 267–71, 281–2, 287–8
well-ordered society, 185–8
wide vs. narrow morality, 12, 257, 287
Wittgenstein, L., 135, 241